Wendell Berry and Religion

Heaven's Earthly Life

Edited by Joel James Shuman
and L. Roger Owens

THE UNIVERSITY PRESS OF KENTUCKY

Editorial and Sales Offices: The University Press of Kentucky
663 South Limestone Street, Lexington, Kentucky 40508-4008
www.kentuckypress.com

13 12 11 10 09   5 4 3 2 1

Library of Congress Cataloging-in-Publication Data

  Wendell Berry and religion : heaven's earthly life / edited by Joel
James Shuman and L. Roger Owens.
      p.   cm. — (Culture of the land)
  Includes bibliographical references and index.
  ISBN 978-0-8131-2555-8 (hardcover : alk. paper)
  1. Christianity. 2. Berry, Wendell, 1934–   I. Shuman, Joel James.
II. Owens, L. Roger, 1975–
BR50.W398 2009
277.3'082092—dc22

                          2009018235

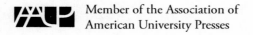

Contents

Joel James Shuman

Introduction

Placing God in the Work of Wendell Berry

God saw everything that he had made, and indeed, it was very good.
—Gen. 1:31

We declare to you what was from the beginning, what we have heard, what we have seen with our eyes, what we have looked at and touched with our hands, concerning the word of life.
—1 John 1:1

I take literally the statement in the Gospel of John that God loves the world. I believe that the world was created and approved by love, that it subsists, coheres, and endures by love, and that, insofar as it is redeemable, it can be redeemed only by love. I believe that divine love, incarnate and indwelling in the world, summons the world always toward wholeness, which ultimately is reconciliation and atonement with God.
—Wendell Berry, "Health as Membership"

The title notwithstanding, this is not a book *about* Wendell Berry. It is not a biography, nor does it attempt a systematic critical analysis of his writing. As interesting and significant as those projects might be, they will have to be undertaken by someone else.[1] Rather, these essays are intended to be contributions to an ongoing conversation, in what I take to be the best and fullest sense of the term, meaning that they have to do, not simply with the exchange of discourse, but also with being among a particular group of persons, over time and in a particular place.[2] In this case, the place and the persons in question are the Christian community—the church catholic[3]—and some of its members who recognize in the work of Wendell Berry a kind of wisdom that might help them and their fellow Christians work, live, and think more faithfully in a world that, to the extent it recognizes their Christianity at all, finds it increasingly unpalatable.

The authors of these essays are all Christians who understand themselves to be writing in conversation with the work of a fellow Christian about things that matter. Yet, beyond the authors of these essays, it is unclear how many of the significant number of people who read Wendell Berry understand him as a Christian author. Indeed, Berry is often explicitly critical of Christianity in his work, especially with respect to the complicity of modern North American Christianity in the violent exploitation of the earth and its inhabitants by consumer capitalism and military-industrialism.[4] That Berry is not frequently seen as a Christian writer, or that many self-identified Christian readers probably find him stranger than they do their own beliefs, says more about how attenuated Christianity has become in the popular imagination than about how well Berry's work synchronizes with the mainstream of contemporary North Atlantic culture, whether secular or Christian.

As eclectic as the authors of these essays are, and in spite of whatever theological differences they may have with Berry or one another, they all share with him certain common convictions. First, all would agree that Christianity has often been insufficiently attentive to earth and flesh and so has seldom been fully able to resist the temptation represented by some form of the ancient heresy called *Gnosticism.* Second, all would agree that the highly privatized, excessively therapeutic Christianity of North American modernity is especially guilty in this respect. Finally, all would agree that genuine Christian faithfulness *and* genuine human flourishing demand a decisive, explicit rejection of all things Gnostic, a demand that requires Christianity to be understood as a good deal more than individual belief about the possibility of self-transcendence—that is, "pie in the sky in the sweet by-and-by."

Gnosticism refers broadly to a variety of ancient and modern departures from Christian orthodoxy that have in common the assumption of a fundamentally *dualistic* account of reality, most often based in some variety of radical distinction between matter and spirit (or soul, or mind). Generally speaking, Gnosticism, which Harold Bloom has called "the American religion,"[5] holds that the material creation—the human body and the earth and the creatures on which human bodies depend for their existence—is, ultimately, unimportant. At best, it views materiality as morally inconsequential and significant only in a temporary, strictly utilitarian sense; at worst, it understands the very existence of materiality as a transient manifestation of the human soul's alienation from God. The limits inherent in materiality are to be ignored, struggled against, or fled, as much and as soon as possible. This earthly life is a simulacrum, or a test, or perhaps even a fleshy prison. What truly matters is the life to come, in which we will have shed our bodies and exist as pure spirits in perfect union with a purely immaterial God. In the meantime, well, at least we have several hundred channels of cable television and shopping malls and the Internet to keep us distracted.

Like a lot of heresies, Gnosticism is a sometimes subtle distortion of orthodoxy. According to Christian tradition, it *is* true that creation has been alienated from its Creator. Life in this world, characterized by exploitation, violence, suffering, sickness, and death, falls well short of the promised Kingdom of God. This side of the consummation of God's work, it always will. Yet the limitations inherent in the materiality of creation are neither cause nor evidence of this alienation, and God's redemptive work neither requires nor encourages a flight from this life or this world. God, who delights in creation and desires its well-being, has given humanity the gift of sharing in that delight. That humanity has often failed to recognize the goodness of God's gift is overshadowed by the fact that God's intention for creation remains one of thoroughgoing redemption. Moreover, God's redemptive work is and always has been "fleshy," which is to say that it is a gift given *to* the material creation *in* and *through* particular members *of* the material creation. As Dante writes at the beginning of the *Paradisio:*

> The glory of Him who moves all things rays forth
> through all the universe, and is reflected
> from each thing in proportion to its worth.[6]

Creation is good, not simply because it is made and sustained by the God who is goodness itself, but also because it is the freely chosen theater and medium of that God's action. As the third-century theologian Athanasius of Alexandria said in the classic anti-Gnostic essay *On the Incarnation of the Word of God,* creation is in some analogous sense God's *body.*[7]

The idea that the God who saves is lovingly at work, in and through material creatures who live as members of the material world, suggests that there is plenty to be done by the women and men whose desire is to live well and in harmony with the proper order of things and their Creator. Yet this is not as easy as it might at first sound, for, as history and the present state of world affairs make all too evident, humankind has through the years done a lot of really bad work. This is a persistent theme in Berry's writing: the wholeness toward which God beckons creation requires that women and men be engaged in good work, yet not all work is good. Some work perpetuates and accelerates creation's alienation from its true good: "Works of pride, by self-called creators, with their premium on originality, reduce the Creation to novelty—the faint surprises of minds incapable of wonder. . . . Pursuing originality, the would-be creator works alone. In loneliness one assumes a responsibility for oneself that one cannot fulfill. . . . There is the bad work of pride. There is also the bad work of despair—done poorly out of the failure of hope or vision. Despair is the too-little of responsibility, as pride is the too-much. The shoddy work of despair, the pointless work of pride, equally betray Creation. They are wastes of life."[8]

The theological name for such wastes of life is, of course, *sin,* one aspect of which is the failure of women and men to discern God's ongoing presence in and to all creation. Athanasius, to whom I refer above, argues that, apart from human sin, all women and men possess the capacity to know God at work, both in themselves and in the rest of creation. Yet, he says, "men's carelessness, by little and little, descends to lower things," such that humankind is, apart from God's gracious intercession, destined ultimately to destroy itself and a good part of creation.[9]

This is, of course, the crux of Christianity—that God has, in and through the history of a particular people, been at work tending to creation, working to restore it to the wholeness for which it was originally intended. Christians believe that the center of this history is the Incarnation—the life, death, and resurrection of Jesus of Nazareth, the very logos of the Creator. Jesus' resurrection from death is the ultimate sign of God's care for creation, signaling the ultimate triumph of creative love over destructive hate. Yet to focus exclusively on the resurrection is to overlook the significance of Jesus' life and teaching. It is, says Athanasius, "by the works of his body [that Jesus teaches them] so that they who would not know him from his providence and rule over all things, may even from the works done by his actual body know the Word of God which is in the body, and through him the Father."[10] God became a particular human person living in a particular place and time, and the things that person said and did in, through, and with his body made God present to creation in a unique and unrepeatable way.

Nor has that presence ceased. Not incidentally, the New Testament describes the gathered Christian community as, among other things, the "Body of Christ." Jesus has, according to Scripture, ascended into heaven and no longer walks the earth. Yet his life and teachings continue to be bodily present to the world through the gathered community of his disciples as they faithfully rehearse and perform his story. The name traditionally given to that rehearsal is *liturgy,* from a Greek word meaning roughly "to work publicly for the common good." Christians are called collectively to become Jesus' manifest incarnate presence to creation by working together publicly for creation's good.

Indisputably, Christians have not always worked for the common good of creation. Indeed, they have more than occasionally, and not always with good intentions, worked for its destruction. Yet this is an expression not of Christianity but of Christian unfaithfulness, the failure of Christians to follow in the steps of the one they call *Lord.* That the earth continues abundantly to bless us in spite of these failures is but a sign that God's love exceeds our callousness and ineptitude. That confession, absolution, penance, and instruction remain significant parts of the Christian liturgy signals our hope concerning God's willingness to continue, in spite of our failures, the work of transforming us and remaining present to the world through our work. These essays should be read, I believe, from this perspective; as the attempts of members of Christ's body to discern together with one of our fellow members how to move forward, to try yet again to say something useful and interesting about the good work to which we and all women and men have been called.

Part 1: Good Work

This book divides into four parts, the first of which is called "Good Work." "Good work," Wendell Berry says, "finds the way between pride and despair. It graces with health. It heals with grace. It preserves the given so that it remains a gift."[11] This is a persistent theme in Berry's writing: women and men are created to work and to do so well. Properly understood, work does not simply make possible the continuation of human existence; it is also potentially a source of pleasure and satisfaction and a means by which humans may rightly connect: to their Creator, to each other, and to the rest of creation. Thus, part of the great pathos of modernity is its uncritical emphases on efficiency and utility, which Berry rightly understands to involve a disparagement of work as a human discipline. Such disparagement leads inevitably to the failure of people to work well. One might well say that part of God's redemptive work is to call women and men back to the task of good work—work that is peaceable and compassionate toward other persons and the rest of creation. The essays in this part are all reflections on what have traditionally been called the *professions,* teaching, medicine, law, and ministry, and on the institution in which professionals are trained, the university. Their authors are all accomplished practitioners of their respective crafts, each of whom recognizes in his field of endeavor a history of failure that has, nonetheless, failed to destroy the discipline's capacity to do significant good in the world. Each draws on Berry's work in an attempt to imagine what it would look like for their professions to recommit to working for the common good.

Any consideration of how the professions might recommit to working for the common good has necessarily to take into account the way those professions train their members. The essays in part 1 of the book do just that. The first, written by the eminent theologian Stanley Hauerwas, asks Berry to help him imagine what a Christian university might look like. Hauerwas concludes that it would have to be characterized first of all by propriety and truthfulness and that only through a firm commitment to these standards can it be saved from being beholden to corporations and their influence on the career interests of students, which are destructive of long-term fidelity to people and place. Similarly, Brian Volck, a pediatrician who teaches in the medical school at the University of Cincinnati, suggests that, if medicine is to remain the profoundly moral practice it has traditionally been, it must find a way to train its students genuinely to care for their patients as human persons, which surely will require a turn away from the technology-centered hyperspecialization characterizing so much of contemporary medicine.

Richard P. Church, an attorney, theologian, and farmer from the North Carolina Piedmont, considers in his essay the practice of law. He enters into an imaginative conversation with the attorney Thomas Shaffer, a persistent Christian critic of the procedural ethics typical of American jurisprudence, and the fictional Wheeler Catlett, the resident lawyer of Berry's Port William membership. In Shaffer, Church sees a lawyer who has considered carefully what it would mean for a Christian attorney to practice law in a manner faithful to his or her most basic theological convictions, while, in Catlett, he sees a life in community that both exemplifies and makes possible such faithfulness.

Kyle Childress, who for more than fifteen years has been the pastor of the

Austin Heights Baptist Church in Nacogdoches, Texas, is the author of this part's concluding essay. Austin Heights is a relatively small congregation, and Kyle is an erudite, gifted minister who has frequently been asked when he is going to move on to a "better" position in a larger church. Developing Berry's distinction (borrowed from Wallace Stegner) between perpetually upwardly mobile "boomers" and faithful, contented "stickers," Kyle shows that genuinely good work demands not simply highly developed technical skill but also long-term fidelity to the people and place for whose good that work is to be done.

Part 2: Holy Living

One of Berry's ongoing concerns is the health of people and places and the ways modern life threatens both. The authors in this second part of the book, "Holy Living," join Berry in recognizing this as a theological concern. "The word 'health,'" he notes, "comes from the same Indo-European root as 'heal,' 'whole,' and 'holy.' To be healthy is literally to be whole; to heal is to make whole. I don't think mortal healers should be credited with the power to make holy. But I have no doubt that such healers are properly obliged to acknowledge and respect the holiness embodied in all creatures, or that our healing involves the preservation in us of the spirit and the breath of God."[12] Among the most repeated biblical exhortations to the people of God is the proclamation that they should be holy. Those of us living today, when religion has been sequestered largely to the sphere of the private, can when we hear the word *holy* scarcely help think primarily of religiosity; a "holy" person is one whose personal religious behavior is especially evident and who refrains from certain (often trivial) proscribed activities. But this is a horribly reductive account of holiness, which, as Berry points out, shares a common linguistic heritage with the words *heal, health,* and *whole.* In this broader sense, a holy person is one attentive to his or her existence as a member of creation, which is constituted by an intricate constellation of dependences. Both health and holiness, then, have to do with living well in relationship—to other persons, other creatures, and God. The essays in this part of the book all focus in some way or another on better living in relationship.

In this part's first essay, Elizabeth Bahnson argues that Christian women have good reasons to be suspicious of hormonal contraceptives. This is hardly a novel position; Catholic teaching has, since the promulgation of the 1968 papal document *Humanae vitae,* proscribed the use of all "artificial" contraceptives, primarily on the grounds that they violate the natural moral order given by God. The argument that Bahnson makes is analogous, but sophisticatedly nuanced. Citing her own personal experience with oral contraceptives as well as an emergent body of medical and scientific research, she suggests that Christians should not use oral contraceptives because they are ultimately unhealthy, which is to say that they violate the wholeness of the bodies of women who use them and threaten the integrity of the ecosystems on which those women and their families depend for life.

Elizabeth's husband, Fred, with whom she operates a small farm in the North Carolina Piedmont, contributes the next essay. Fred Bahnson manages the Anatoth Community Garden in Orange County, North Carolina, and argues that seemingly insignificant projects like community gardens are, in fact, important gestures in defiance of the modern food industry, which is part of a political economy that depends on violent, exploitative, and ultimately unsustainable practices. Like the Jewish exiles in Babylon to whom the prophet Jeremiah wrote in the sixth century B.C.E., Christians have an obligation to "seek the *shalom* of the city where I have sent you into exile" (Jer. 29:7). Bahnson shows how Anatoth is a means by which those who work there seek the *shalom* of their own cities while anticipating the consummation of God's kingdom and the coming of the heavenly city.

The first two essays in this part presume what the third makes explicit, which is that the earth is God's provisional gift to humankind, which is charged with its proper stewardship, what Berry calls its "usufruct." The Old Testament scholar Ellen F. Davis suggests that the "agrarian" viewpoint held by Berry and his friends is as old as God's instructions to the Israelites when he brought them out of Egypt and settled them in the land of Canaan. For Israel, Davis says, being holy meant using the land well and treating it as the gift it was, practices that set the Israelites apart from their apparently more sophisticated neighbors to the south and east. The Torah is full of instructions on precisely how to do this, and Davis shows the relevance of those instructions to those who would aspire to holy lives in a more contemporary context.

Ultimately, the land must be treated well because it belongs to God and is given to us as a gift and a loan. More immediately, however, we are charged to care for the land because the health of our bodies depends on that care. Our bodies are not simply contiguous, but continuous with the places they inhabit. In my own essay, I draw on Berry's criticism of modern medicine's uncritical use of the machine metaphor as a way of understanding and treating the human body. Taken too literally, that metaphor disregards the manifold relationships on which the body depends for its flourishing. As an alternative, I propose we begin thinking and speaking of the body not as a machine but as a beloved and ecologically interconnected "landscape of flesh."

This part concludes with an essay that takes one of our most common assumptions and turns it upside down. In "The Dark Night of the Soil," Norman Wirzba argues that the popular understanding of mysticism as a purely introspective flight from the everyday is deeply problematic. In the most basic sense, Wirzba maintains, mysticism involves neither esotericism nor excessive introspection. Rather, mysticism is a careful, cultivated attention to God's presence in and to the world. To see the world through the eyes of the mystics, he says, is to see it clearly, as God intends us to see it. Thus, a cultivation of the practice of seeing clearly—again, one of the persistent themes in Berry's essays and poetry—is a necessary step on the way to learning to live peaceably as a member of creation.

Part 3: Imagination

The task of theology is in good measure an enterprise of the imagination. "A man cannot despair," Berry writes, "if he can imagine a better life, and if he can enact something of its possibility. It is only when I am ensnarled in the meaningless ordeals and the ordeals of meaninglessness, of which our public and political life is now so productive, that I lose the awareness of something better, and feel the despair of having come to the dead end of possibility."[13] The writers represented in the first two parts of the book tend, with a few notable exceptions, to focus on Berry's work as an essayist, a concentration understandable given the essays' richness as a source of social critique. Yet Berry's fiction and poetry are equally rich sources of wisdom about how better to live and work, for it is here that we discover Berry at his most fecund theologically. It is in poetry and fiction that Berry explores questions theologians would call *eschatological*, meaning having to do with the present and ultimate fulfillment of God's intent for creation. The authors of the essays in this third part of the book, "Imagination," rightly see that Berry's fiction and poetry (as well as his essays) help us live better by allowing us to imagine a better way to live; hence, they work to parse Berry's views on love, forgiveness, hope, and life eternal.

D. Brent Laytham sees in Berry's fictional Port William membership, especially as described by the eponymous protagonist of the novel *Hannah Coulter,* a particularly profound instance of what Christian tradition has called the *communio sanctorum,* the "communion of saints." Laytham argues that the membership's stubborn, active remembrance of its departed members gives the community both a continuity across time and the hope that extends beyond time into God's eternal future. Such remembering, Laytham insists, is fundamentally bound to place, and, in this, he draws interesting connections between Berry and the ancient Christian practice of venerating relics of the saints. Philip A. Muntzel continues Laytham's exploration of hope in Berry by noting significant similarities between Berry's "earthy" account of hope and that of Saint Thomas Aquinas. Both Laytham and Muntzel suggest that Berry, who refuses entirely to project hope into a time beyond history, holds a position largely consistent with the best of Christian teaching.

The next essay, by Scott Williams, tells the disturbing story of mountain-top-removal coal mining, a practice that is enjoying significant growth, especially in Appalachia, as petroleum supplies dwindle and become more expensive. Williams suggests that the apparently trivial act of flipping an electric switch implicates every modern person in a troublesome history of largely invisible violence—that of mining the coal used to generate the steam driving the turbines of the plants generating our electricity. He deftly anticipates the common rejoinder to pointing out such complicity, which is that it is inevitable, for who among us would seriously argue that electricity does not make the world a better place? Yet, for Christians, says Williams, who hold fast to the hope that God ultimately will finish the work he has begun in the resurrection of Jesus, "there is no inevitable violence." To think otherwise is simply to lose faith, which is nothing less than a failure of imagination. God has given us the capacity of imagination in part that we might escape the illusion that violence is inevitable.

The part concludes with an essay by my coeditor, L. Roger Owens. This book is Roger's idea, and his essay captures the spirit of both the book and his own work to discern how to be faithful to where God has placed him. As a United Methodist minister and a promising scholar with a Ph.D. in theology, Roger chose the rural parish over the university classroom, determined to be a pastor-scholar whose work was of use to the particular women and men to whom God sent him. In his essay, he uses Berry's work to show that the proclamation of the Christian Gospel cannot be other than local and particular.

Part 4: Moving Forward

The book concludes with an essay by Charles R. Pinches engaging the ongoing debate among Christians regarding how best to engage the realm commonly referred to as *political.* Pinches suggests that Berry's accounts of memory, work, and membership offer a way forward that avoids the misguided division of Christians into withdrawn, tribal "sectarians" and cosmopolitans adept at engaging the secular on its own terms.

And so the conversation continues. Begun long ago in a thousand Port Williams, faithfully carried by innumerable women and men whose lives have evidenced their refusal to abandon hope, it points beyond itself toward the redemption of creation, to a new heaven and a new earth, and a new Jerusalem, and, of course, a new Port William.

Notes

1. Indeed, they have been. See, e.g., Jason Peters, ed., *Wendell Berry: Life and Work* (Lexington: University Press of Kentucky, 2007).

2. Interestingly, the *first* of nine definitions for the word *conversation* offered by the *Oxford English Dictionary* is "the action of living or having one's being *in* a place or *among* persons," suggesting that the interchange of discourse suggested by the seventh definition necessarily depends on the having in common suggested by the first.

3. I offer here the definition of the *church catholic* that I give to my students: it is the visible gathering of all who confess "Jesus is Lord."

4. For what I take to be a wonderful summary of his view on this question, see Wendell Berry, "God and Country," in *What Are People For?* (New York: North Point, 1990), 95–102. There he writes: "One must ask, then: is this state of affairs caused by Christian truth or by the failures and errors of Christian practice? My answer is that it is caused by the failures and errors of Christian practice. The evident ability of most church leaders to be 'born again in Christ' without in the least discomforting their faith in the industrial economy's bill of goods, however convenient and understandable it may be, is not scriptural" (98).

5. Harold Bloom, *The American Religion: The Emergence of the Post-Christian Nation* (New York: Simon & Schuster, 1992). Although Berry does not, to my knowledge, use the words *Gnostic* and *Gnosticism* in his writings, his opposition to the *notion* permeates his work, most obviously in the programmatic essay "The Body and the Earth" (in *The Unsettling of America: Culture and Agriculture,* 3rd ed. [San Francisco: Sierra Club Books, 1977]), the introduction to *The Hidden Wound* (1970;

reprint, San Francisco: North Point, 1989), and the more recent "Health as Membership" (in *Another Turn of the Crank* [Washington, DC: Counterpoint, 1995]).

6. Dante Alighieri, *The Divine Comedy*, trans. John Ciardi (New York: New American Library, 2003), 596.

7. Athanasius of Alexandria, *On the Incarnation of the Word of God* (Willits, CA: Eastern Orthodox Books), 65.

8. Wendell Berry, "Healing," in *What Are People For?* (New York: North Point, 1990), 9–10.

9. Athanasius, *On the Incarnation,* 19 (see generally 19–23).

10. Ibid., 23.

11. Berry, "Healing," 10.

12. Berry, "Health as Membership," 86–87.

13. Wendell Berry, "An Entrance to the Woods," in *Recollected Essays: 1965– 1980* (1981; reprint, San Francisco: North Point, 1998), 240.

Part 1

Good Work

Stanley Hauerwas

What Would a Christian University Look Like?

Some Tentative Answers Inspired by Wendell Berry

The Challenge Before Us

"There are also violent and nonviolent ways to milk cows," I observed in a sermon on the occasion of the installation of Dr. Gerald Gerbrandt as president of the Canadian Mennonite University on September 28, 2003.[1] I made the comment to commend the parochial character of the Canadian Mennonite University. The Canadian Mennonite University, as its name suggests, is Mennonite and Canadian, and you cannot get more parochial than that. My comment about milking, therefore, was meant to praise why such a university would have no reason to distinguish between theoretical and practical forms of knowledge.

My sermon—and I think it important to observe that this is a university that assumes it is appropriate to have a sermon as part of its inaugural event for its first president—expressed my hope that the Canadian Mennonite University would not be just another "Christian liberal arts college." I think it is now clear that Christian liberal arts colleges have turned out to be more liberal than Christian. It is not my particular interest in this essay to try to understand why the Christian liberal arts college has failed to sustain itself as Christian; rather, I begin to explore what a Christian university might look like.[2]

To "begin to explore what a Christian university might look like" is, of course, a far too grand project. What I am really interested in is to try to spell out what difference there may be between violent and nonviolent ways to milk cows. The focus on milking cows might suggest I assume that university curricula should not be determined by presumptions about the necessity to sustain "high culture." I think it important, however, that universities teach Plato, Aquinas, Dante, and Darwin because I think one of the tasks of the university is to be a memory of a people. But too often Christian justifications of the university focused on the need to preserve the "classics" of Western civilization have created universities that serve class interests more than Christian purpose. Why and how Plato is read at the Canadian Mennonite University may be quite different than why and how Plato is read at Duke University.

I think, moreover, Wendell Berry's criticism of the university is very important to help us understand the difference between violent and nonviolent ways to milk cows. Berry is an unrelenting critic of the contemporary university. I am deeply sympathetic with his criticisms of the university as we know it, but his criticisms are so radical it is not unreasonable to conclude that he has no hope that the university can be reclaimed for humane—much less Christian—purposes. I hope to show that his work also suggests how we need to begin to live and, thus, think if we are to begin to imagine what a university shaped by Christian practices might look like.

I have, like Berry, often been a critic of the contemporary university. Of course, to be a critic of the university is to mark oneself as a university person. After all, universities are often associated with people who believe thinking means you are "critical." So, critics of the university often discover that their criticisms of the university are criticisms that only people trained at universities could produce. Therefore, our very critiques reproduce the practices that we critique. The truth of the matter is that, in America, it is very hard to sustain a life of study without being parasitic on the university. I am more than willing, therefore, to acknowledge that my criticisms of the university, I hope, reveal my profound love of the university.

I hope I am a Christian, but the university has been more my home than the church. I went to Southwestern University in Georgetown, Texas, in September 1962. As they say, "the rest is history" because, from that time to the present, I have always lived in a university. The only way I know to make a living is to be at a university. I did not necessarily set out to be a university person. My life just worked out that way. I was brought up to be a bricklayer—honest work. I have tried not to forget what it means to be in the trades, but, for better or worse, I am an academic.

After Southwestern, I spent six years at Yale Divinity School and Yale Graduate School, where I received the bachelor of divinity degree and my Ph.D. I taught two years at Augustana College in Rock Island, Illinois, and fourteen years at the University of Notre Dame, and I am now in my twenty-second year of teaching in the Divinity School at Duke. My life has been made possible by people who care about sustaining the university. I no doubt owe the university more than I know.

Yet the history recounted in the last paragraphs is not one characteristic of those who have sought to have an academic career. I have always served the university. Because I am a Christian, I have worked to allow myself to be used by, as well as to use, the university. I am a theologian. Theology is not generally considered a legitimate field in the university. Of course, that was not the official position at Augustana or Notre Dame. Lutherans and Catholics still thought and think that theology should matter, though how it matters is in dispute. Theology is tolerated at Duke because we are a divinity school, but the Divinity School is regarded by many at Duke as a "cultural lag." Theologians in the modern university bear the burden of proof, which turns out to be very good for theology because, if you are a theologian, you need to know what your colleagues in other disciplines know even though they do not have to know what you know.

Yet my identity as a theologian means I have always been in the university but not of it. Berry has been more out of the university than in the university. Berry, of course, would not be Berry without the university. He is a graduate of a university. He has a graduate degree. He has taught at the University of Kentucky and other universities from time to time. But he has clearly chosen to think and write outside the university. I may, therefore, have more of a stake in making the university work than Berry has. Nonetheless, I hope to show how he can help us begin to rethink what a university might look like in order to be of service to the church. Having said this, I should warn the reader that I may also be using Berry's work to sustain a project that Berry thinks hopeless.

Berry on the University

"Abstraction is the enemy *wherever* it is found."[3] If any sentence could sum up Berry's work and, in particular, his criticism of the modern university, it is this one. In order to appropriately appreciate his criticism of abstraction, however, it is wise, I think, to attend to his early but very important essay "Standing by Words." Berry is very careful not to reproduce dualisms that only create the problem he is trying to help us avoid. He is not, for example, advocating subjectivity as an alternative to objectivity, nor is he recommending the particular over the universal. Rather, he is trying to help us resist our tendency to speak nonsense.

Berry seldom betrays any knowledge of philosophy or philosophers. I suspect that, like many poets, he is suspicious of philosophers. But his understanding of language, the criticism of the abstractions that we are taught to speak at universities, cannot help but remind some of us of lessons we have learned from Wittgenstein. In "Standing by Words," Berry argues that the disintegration of communities and persons in our time is a correlative of the loss of accountability in our use of language. According to Berry, for any statement to be complete or comprehensible, three conditions are required:

1. It must designate its object precisely.
2. Its speaker must stand by it: must believe it, be accountable for it, be willing to act on it.
3. This relation of speaker, word, and object must be conventional; the community must know what it is.[4]

Berry suggests that these common assumptions are becoming uncommon through the development of specialization. As a result, language is increasingly seen as a weapon to gain power over others or as a medium of play. Some—even poets such as Shelley—think our task is to heighten the subjectivity of language in order to resist objectification. Yet, when that unhappy choice is accepted, only pathos can result, making language nothing more than a medium of self-pity.

It is extremely important to note that Berry is not denying the need for generalization. There is truth in T. S. Eliot's claim that "the particular has no language"—but there are, nonetheless, two forms of precision that allow the particular to be communicated.

The first is the precision in speech of people who share the same knowledge of place and history: "The old hollow beech blew down last night." Berry calls this *community speech,* which he praises because it is precise and open to ongoing testing against its objects. Such speech is the "very root and foundation of language."[5]

The second form of precision is that which "comes of tension either between a statement and a prepared context or, within a single statement, between more or less conflicting feelings, or ideas."[6] To illustrate this form of precision, Berry contrasts Shelley's complaint against our mortality, "I could lie down like a tired child," with Robert Herrick's, "Out of the world he must, who once comes in," observing that the latter satisfies our need for complexity and, thus, does justice to our actual experience.[7] Such precision is hardwon, requiring us to battle against our proclivities to engage in fantasies.

One form such fantasies take is the production of sentences that try to be objective by avoiding all personal biases and considerations. Berry thinks scientists often use such language. He gives the example of conversations transcribed during the Three Mile Island crisis as members of the Nuclear Regulatory Commission worked to "engineer a press release" to avoid frightening the public that a meltdown might happen. Thus, one commissioner suggests they say "in the unlikely event that this occurred temperatures would result and possible further fuel damage." Berry observes that what is remarkable and frightening about such language is the inability of those who so speak to acknowledge what it is they are talking about.[8]

The perversion of speech illustrated by attempts to be objective serves the political purpose of securing the power of those who use it without their being held accountable. They say such speech aims to bring people together for some common project. Accordingly, they try to create the illusion we all speak the same language: "[This means] either that they will agree with the government or be quiet, as in communist and fascist states, or that they will politely ignore their disagreements or disagree 'provisionally,' as in American universities. But the result—though power may survive for a while in spite of it—is confusion and dispersal. Real language, real discourse are destroyed. People lose understanding of each other, are divided and scattered. Speech of whatever kind begins to resemble the speech of drunkenness or madness."[9]

Berry offers another example of this passion for objectivity that, interestingly enough, has to do with cows. In an article entitled "The Evolution and Future of American Animal Agriculture," G. W. Salisbury and R. G. Hart argue for the importance of the transformation of American agriculture from an art to a science. Art, they suggest, is concerned only with the "hows," science with the "whys." Accordingly, they recommend that a cow be described as an "appropriate manufacturing unit of the twentieth century."[10] Berry notes that such language relieves those who use it of any accountability indicated by a farmer's statement: "Be good to the cow, for she is our companion."[11]

The latter sentence requires a world that is organized in the hierarchical sequence of nature, agriculture, community, family, person. Such a hierarchy is based on the assumption that these systems are interrelated and that whatever affects one will affect the other. The former sentence reverses this hierarchy so that it runs from industrial economy, to agriculture, to dairy, to dairyman. This latter hierarchy is meant to disintegrate the connecting disciplines, turning them into professions and professions into careers. Berry's subsequent criticism of the university can now be seen as the development of his concern that in the university we are taught to speak in a manner in which we are no longer able to "stand by our words." Thus my claim that the two questions you cannot ask in the modern university are, "What is the university for?" and "Who does it serve?" That the university has no "learned public" to serve—and a learned public might be one that milks cows—is at the heart of our problem.

Berry thinks the modern university is at least one of the institutions that should be held responsible for the corruption of our language. The university at once legitimates and reproduces the disintegration of the life of the mind and of communities through increasing specialization. According to Berry:

> The various specialties are moving ever outward from any center of interest or common ground, becoming ever farther apart, and ever more unintelligible to one another. Among the causes, I think, none is more prominent than the by now ubiquitous and nearly exclusive emphasis upon originality and innovation. The emphasis, operating within the "channels" of administration, affects in the most direct and practical ways all the lives within the university. It imposes the choice of work over life, exacting not only the personal costs spoken of in Yeats' poem ("The Choice"), but very substantial costs to the community as well.[12]

Specialization of the disciplines, however, is crucial if the university is to receive the support it needs from a capitalist society. If universities are to grow—and the assumption is that they must always grow—they will need money. But it is equally important that they accept the fundamental economic principle of the opposition of money to goods. Berry, who otherwise betrays no Marxist sympathies, seems to know in his bones that there is no abstraction more abstract than money. Not only is labor appropriated from the worker in the name of money, but the worker is also expected to use that money to buy goods that cannot be represented by money.

The incoherence of university curricula reflects the university's commitment to legitimate the abstraction effected by money. For example, it is crucial that the university ensure that learning be organized not as a conversation between disciplines but rather as a place where disciplines are representatives of competing opposites. As a result, accountability is lost. The sciences are sectioned off from one another so that they might serve their respective corporations: "The so-called humanities, which might have supplied at least a corrective or chastening remembrance of the good that humans have sometimes accomplished, have been dismembered into utter fecklessness, turning out 'communicators' who have nothing to say and 'educators' who have nothing to teach." Indeed, universities no longer are sources of literacy. Accordingly, the English department itself has become a specialty, and, even in those departments, writing has become a subspecialty of the freshman writing program. The result is the clear message that to write well is not necessary.[13]

Berry confesses he has no idea how the disciplines might be reorganized, but he is doubtful that anyone knows how to do that. However, he is convinced that the standards and goals of the disciplines need to be changed. He observes:

> It used to be that we thought of the disciplines as ways of being useful to ourselves, for we needed to earn a living, but also and more importantly we thought of them as ways of being useful to one another. As long as the idea of vocation was still viable among us, I don't believe it was ever understood that a person was "called" to be rich or powerful or even successful. People were taught the disciplines at home or in school for two reasons: to enable them to live and work both as self-sustaining individuals and as useful members of their communities, and to see that the disciplines themselves survived the passing of the generations.[14]

The incoherence of university curricula reflects the acceptance of the assumption that there is nothing odd about unlimited economic growth or consumption in a limited world. Education is now job preparation for a career in a profession.[15] But work, whether it is done in the academy, a profession, or industry, is now designed so that the workers are separated from the effects of their work. They are permitted "to think that they are working nowhere or anywhere—in their careers or specialties, perhaps, or in 'cyberspace.'"[16] The university, therefore, becomes a home for the homeless, those whom Wallace Stegner calls the "boomers."[17]

The dominance of science in the modern university reflects the captivity of universities to industrial societies. For the abstractions of science are readily assimilated to the abstractions of industry in which

> everything is interchangeable with or replaceable by something else. . . .
> One place is as good as another, one use is as good as another, one life is
> as good as another—if the price is right. This is the industrial doctrine
> of the interchangeability of parts, and we apply it to places, to creatures,
> and to our fellow humans as if it were the law of the world, using all the
> while a sort of middling language, imitated from the sciences, that can-
> not speak of heaven or earth, but only of concepts. This is the rhetoric
> of nowhere, which forbids a passionate interest in, let alone a love of,
> anything in particular.[18]

For Berry, the assumption that education is the solution to all our problems is a correlate to the increasing violence of what is taught. Berry thinks
the violence of education is, as we should suspect from his analysis in *Standing
by Words,* to be found in the destruction of language and community. He
observes: "Education has become increasingly useless as it has become increasingly public. Real education is determined by community needs, not by
public tests."[19]

This distinction between community and public may seem odd given the
assumption that the public names the goods of the community, but Berry
understands the term *public* to mean simply all people abstracted from any
personal responsibility or belonging. Thus, a public building is one that belongs to everyone, but no one in particular. A community, in contrast, "has
to do first of all with belonging": "It is a group of people who belong to one
another and to their place. We would say, 'We belong to our community,' but
never 'We belong to our public.'"[20]

Berry does not deny that under certain circumstances the public and the
community might be compatible, but within the economic and technological
monoculture in which we live they cannot help but be at odds. A community
is centered on the household, which means it is always concerned with a place
and time. The public, when it is rightly formed, is concerned about justice and
is centered on the individual. The problem we confront is that the emphasis on
individual liberty has made the freedom of the community impossible.
Paradoxically, as a result, the more the emphasis has been on individual freedom, the less liberty and power have been available to most individuals.[21]

In the novel *Hannah Coulter,* Berry describes the effects of the university
on Caleb Coulter, the son of Hannah and Nathan. Hannah and Nathan are

hardworking farmers who have managed to create a life from an unforgiving ground. Caleb was the last born of their three children, all of whom went to college. Hannah observes that you send your children to college in order to do the best for them, but neither do you want to burden them with your expectations. She confesses that you hope they will go away and study and learn and then come back and you will have them for a neighbor. However, she observes, while their children were at the university, there always "came a time when we would feel the distance opening to them, pulling them away. It was like sitting snug in the house, and a door is opened somewhere, and suddenly you feel a draft."[22]

Caleb even became Dr. Coulter, a professor who taught agriculture to fewer students who were actually going to farm. Hannah describes him this way:

> He became an expert with a laboratory and experimental plots, a man of reputation. But as I know, and as he knows in his own heart and thoughts, Caleb is incomplete. He didn't love farming enough to be a farmer, much as he loved it, but he loved it too much to be entirely happy doing anything else. He is disappointed in himself. . . . Caleb is well respected, and I am glad of that. He brings me what he calls his "publications," written in the Unknown Tongue. He wants me to be proud of them. And I am, but with the sadness of wishing I could be prouder. I read all of his publications that he brings me, and I have to say that they don't make me happy. I can't hear Caleb talking in them. And they speak of everything according to its general classification. Reading them always makes me think of this farm and how it emerged, out of "agriculture" and its "soil types" and its collection of "species," as itself, our place, a place like no other, yielding to Nathan and me a life like no other.[23]

The novel *Hannah Coulter* expresses Berry's deepest worry about the contemporary university: what an education does to people. It is a mistake to accuse him of being antitechnological or against all forms of specialization. His problem with technology and specialization is that they tend to become ends in themselves, producing people with no ends. As he puts it in the essay "Health as Membership": "[I am not] 'against technology' so much as I am for community. When the choice is between the health of a community and technological innovation, I choose the health of the community."[24] Technology, particularly in industrial economies, too easily becomes abstracted from the purposes that it was to serve.

Nor is Berry against science. Science has a proper place in relation to the other disciplines, particularly when all the disciplines are equally regarded and given equal time to talk no matter what the market may be in jobs or intellectual property. Indeed, it is the task of the university to foster such a conversation between disciplines so that our whole humanity may be embodied in and by the university. So Berry thinks the university has an appropriate task, but he is simply doubtful that any university presently in existence is committed to accomplishing that task.[25]

That task, moreover, requires that "a system" exist that secures the conviction that the truth can be known, but never all truth. Such a conviction Berry calls *religious* to indicate that the world in which we find ourselves is a mystery making possible accountable speech and behavior. For I hope it is now clear that Berry's criticisms of the university are but an extension of his concern that we hold one another accountable for what we say. From his perspective, the university has become the source of abstract speech that is no longer accountable to any community of purpose. Berry does not claim that the fate of the modern university is the result of the loss of mystery, but he is sure that all "answers" put forward in the university

> must be worked out within a limit of humility and restraint, so that the initiative to act would always imply a knowing acceptance of accountability for the results. The establishment and maintenance of this limit seems to me the ultimate empirical problem—the real "frontier" of science, or at least of the definition of the possibility of a *moral* science. It would place science under the rule of the old concern for propriety, correct proportion, proper scale—from which, in modern times, even the arts have been "liberated." That is, it would return to all work, artistic or scientific, the possibility of an external standard or quality.[26]

His criticisms of the university are clearer than the alternative Berry offers. That is probably the way it should be. Who knows what a Berry-inspired university might look like? It may well sound too artsy, but Berry, I think, would want the center of a university to be the practice of poetry. For only through poetry—speech tied closely to community, place, and time—can we avoid the abstractions that have become our way of life.

Berry reports that he was raised by agrarians but that he did not know he was an agrarian until he was a sophomore in college. He seems to think it a good thing he was taught he was an agrarian. Indeed, he seems to indicate that learning he was an agrarian was a poetic development. Learning he was an agrarian meant he was able to distinguish between industrialism, which is based on monetary capital, and agrarianism, which is based on land. Moreover, it was partly his education that made it possible for him to trace the lineage of agrarian thought through Virgil, Spenser, Shakespeare, and Pope. According to Berry, it is from poets like these you learn you should not work until you have looked and seen where you are in a manner that honors nature not only as your grandmother but as your teacher and judge as well.[27]

As critical as Berry is of the university as we know it—and certainly any of us who live in the university recognize the university exists that he criticizes—he still remains a lover of the university. After all, it was in a university that he learned to read Virgil, Spenser, Shakespeare, Pope, and Jefferson. Yet he seems to hold out little hope that the kind of university he would like to exist could be a reality. No doubt, he assumes that his university might exist in pockets of any university but that such an existence depends on people existing who defy the abstractions that are so tempting. It would be silly to suggest that the church might offer the possibility of making a Berry-like university a reality, but I at least want to explore how we might imagine that possibility.

Why Berry Needs a Church

Christians are a people who worship the God of the Jews. We are a people who worship Jesus, the Messiah, and the Incarnation of the Word of God. The God we worship is flesh, such that our cardinal action is to eat and drink the body and blood of Christ. The God we worship is, therefore, known only through a story as concrete as "The old hollow beech blew down last night." We learn about the old hollow beech by being told by another it was blown down. In similar fashion, we know about Jesus by being told by another. Witness is constitutive of the character of what Christians believe. For the Christian witness to be truthful requires that Christians distrust all abstractions not disciplined by the Word that is Christ.

However, well before the development of the kind of abstraction Berry finds so destructive, Christians developed their own form of abstraction. Jesus commanded his disciples: "Go therefore and make disciples of all nations, baptizing them in the name of the Father and of the Son and of the Holy Spirit, and teaching them to obey everything that I have commanded you" (Matt. 28:19–20). Jesus' command to be a witness to the nations, a task that should force Christians to recognize as well as criticize the infinite and unending forms of abstraction, has also tempted Christians to confuse the pretentious universalism of *the nation* with the Gospel.

The politics of Christian abstraction has taken many different forms. But at least one name for such a politics is *Constantinianism.* Constantinianism is the attempt by the church to use the power of the state (and *the state* is an abstraction) to impose the Gospel on others without the vulnerability of witness. Because the church is obligated to be a witness to all nations, it has sometimes confused the universalism of the speech of empire, speech that by necessity is shaped by abstraction, with the concreteness of the Gospel.

Christians, particularly in modernity, have forgotten that our name for universal is *catholic* and that the office that enacts the catholic character of the church is called *bishop.* The task of the bishop is to ensure that the stories that make a church the church are shared by other churches across time and space. Therefore, our speech is tested by how other Christians have learned to speak to one another as well as to those who do not speak as we speak. Theologians are servants to the bishop charged with the task of maintaining the memory of the church so that the church may be one. Theologians are, therefore, "answerable to a specific locality or very often multiple specific localities, such that [their] sense of perpetuating a history must be combined with [their] sense of carrying out an archaeology and mapping a geography."[28]

If Christians are to support the development of a Berry-like university, we will need to be freed of our Constantinian pretensions. That freedom, moreover, will come only by the intensification of the catholic character of the church. For the abstractions that bewitch our speech as Christians can be located and resisted only by word care made possible by being challenged by our brothers and sisters across time and place. As John Howard Yoder has observed, the alternative to the confusion of paganism and Christianity so often the result of Constantinianism is "the concreteness of the visible community created by the renewed message. The alternative to hierarchical definition is local definition."[29]

Modern universities, whether Christian or secular, have been servants of the emerging nation-state system. That nation-state system, moreover, has been the enemy of locality. Local communities are not and cannot be efficient given the need to organize "populations."[30] The abstractions Berry identifies as the enemy are those necessary to legitimate the public organizations that claim to serve our interests. The very language of "interest," of course, is but an exemplification of the kind of abstraction he deplores.

Berry's appeal to a religious sense of mystery for maintaining some sense of the whole is important, but a sense of mystery cannot be sustained in the absence of a community in which the mystery is materially enacted. A university able to resist the mystifications legitimated by the abstractions of our social order will depend on a people shaped by fundamental practices necessary for truthful speech. In short, without a church capable of demythologizing the false idealism that possesses our imaginations, there is no possibility that a university capable of educating a Caleb Coulter who might return home can actually exist.

These are, of course, highly theoretical remarks. Do they have any implications for what a church-based university might look like? Some are beginning to try to imagine what such a university might entail. For example, many of the essays in the collection *Conflicting Allegiances: The Church-Based University in a Liberal Democratic Society* are not content to explore how the contemporary university might be reformed to be more responsive to Christian practice. As Michael Budde puts it: "The purpose of ecclesially based higher education is to make participants more fully into disciples shaped by the priorities and practices of Jesus Christ; to help them discern their vocation as members of the transnational body of Christ; and to contribute to the mission of the church—to help the church serve more fully and faithfully as a foretaste of the promised kingdom of God, on earth as in heaven."[31]

Budde observes that this is a difficult task because our imaginations are possessed by what we assume are normative assumptions about higher education. So, for example, the very language of *higher* may be misleading just to the extent it presumes that knowing how to milk is not a "higher" knowledge. Budde, however, would readily agree that the use of *higher* to distinguish university subjects from the knowledge represented by the act of milking is part of the problem. Accordingly, many of the essays in *Conflicting Allegiances* challenge the (dis)organization of knowledges characteristic of the contemporary university. For example, Therese Lysaught asks what form the life sciences might take if they were organized on the principle that Christians are obligated to love our enemy, even the enemy called *death*.[32]

The problem is not whether we lack the imagination to begin to think what a university shaped by Christian practice might look like but rather whether a church exists that can provide the material conditions that might make such an alternative university possible. By *material conditions* I mean not just money but also whether churches are constituted by the practices, that is, by habits nurtured by worship, that require the development of knowledges that can challenge the abstractions that are legitimated in and by the current university. Have Christians learned to milk nonviolently? So, oddly enough, we will not know how to think about the character of the university without thinking about the character of the church.

But we cannot wait. Many of us, as I suggest above concerning my own life, continue to teach in universities that exemplify the pathologies Berry describes. Should Christians continue to teach in universities, including those often identified as "church-related," in which students are shaped by abstractions that serve quite a different reality than that of the church? Do Christian academics, in spite of their criticisms of the university, legitimate those universities by their very presence?

Any attempt to justify Christian participation in the university as we know it is an invitation to self-deception. Yet, in his 2004 Oxford University Commemoration Day sermon, Rowan Williams provides some helpful reminders that can point us in a constructive direction. Williams observes that Oxford began as a cell of the Catholic Church for the study of canon law, but, by the fourteenth and fifteenth centuries, its survival depended on forming people who would govern the kingdom. He notes that this will confirm the worst fears of some who assume that Oxford is primarily an institution committed to serving the elite. Yet he points out that it was assumed "that to govern a kingdom you needed to know how language worked, what the difference was between good and bad arguments, and how you might persuade people to morally defensible action."[33] Accordingly, you needed tools of thought that were organized in a hierarchy of learning.

Williams acknowledges that much has changed at Oxford. An abstract understanding of rationality has displaced what many now consider the authoritarian character of the medieval university. Yet Williams argues that, to the extent the university maintains a commitment to disciplined argument, there remains a sense of the capacity to respond with justice and accuracy to the inner structure of creation, thus testifying to the divine image constitutive of each of us. He therefore thinks he is justified to "insist upon the university's role in nourishing honest and hopeful speech, for the sake of a properly reasonable culture and politics." He therefore concludes that what the church has to say to the university is:

> Don't be afraid of assuming that your task is to equip people to take authority. In a democratic age, this is not the authority of a royal counselor or imperial proconsul; it is the authority of the literate and educated person to contribute to the public reason. And don't be afraid in encouraging in whatever way is available the calling both to scientific research and to public service, administration and politics and social care; law and medicine, those ancient and persistent elements in the pattern of public life; the service, in one calling or another of the Body of Christ. Avoid the false polarization between disinterested research and the world of target setting and assessment; remember that all properly intellectual work can be a form of witness to public values.[34]

I have no idea whether Berry would find Williams's understanding of the task of the university compatible with his understanding of what universities ought to be about. However, I suspect he might find congenial Williams's suggestion that the university's task is to train literate people capable of recognizing the difference between a good argument and a bad argument. No doubt, the study of poetry helps the development of such a skill, but so can the study of a science. I am sure, moreover, that at every university poets and scientists exist who are committed to such a task. What remains unclear is whether a people exist who care whether such poets or scientists exist. At the very least, Christians are obligated to care because we believe we have been given the great privilege to stand by the Word.

"To stand by the Word," moreover, might help us maintain the connection between those who labor within the university and those who labor outside it. Fritz Oehlschlaeger, in a letter responding to my essay "Theological Knowledge and the Knowledges of the University," observes that, even at its most strenuous, intellectual work is not as difficult as physical labor. How, then, he asks, can we ever justify those like ourselves who think the work we do in the university is important? Oehlschlaeger, who teaches in the English Department at Virginia Tech, responds to this question by observing:

It seems to me this requires active memory and recognition by the intellectual of the labor that sustains his/her ability to pursue knowledge. The best way to ensure this is for the intellectual to come into the presence of others, to make offering with them of their labor, and to receive the truly priceless food provided by the One whose love can only be understood as pure gift. Thus we learn that utility in meeting needs can never be a sufficient standard, as we cannot produce the very thing we need most. And the Eucharist perhaps also disciplines the intellectual to recognize his bonds to those whose labors make his work possible—so that any pursuit of knowledge for its own sake carries also the memory of the labor that sustains it. Intellectuals formed within a community nourished by the milk of Jesus seem much more likely to think of what they do as requiring a community to receive it. . . . Maybe there's a role, then, for Christian intellectuals who might mediate among the disciplines and between disciplines and public in ways that would not occur to the market-driven knowledge-producers on today's faculties.[35]

"Maybe there's a role" is, I hope, hopeful speech.

Notes

This essay first appeared in Stanley Hauerwas, *The State of the University: Academic Knowledges and the Knowledge of God* (Oxford: Blackwell, 2007).

1. The sermon, entitled "On Milk and Jesus," can be found in my *Disrupting Time: Sermons, Prayers, and Sundries* (Eugene, OR: Cascade, 2004), 142–48.

2. For my analysis of some of the developments surrounding the relation of the church and the university, see my "How Risky Is the Risk of Higher Education? Random Reflections from the American Context," *Communio* 30, no. 1 (Spring 2003): 79–94, and "Pro Ecclesia, Pro Texana: Schooling the Heart in the Heart of Texas," in *The Schooled Heart: Moral Formation and American Higher Education*, ed. Michael D. Beaty and Douglas V. Henry (Waco, TX: Baylor University Press, 2007).

3. Wendell Berry, "Out of Your Car, Off Your Horse," in *Sex, Economy, Freedom, and Community: Eight Essays* (New York: Pantheon, 1992), 23.

4. Wendell Berry, "Standing by Words," in *Standing by Words* (Washington, DC: Shoemaker & Hoard, 1983), 25.

5. Ibid., 33.

6. Ibid., 34.

7. Ibid., 35.

8. Ibid., 38.

9. Ibid., 40.

10. G. W. Salisbury and R. G. Hart, "The Evolution and Future of American Animal Agriculture," *Perspectives in Biology and Medicine* 22 (1979): 394–409.

11. Ibid., 43–44.

12. Wendell Berry, *Life Is a Miracle: An Essay against Modern Superstition* (Washington, DC: Counterpoint, 2000), 61. Yeats's poem (quoted in ibid., 56) reads:

The intellect of man is forced to choose
Perfection of the life, or of the work,
And if it take the second must refuse
A heavenly mansion, raging in the dark.
When all that story's finished, what's the news?
In luck or out the toil has left its mark:
The old perplexity an empty purse,
Or the day's vanity, the night's remorse.

13. Ibid., 123 (quote), 68.

14. Ibid., 130.

15. Wendell Berry, "Conserving Communities," in *Another Turn of the Crank* (Washington, DC: Counterpoint, 1995), 13–14.

16. Wendell Berry, "Going to Work," in *Citizenship Papers* (Washington, DC: Shoemaker & Hoard, 2003), 33.

17. Stegner cited in Wendell Berry, "The Conservation of Nature and the Preservation of Humanity," in *Another Turn of the Crank*, 82. Berry reports boomers are people "who expect or demand that the world conform to their desires. They either succeed and thus damage the world, or they fail and thus damage their family and themselves" (ibid.).

18. Berry, *Life Is a Miracle*, 41–42. Berry's characterization of science unfortunately too often is accurate, but science can be one of the most exciting disciplines through which to see the beauty of the particulars.

19. Wendell Berry, "Sex, Economy, Freedom, and Community," in *Sex, Economy, Freedom, and Community*, 123.

20. Ibid., 147–48.

21. Ibid., 147–55.

22. Wendell Berry, *Hannah Coulter* (Washington, DC: Shoemaker & Hoard, 2004), 120.

23. Ibid., 131–32.

24. Wendell Berry, "Health as Membership," in *Another Turn of the Crank*, 90.

25. Wendell Berry, "Is Life a Miracle?" in *Citizenship Papers*, 189.

26. Berry, "Standing by Words," 49–50.

27. Wendell Berry, "The Whole Horse," in *Citizenship Papers*, 118–19.

28. John Milbank, "The Last of the Last: Theology in the Church," in *Conflicting Allegiances: The Church-Based University in a Liberal Democratic Society,* ed. Michael Budde and John Wright (Grand Rapids, MI: Brazos, 2004), 250.

29. John Howard Yoder, "The Disavowal of Constantine: An Alternative Perspective on Interfaith Dialogue," in *The Royal Priesthood: Essays Ecclesiological and Ecumenical,* ed. Michael Cartwright (Grand Rapids, MI: Eerdmans, 1994), 253.

30. For my analysis of the significance of the creation of the nation of "populations," see my "The Christian Difference; or, Surviving Postmodernism," in *A Better Hope: Resources for a Church Confronting Capitalism, Democracy, and Postmodernity* (Grand Rapids, MI: Brazos, 2000), 35–46.

31. Michael Budde, "Assessing What Doesn't Exist: Reflections on the Impact of an Ecclesially Based University," in *Conflicting Allegiances,* 256.

32. Therese Lysaught, "Love Your Enemies: The Life Sciences in the Ecclesially Based University," in ibid., 109–27.

33. Rowan Williams, "Oxford University Commemoration Day Sermon, University Church of St. Mary the Virgin, Oxford" (sermon delivered June 20, 2004), available at http://www.archbishopofcanterbury.org1205?q=%22your+task+is+to+equip+people+to+take+authority%22.

34. Ibid.

35. Fritz Oehlschlaeger to the author, September 21, 2004. Oehlschlaeger has begun the difficult task of thinking what a Christian reading of literature might mean. See Fritz Oehlschlaeger, *Love and Good Reasons: Postliberal Approaches to Christian Ethics and Literature* (Durham, NC: Duke University Press, 2003). See also my "Theological Knowledge and the Knowledges of the University: Beginning Explorations," in *The State of the University: Academic Knowledges and the Knowledge of God* (Oxford: Blackwell, 2007).

Brian Volck

Mr. Berry Goes to Medical School
Notes toward Unspecializing a Healing Art

In a literature and medicine elective I help teach, fourth-year medical students read fiction, memoirs, essays, and plays more or less about health, disease, physicians, and patients. Our purpose is not to teach literary theory but to connect these works with the lives of our doctors in training. Most attempts are encouraging; some less so. From the beginning, we've read works by Wendell Berry. They are not well received.

One student, a budding surgeon, dismissed Berry's "Health Is Membership" as the "most revolting thing I've ever been forced to read." Others were troubled with Berry's attention to—as they saw it—*trivial* details of hospital experience, such as poor food and bad sleeping conditions. The strongest objections, however, focused on his criticism that, in emphasizing technological solutions derived from fallible and frequently misapplied science, medicine destroys human connections between patients, communities, and the land. "Who does this Kentucky farmer think he is, telling me how to be a doctor?" said one student, who would soon be an internist. To Berry's claim that "medicine is an exact science until applied,"[1] one doc, training in emergency care, countered: "Medicine *is* an exact science, and it's getting more exact all the time!" A second-generation immigrant, destined for psychiatry, went further, pounding her fist on the table as she declared: "The reason American medicine's the best in the world is capitalism!" She did not elaborate, nor did I ask by what criteria she assessed America's medical superiority, though I might have referenced many public health measures, such as infant mortality, teen pregnancy, and health care access, in which the U.S. world ranking is absolutely shameful.

Still, I was grateful our students were responding to the essay, if not necessarily as I would have liked. I also learned that challenging ideas are better received in story form than as direct statement, which may account for the enduring power of parables. While there were complaints about medically "unrealistic" descriptions in "Fidelity," a story in which family members rescue the dying Burley Coulter from a Louisville hospital so that he may die with his people in his own country, the narrative spawned less protest than the essay. Yet it was clear that students about to begin the long, often grueling years of residency training are poorly disposed toward criticism of the profession, even if medical practice has precious little to profess these days.

Occasionally, I'm heartened by a student who takes a real liking to Berry's work. One recalled his own days on a Kentucky farm and how he relished walking the woods in peace after a frenetic week in the hospital. I've even found residents reading Berry on their own, though they tend to be an odd sort in this business. After all, they're reading something other than online medical references and journal articles, and a resident's schedule rarely permits leisure reading. Some come from small towns or farms; most find Berry attractive because he offers an alternative voice to that of the mainstream medical industry. Not that they buy all of Berry's critique, however. I spoke with one young doctor while on a medical trip to Honduras, and he said: "Yeah, I really like what he has to say. Except that short story about stealing the guy from the hospital. That was just wild."

Autonomy

Is Mr. Berry too wild for medical school? There is, in fact, very little about medical education or practice in the United States to suggest that health has anything to do with membership or community. Families visiting my university-affiliated office come from an array of economic and ethnic backgrounds. Most of my patients can't afford private medical insurance. Some travel many miles to be seen and wait for their appointment in a lobby full of strangers. At best, my patients and I weave in and out of each other's lives. Our embodied interactions are less communal encounters than isolated vignettes, scenes within larger, unrelated dramas.

So it's a personal experience of absent community—a wholeness ruptured by the North American obsession with individual health—that I bring to the classroom when we read Wendell Berry. On a busy afternoon, for example, after saying good-bye to a mother who brought her healthy newborn in for a first visit, I walk down the hall and grab the next chart: a fifteen-year-old male, here for a sports physical. Entering, I find he's alone, staring at me from his seat atop the exam table, arms crossed, looking annoyed. He's more wiry than muscular, with a heavy dose of mistrust and insecurity in his stony glare. I take a seat, start asking questions. His answers are telegraphically brief: no problems, school's boring, basketball this winter. To stay in playing form, he avoids tobacco but doesn't refuse marijuana, preferring it to alcohol. We talk about this; I give him the facts as I know them, along with pointed advice I both hope and doubt that he'll take. He's learned much from the economy, from movies, television, and music. I ask him to talk with his parents, but he says that his mother has her own troubles and he hasn't seen his father in months. Teachers and counselors aren't his crowd. He's experienced, used to making his own decisions.

I ask, "When's the last time you had sex?" He glares and spits out a line he's probably been rehearsing since his arrival: "I was supposed to get some this afternoon, and you're keeping me from it." I figure he's showing off, though I don't doubt he's seen far more than I did at his age. My job, according to experts in my field, is to suggest other ways of behaving (knowing full well that he has little incentive to change) and provide him with technologies to reduce the harm he causes himself and others. We talk safe sex, protection, and birth control. It's old news to him. He knows where to get condoms, shows no interest in contraception. I don't mention how rarely a teen mother in my practice seeks child support from the baby's father. I ask instead what he wants from life, which turns out to be an NBA career, lots of consumer electronics, and a great deal of autonomy. His eyes tell me I'm pressing too hard. He sees no need for advice or life counseling. I'm here as his pediatric specialist, period. He wants what he came for. At the end of the visit, I sign his sports form—he is, after all, physically able to play—and urge him to make an appointment so we can discuss these things over again. If he returns, I'll be shocked.

I step into the hallway, where the office social worker has been waiting for me. The functionally illiterate mother I referred to her last month has failed again to bring her child in for an appointment with me. The social worker asks how hard we should press to locate her, reminding me we don't have a working telephone number for this family. Perhaps they've moved. We simply don't know. What we do know is that County Child Protective Services is stretched too thin to assist in cases like this, with no evidence of abuse or significant medical neglect. A family simply needs help, and I don't know where to find that. Now I don't even know where in this medium-sized city to find the family. At such times, I remember my wife's comment during her course work in public health: "Why did I waste my time becoming a doctor when the real health problems have nothing to do with stuff learned in medical school?" I hope this mother and her child are OK, that some neighbor looks in on them, takes care of them. I hope, but I've seen too much of life in the city to count on it.

I return to the doctor's charting room, where one of my colleagues mentions another of my patients, a sixteen-year-old girl named Crys, whom he saw in follow-up yesterday, when I was out of the office. I've never met Crys's father. Her grandmother used to bring her in when she was younger, but Crys resented her grandmother's "nosiness." Now she comes alone. If it's something serious, she brings her mother. I've spent much time with Crys, investigating her many physical complaints, and reinforcing the importance of "good choices," a consumer phrase she's comfortable with. Sex holds little mystery for her. Sex, apparently, is something the men in her life expect from her, even if she gives no hint of enjoying it, so we focus on protection and birth control. We've talked over a number of methods, and she's tried several, with lots of encouragement and scheduled follow-up visits. There is no knowledge deficit with Crys; she knows more about contraception in her midteens than I did entering medical school. The news from my colleague is that he's made an appointment for her with the teen pregnancy clinic. She might keep this baby. Of course, that's what the girl told me a year ago, just before her first abortion. I remember taking a long time then with her and her mother, asking about community supports—extended family, friends, adoption agencies, church. They listened to what I said and kindly told me that none of these fit their needs.

I suspect I'm sounding prudish right now, another amateur moralist muttering about social chaos and sexual licentiousness. But a baby doctor can't help but notice how much sexual behavior says about the health of a community. I'm not so naive as to imagine that teen sexual abstinence has been a historical norm. Long before Montagues and Capulets just said no, long before the word *adolescent* came into use, and long, long before this particular consumer demographic was scientifically mapped for maximal corporate exploitation, teenagers have been, to use the fashionable term, sexually active.

What troubles me, however, is the way in which the experience of sex is now shaped by consumer expectations—a technologically modified activity divorced from sustained concern for people or place.

Adolescents didn't make this up; they learned it from parents who, with the aid of specialized knowledge and technology, converted the household from a place of production situated within a community to an autonomous zone of consumption. When I ask young children where their food comes from, very few know that farmland precedes the grocery store. Most of my patients can tell me more about singers and sports stars than about their next-door neighbors. Mothers kiss their children on the steps of the day-care center, hoping they'll be well looked after while Mommy's at school or work. Fathers—the few involved in their children's lives at all—are similarly caught in a brutal economy of getting and spending. But when, amid this frantic, autonomous using up of manufactured products and contrived experiences, do children find the time to ponder the mystery of their own lives or cultivate affection for the things of this world? How does anyone learn to love? It comes as no surprise, then, that whatever goes on behind closed doors between not quite adults just learning the obscure and complex power relations complicating every process of consent should be understood as nobody else's business. It also comes as no surprise that marginalized families, like the illiterate mother and her baby, vanish in an economy more concerned with exchange value than with the value of other lives. I fear too many think that love, like sex, comes naturally, as if a practice so complex demanded anything less than a people's sustained effort. Like other worthwhile human practices—peace or health, for example—love is hard work. To thrive, it has to be given far more than a chance. An impoverished attitude toward the social dimension of sex is just one sign of the division of health from community.

My patients generally buy the heavily advertised American dogma of autonomy. So do their parents, seeing autonomy as central to health, with the corresponding fear that incapacity and age inevitably turn each of us into "a burden." That we might already burden the world with our heedless consumption or burden our neighbors with our unlimited material demands is never explored.

Where, then, would community and membership fit in this understanding of health as functional autonomy? I'm still looking. North Americans generally bristle at all but voluntary, provisional, self-determined membership. I've heard specialists in adolescent care talk about encouraging a desire for intimacy in their patients as an antidote to casual hooking up. I'm not clear what *intimacy* might mean to some of my patients. Judging from the noxious spam clogging my email account, it has less to do with affection than with pharmacologically enhanced penis size.

An endlessly famished craving for autonomy leaves my patients disconnected from one another, increasingly defenseless against the scientifically calibrated power of advertising and the demands of a rapacious economy. The unstated price of our autonomy is an estranging solitude, a loneliness hidden even from ourselves by the diverting entertainments of iPods, video games, and cyberporn. This is the realization that I bring along when reading Wendell Berry. That's why, I suppose, I sit up and pay attention when he writes in an aphoristic essay on, of all things, the specialization of poetry: "To be autonomous . . . is to be 'broken off' and separate."[2] For Berry, the state of our literature reflects the state of our land, our economy, our neighborhoods, and our bodily health.

Specialization

Berry's interest in "unspecializing" is not limited to poetry or medicine. Specialization is a hallmark of technology-dependent economies: complex mechanisms require specialized knowledge with which to manage successes and, even more important, failures. Technology and specialized knowledge promise control over certain aspects of my world, such as the rapidity with which I write and communicate or the relative ease with which I probe my patient's bodies, using precise and increasingly expensive medical testing. At the same time, I'm vulnerable to sudden equipment failures beyond my ability to understand, much less repair. Unlike Berry, I write with a computer. If things go wrong, I fiddle with settings, reboot, or call a technical service number. Beyond that, I'm helpless. I could study the software loaded into the complex circuitry hidden by my screen, but the digital clock warns me that time is short; I have more pressing things to do. Similarly, the computer specialist bringing her children to my pediatric office is, no doubt, quite capable of understanding the diagnostic and therapeutic rubrics I use were she to carve time from her already overscheduled day to study them. She will, however, likely rely on my specialized learning to make a plan. Each has what the other wants, and we're willing to pay for the service. Technology and specialization take away power and control even as they give.

I am a pediatrician, specializing in the medical care of children. I considered a host of pediatric subgenres before accepting that I was and would remain a generalist among "baby doctors." My students are also well on their way to specializing, choosing fields within which many will later subspecialize. It makes sense within the complex medical system to narrow one's focus, mastering the powerful tools of a single, well-defined discipline. The best subspecialists remain keenly interested in general care, but professional, intellectual, and economic pressures drive all but a very few to limit their practice. The effect on the imagination is rather like the story of the elephant and the blind men, each of whom understood the elephant to be that part of the animal they had touched and, in a fashion, comprehended: the tusk, the trunk, the flank, the tail. As the joke goes, a nephrologist sees the heart as a pump supplying the kidneys with blood. Having dismembered the body into its component systems, it's but a simple step to envision it as a machine assembled from smaller, systemic modules. In this view, the heart is not just like a pump; it is one. Indeed, it can be replaced by a machine pump, though not for long and only at an astonishing cost. Likewise, kidneys are conceptually transformed into enormously complex filters, the eye a camera, and the brain a meat computer. Yet, as the Kentucky farmer reminds the body's technicians: "The body is in most ways not at all like a machine. Like all living creatures and unlike a machine, the body is not formally self-contained; its boundaries and outlines are not so exactly fixed. The body alone is not, properly speaking, a body. Divided from its sources of air, food, drink, clothing, shelter and companionship, a body is, properly speaking, a cadaver, whereas a machine by itself, shut down or out of fuel, is still a machine."[3]

The paradox of specialized medicine, then, is that enormous power is gained from understanding the complexities of the body in increasing isolation while the social body withers as the communal context of health is stripped away and ignored. The person assuming the role of patient (from the Latin *patiens*, "to suffer") is measured, medicated, and, in a fashion, nourished in isolation from the land that produces the food we eat. Not surprisingly, such isolation and misplaced confidence in technology disturb the totality of human experience, including our language. Specialized technique requires useful vocabulary: words producing desired effects. Doctors are, after all, highly trained professionals. But what my patients and their parents often want, in addition to expertise, is usable information in understandable language in order to make informed decisions about care. Highly specialized information is translated into laymen's terms—how vocabulary reveals our pretensions!—while words springing from whole continents of human experience are banished from the medical encounter: *love, friendship, mercy.* Clumsy attempts to reintroduce words like *intimacy* quickly go astray. Intimacy, like love or friendship, can be a starting place, a journey, and a destination (concepts rendered meaningless without a particular place in the created world to stand on), but it is none of these things when grafted onto a purely instrumental activity. As for *mercy,* I've heard the word used in a medical context but once: in that appalling oxymoron *mercy killing,* an unscientific term now sanitized for public use as *physician-assisted suicide.*

What the Kentucky Farmer Knew (and I Had to Learn)

Unlike our medical students, I came to Berry's work after several years in the profession, already mystified by medicine's absurdities. Berry made explicit what I, at best, half understood, revealing the mischief arising when technology-dependent, specialized medicine separates bodies from their properly communal context. Of course, Berry isn't the only one to find something amiss in modern medicine, though others often misdiagnose the problem. The contemporary emphasis on individualized health assumes that patient isolation is a side effect best treated homeopathically, using increments of the existing malady. The wounds created by illusions of autonomy are patched over with new choices for the autonomous medical consumer: LASIK, open-sided MRI, doctor-approved complementary medicine, and birthing rooms remodeled to resemble suburban boudoirs.

Yet this banquet of choice is typically available only to a fortunate few living in technology-rich Northern countries. The way in which specialized, technology-dependent medicine obscures and destroys embodied connection is clearer in the so-called developing world. There is an implicit assumption in our terminology that *developed* is superior to *developing,* which may be true in some respects. I'm pleased that my doctor has all the medicine and equipment she needs to care for me, and one should avoid unnecessarily privileging the primitive. But the implied trajectory of what is called *development* assumes that Northern countries are models, goals toward which the rest of the world should aim. At the same time, such terminology hides the real toll that technology and development take on the lives of those not directly benefiting from them.

I travel yearly to Honduras, where the organization I work with has a permanent clinic, staffed by Honduran physicians and dentists. Every project is decided on, planned, and carried out as a community, a cooperative effort of local Hondurans and visiting North Americans. When I'm there, I'm simply a doctor, not a specialist. No one asks at what age patients must be referred elsewhere; I provide medical care for all comers.

Nor can I limit my attention to things I learned in medical school. On a recent trip, I assisted with patient care while another university team began the complex task of establishing a new clinic in a mountain village. The building we met in had a wood stove and a few electric lights but no running water. We joined the villagers in line to use the town pump, stewarding every drop for our drinking, cooking, and bathing. Yet to the side of the town square was, of all things, an Internet café. After long hours treating intestinal parasites, bandaging machete wounds, or delivering babies by flashlight, we paid a few lempiras and left behind the distressing confines of material reality. Perhaps the Internet had delivered on its promise: we were instantly in touch with the world. Yet that was—and has always been—a con, an illusion. For all the excitement of e-mailing loved ones, there was, in fact, no one to touch, nothing present to us save a plastic box, a glowing screen.

Late one afternoon, a group of us visited a *pulperia* and bought choco-bananas: chilled, chocolate-covered fruit sold on a stick for less than a quarter. Kevin, one of the residents, struck up a conversation outside the shop with a woman holding a rather thin-looking infant. He learned that the baby was the woman's nephew, the mother of whom had died soon after the baby's birth. The father, we were told, was unreliable and rarely around, so the baby's aunt had taken the infant in. She had no money for formula and lived several hours' walk from town. They were very poor; reliable food and water were hard to come by. Kevin borrowed my equipment and examined the baby. He had an ear infection, was mildly dehydrated, and almost certainly had parasites stealing whatever food he swallowed. Our makeshift pharmacy was just up the hill, from which we gathered medicines and rehydrating solution for the baby to drink. We had very little baby formula but could get some from our main clinic two hour's drive away. Kevin explained all this to the grateful woman, now crying as she held the baby to her chest. He arranged for her to come by the government health center the next day, where he would reexamine the child and have formula. We would introduce her then to the local health workers, who could explore other ways to support her. We stayed to talk with her a while, then headed back up the hill, feeling less self-congratulatory that we'd done a good deed than worried we hadn't done nearly enough.

Most of the human needs we encounter are beyond a doctor's power to satisfy. The lasting solution to diarrhea and parasites isn't medicine but readily available clean water. Chronic malnutrition won't be eliminated with IVs and high-dose multivitamins but with reliable and affordable food. Crushing poverty demands new ways to make a living that won't cripple bodies or wound the land. We have no medicine for such things. No individual does. What is so patently obvious to me when in rural Honduras is that community is vastly more important than technology.

That same evening, I joined Sarah, one of the nurses, on the tiled landing of the municipal building our group was using as the women's dormitory. We sipped Honduran coffee and talked over the day's events, looking down on the town square and up to the rugged hills surrounding us. Even in the dry season, the slopes are green and lush in the raking evening light. It was a perceptual trick I'd learned on my first trip to Honduras: things look beautiful at a distance; it's only close up that you see the suffering. Sarah pointed out the trash littering the town square: plastic bags, boxes, popsicle sticks, and paper scattered like treats for an Easter-egg hunt. The few trash cans, prominently labeled with slogans about keeping the village beautiful and healthy, were overflowing. Sarah asked what it would take to instill enough pride in the townspeople for them to care about appearances. I wondered, in response, whether the litter didn't cast judgment as much on American culture, throwaway items being visible markers of our economy that increasing access to electronic media taught the locals to emulate. In my experience, Hondurans aren't necessarily inclined to conserve when consumer products make careful husbandry momentarily unnecessary. Given the choice, they'll throw away plastic wrapping as thoughtlessly as their wealthy neighbors to the north. Compared to North Americans, however, they are less likely to forget the earth's material limits, if only because they lack the wealth and mobility to do so for long. Necessity and scarcity are demanding tutors.

At the end of the brigade, on the bus ride north to the airport, we passed hundreds of banana trees and vast fields from which sugar cane had been harvested. The first time I saw this fertile valley—six years earlier—was shortly after the catastrophic floods accompanying Hurricane Mitch. Then, the corporately owned fields lay barren while displaced locals occupied shantytowns snaking along the highway median from San Pedro Sula—the business and HIV capital of Honduras—to El Progreso, a city of uncommon squalor.

This time, however, the plantations were flourishing, and the once-displaced locals had resumed their accustomed invisibility. A copy of Berry's *Citizenship Papers* in my hand, I was in the mood to raise irksome questions. Which, I wondered, was more strange: a village with no running water sporting an Internet café or a country with entire valleys devoted to large-scale monoculture for export still struggling to feed its own people? Some Hondurans living in the fertile Valle de Sula were, no doubt, employed by the multinational corporations supplying the wealthy North with inexpensive fruit and sugar. Doubtless, too, Honduran government officials and private citizens profited from this arrangement. Still, I had difficulty understanding why the underfed children I treated the day before did not benefit from the land's agricultural abundance. Perhaps the world economy is best served using this rich bottomland as one exploitable resource among others around the globe; I lack the macroeconomic language and training to refute such assertions. This, however, was quite clear: one part of the world suffered harm for the benefit of another.

The smell of burning sugarcane hung in the air as we stepped off the bus at the airport. There had been more rain than anticipated in the dry season, and the cane fields were being torched later than usual. The result was a particulate haze dense enough to ground commercial jet traffic. The plane we were supposed to board never landed in San Pedro Sula, having been redirected to the States. As trip leaders scrambled for alternatives, others asked what was going on. When I explained about the burning cane fields, one of our crew said, knowingly: "So we're trapped here because of their economy." A voice, sounding rather like a Kentucky farmer, spoke sharply in my head: "No, we're trapped because of *our* economy." No matter what my colleague and I had done for the people of Honduras, we were sugar consumers, and the land serving as factory had to be readied for next year's production. Had we remained in the States, the consequences of our habits of consumption, now causing us momentary inconvenience, would have remained invisible. That these same habits might trap others in permanent misery was more than any of us wanted to know.

Fixes and Diversions

In such times, a technologically dependent man like me—taught to believe that specialized knowledge, properly applied, will shape any reality to human desire—hopes that the world's connections and limits can be either transcended or ignored. Trained over many years to consume the things of this world with no thought to their provenance, I join my fellow Americans in pillaging our planet and bodies. "We will invent our way out of any self-created problem," we insist—a fixed, false belief pathognomonic of the technological psychosis. A loose tethering to the realities of life on this planet is required for a people to pursue food and energy policies in defiance of the second law of thermodynamics and to offer as technological fixes—to problems largely of our own making—the still-beckoning catastrophes of bioengineered monoagriculture and Yucca Mountain.

There's no affection for created things in bending nature to our will while ignoring the damage done in the process. Lamentably, Christians have been among the worst in sheer brutality against creation, using up God's good gifts with abandon. Christians should know better. They claim to follow the God revealed in Jesus, a God who so loved the world that he entered it in a living human body. In his healing ministry, Jesus touched people unclean under the law, cured blindness mixing dirt and saliva, visited the sick in their homes. In my far more humble healing art, I use my body and senses to diagnose, treat, and reassure. Placing the diaphragm of my stethoscope on the chest of the febrile child, I listen for the secrets of a heart. I touch the pads of my fingers to a frightened adolescent's wrist, taking her pulse. I watch, amazed at the ferocity with which a hungry infant nurses at his mother's breast. I am one creature working among others, and it has taken me years to understand that only by nurturing a real affection for other creatures can I rightly serve them, much less understand what it means to be healthy.

The Incarnation hallows everything that is made: the earth, our bodies, all living things. Precisely because of this, the long and shameful legacy of Christians defacing Christ-hallowed creation demands an enormous and still unpaid restitution. Even so, history also records that deeper tradition welling up like an underground spring in persons such as Francis of Assisi, who knew every creature, animate and inanimate, as brother or sister. Siblings in a healthy community don't ask reasons why they should care for one another, nor do they permit anyone to abuse family members.

We do well to acknowledge such relationships, make them explicit rather than obscured. Technology's power to mask relationships is, perhaps, its least-appreciated attribute. I was a better doctor when I worked on the Navajo Reservation than I am now, and I am a better doctor in Central America than I am in the States. I can be better present to my patients in places where I'm stripped of the trappings of the medical-industrial complex and we face each other on something like an equal footing. It is important to admit, however, that such na-kedness reduces my effectiveness, at least in the terms North Americans have been taught to measure effectiveness: convenience, longevity, material comfort.

Technology also disrupts time. Technology is usually considered progressive (just as the American eugenics movement and deracinating, off-reservation Indian boarding schools were widely understood in their day as progressive) because it is future oriented. A bold new model is forever on the way and, we are told, will be worth the price current circumstances force us to pay. It is difficult, then, given the "reality-based" claims of applied science, to admit the obvious: the future does not exist. It can't be touched, heard, or smelled. It produces nothing of use. It cannot be loved in the way any sensible thing can be loved. It is held before us, an inedible carrot urging the donkey on as he labors to pull the cart.

The future is, in short, a Gnostic diversion, segregating the dreariness of the material present from an ideal, if insensible, tomorrow. Humans desperately want something better and put nature to the rack to eliminate human suffering, even if suffering is, in the developed North at least, sometimes re-defined to include the simple frustration of desire.

Seeing Creation as a Whole

Saint Augustine, who knew a thing or two about frustrated desire, was in-tially drawn to Manichaean Gnosticism because he believed that it could ex-plain far better than Christianity the gulf between the world he desired and the world in which he lived. The Manichaean subordination of matter to spirit promised a way past earthly limits. Yet, in book 7 of his *Confessions,* Augustine records his late discovery of the created world's goodness. For him, the evil that marred creation merely names a deprivation of the good. From this moment, he takes all creation seriously, no longer segregating the desired from the undesired: "I no longer wished for a better world, because I was thinking of the *whole* of creation."[4]

Though Augustine sometimes seems reluctant to admit as much, the body too is God's good creation, joining us to the earth and to each other, all transformed by the Incarnation. Not that the body is good in itself, in isolation. Its goodness is found in relation to created things, including the land that feeds it and other bodies that love and support it. Augustine, keenly aware of what he called the *ordo amorum,* "the right ordering of our loves," struggled to order his many earthly loves in the light of God's love. Some loves are higher than others, laying greater claim on our lives and actions. For Augustine, everything—including the professions—properly honors and serves higher things. Taking Augustine's cue, Port William's lawyer, Wheeler Catlett, advises the confused detective in "Fidelity" regarding the proper use of the law:

> "But, my dear boy, you don't eat or drink the law, or sit in the shade of it, or warm yourself by it, or wear it, or have your being in it. The law exists only to serve."
> "Serve what?"
> "Why, all the things that are above it. Love."[5]

Wheeler Catlett knows something that his interlocutor, Detective Bode, could not: that things are never as discrete and separable as we wish, that autonomy and specialization, for all their productive power, cause great harm apart from an embodied regard for a contextual whole. Everything is, after all, connected to everything else. Wheeler—who chides Bode after the detective angrily accuses Danny Branch of burying Burley Coulter "somewhere in these end-of-nowhere, godforsaken hills and hollows"—also knows something about finding grace and holiness even in the end-of-nowhere places of the created world.[6] As Berry notes elsewhere:

> There are no unsacred places;
> there are only sacred places
> and desecrated places.[7]

Like a broken clock, Detective Bode could not help but be right on occasion. Danny did, in fact, bury Burley in the hills the old man loved. Danny, who understands the landscape as anything but "godforsaken," returns after the burial to a Port William membership with "the aspect and the brightness of one who had borne the dead to the grave, and filled the grave to the brim, and received the dead back into life again."[8]

"Receiv[ing] the dead back into life again" seems rather much for medicine to take on right now. Perhaps, however, there is something to be learned from a community reclaiming one of its members from a technology-dominated medical industry. Church communities, for example, could behave as a body gathered in Christ, insisting that members remain integral parts of a wholeness even in the alienating technological deserts of hospitals and nursing homes. How so? Not just by physical presence and support, but through liturgical reclamation, such as the anointing prescribed in James 5:14–15. This is not a variety of faith healing used to achieve specific, individual ends through religious ritual. Anointing reminds everyone that the sick person belongs to the community and, ultimately, to God, that a gathered people does not cease to care when technology no longer promises a cure, and that, in community, no one is a burden. Such powerful actions testify that the good found in medical expertise remains subordinate to the good of the gathered body. Highly trained specialists know a great deal about the body as machine, but a community knows and loves its own.

Communities can teach through example the hard work of love, affection, and true intimacy. Sexual responsibility is fostered neither through distributing technological fixes with a nod and a wink nor by demanding that young people practice more control and show more concern for human relatedness than their parents do. Augustine was shaped by the philosophical ethos of late antiquity, which feared that sexual passion corrupts the human desire for the good. Today, perpetually inflamed consumer desire corrupts sexuality and everything else connecting us to one another. Sex is too close to the core of who we are as embodied persons to be a merely private matter. Churches will first have to learn, and then show the rest of the world, what it means to care for other people's children.

Within the hospital itself, medical professionals might insist on providing patients not only with adequate rest and nutritious food but also with a healthy world to which the healed member may return. I need not recount here Berry's many arguments in favor of a local food economy rather than the current system, which treats food as a technologically enhanced commodity. It is sufficient to note that no doctor should prescribe nor any nurse administer a medicine without proper care and attention. Attention to such details as where one's food comes from and how the land in which it grew—and the people who grew it—is treated is a step toward seeing health and creation as a whole.

Awareness that everything affects everything else might include the recognition that seemingly innocuous shopping choices made in the United States compromise the health of whole communities elsewhere on the planet. "Thinking globally while acting locally" can quickly become a self-serving, though comforting, thought for those who have never seriously labored in a particular locality themselves. Immersion into the practices of one particular place is necessary for real knowledge and affection—what the philosopher of science Michael Polanyi calls "indwelling"—to be born.[9] Only with true knowledge and affection for one such place can humans know what it means to love any place at all, just as true friendship is known only by those who have themselves been a friend.

Friendship, affection, love: these are the wholenesses toward which any healthy attempt at unspecializing medicine must gesture. When in Honduras, I particularly enjoy working with our interpreters, Honduran students from a privileged, English-speaking school who volunteer their vacation time to help us. One of them, a loud and funny young woman who liked to dance and tell jokes, was a particular favorite of mine on one trip. She was not conventionally beautiful. She was too fond, I suppose, of good food to ever become a surgically enhanced fashion wraith. But no one could deny that she was beautiful, her entire body overflowing with life, her face unable to hide its delight in nearly everything she saw. She and I often told stories outside the clinic after the last patient had been seen. We laughed nearly as often as we spoke. On our last day in the village, as we gathered our belongings for the trip home, she handed me a postcard, signed by all the interpreters but written in her own hand, that read in part: "Thank you for loving my country and my people."

I had to ponder that awhile. I thought back to my first visit to Honduras after Hurricane Mitch and the people I met who left me forever uncomfortable, no longer at ease in my old North American life. I remembered sawtoothed horizons in the Honduran mountains, the scent of burning cane, the taste of mango fresh from the tree, and voices of welcome and hospitality I'd done nothing to deserve.

I had a fondness for all this, but did I really love them? Was *love* the right word? I've worked in Honduras, in a particular place and with particular people, long and often enough to hazard an answer. I love her country. I love her people.

Which brings us to a starting place.

Notes

1. Wendell Berry, "Health as Membership," in *Another Turn of the Crank* (Washington, DC: Counterpoint, 1995), 106.

2. Wendell Berry, "Notes: Unspecializing Poetry," in *Standing by Words* (New York: North Point, 1983), 80.

3. Berry, "Health as Membership," 94–95.

4. Saint Augustine, *Confessions,* trans. Henry Chadwick (Oxford, 1991), bk. 7, chap. 13 (emphasis added).

5. Wendell Berry, "Fidelity," in *Fidelity: Five Stories* (New York: Pantheon, 1992), 175.

6. Ibid., 189.

7. Wendell Berry, "How to Be a Poet (to Remind Myself)," in *Given: New Poems* (Washington, DC: Shoemaker & Hoard, 2005), 18.

8. Berry, "Fidelity," 188.

9. See Michael Polanyi, *Personal Knowledge: Towards a Post-Critical Philosophy* (Chicago: University of Chicago Press, 1958).

Richard P. Church

Of the Good That Has Been Possible in This World

Lawyering in Port William

On particularly cold and dark mornings, as I milk our four-and-one-half-year-old goat, I like to think I must be the only Duke University law graduate milking a goat this morning. It is not, of course, that I am the only Duke law graduate (or Duke theologian, for that matter) working at 6:00 A.M. I imagine most of us are. It is just that I think that I am the only one doing such enjoyable work. I would take credit for the story of how a Duke law graduate became a farmer, but, like all good stories, mine has been gifted to me. This essay is written in thanksgiving for two storytellers in particular who have told stories that led me from the law to the farm and perhaps back to the law. Or, said differently, this essay seeks to discern how Christians might practice law by considering the work of the novelist, essayist, poet, farmer, and son of a country lawyer Wendell Berry, to whose work this volume is dedicated, alongside that of the lawyer and legal storyteller Thomas Shaffer. In his descriptions of Wheeler Catlett, the lawyer for the Port William membership, Berry offers a vision of the good work that Christians who are lawyers might do, the types of communities necessary to sustain Christians in the law, and the limits that Christians who work as lawyers must ultimately place on the law. Further, his descriptions of Wheeler can be seen as an exemplification of the arguments made by Shaffer as to the task of Christians within the law.[1]

In considering the work of Wheeler Catlett, I focus on three stories in the Port William narrative, none of which suggests immediately that Wheeler is a model lawyer or legal ethicist. In the first, Wheeler fails to achieve the desired disposition of his deceased client's estate and, instead, lends money to a second client to achieve the goals of his dead client's will. In the second, he initially refuses to draft his client's will on the basis of his own beliefs about the propriety of the proposed disposition, a violation of his client's autonomy.

In the third, Wheeler, along with his son Henry, aids a fugitive in evading the law during the ongoing commission of a "crime." While each of these stories raises concerns under standard accounts of legal ethics, each is exemplary of a lawyer who has befriended his clients in such a manner that he might serve them in lieu of the law.[2]

Legal Friendship in Port William

The first short story, "It Wasn't Me," is the story of a failed will. Old Jack Beechum has died. Wheeler drafted his will, which included a substantial bequest to Old Jack's tenants and preferred heirs, Elton and Mary Penn, who have farmed his place since his retirement into Port William. Old Jack's intent was for the sum to be sufficient to cover half the cost of purchasing his farm; however, he failed to specify the price of the farm in anything other than a note to Wheeler, never sent, found on Old Jack's person at his death. Old Jack's daughter, Clara Pettit, who is married to a city banker, estranged from Old Jack and Port William almost from her birth, and likely already unhappy with the inclusion of Elton and Mary Penn in Old Jack's will, insists on a public sale despite her father's wishes with regard to the disposition of the farm.

Like most of Wheeler's clients, Old Jack is more than a client. As Berry describes him: "Old Jack Beechum was Wheeler's client, his kinsman by marriage, and his friend." Wheeler's friendship with Old Jack is built around a shared life together in community, which itself is built on a shared vision of the good practice of farming. Thus, Wheeler is haunted not only by Old Jack's unfulfilled desire for the disposition of his farm but also by his own vision of the good disposition of that land and place:

> The truth is that Wheeler is a seer of visions—not the heavenly visions of saints and mystics, but the earthly ones of a mainly practical man who sees the good that has been possible in this world, and, beyond that, the good that is desirable in it. Wheeler has known the hundred and fifty acres called, until now, the Beechum Place all his life. . . . It is a place with good human life already begun in it, where the right sort of young man and woman could do well. Knowing all this, knowing the farm, knowing Elton and Mary Penn, Wheeler has irresistibly imagined the life they might live there.

Thus, Berry suggests that Wheeler's representation of Old Jack and his good ends for this young couple, for this farm, and "for the good of the world" was a "problem . . . that he inherited, a part of his own legacy from his deceased client and friend."[3]

In the pursuit of this good hope, Wheeler throws his lot in with Elton and Mary Penn. Having vouched for them once before in recommending them to Old Jack as tenants, he now offers his own money to Elton in the midst of the auction, at which the farm sells for one and a half times the price Old Jack had envisioned. Elton resents Wheeler's aid, "[having] become first the inheritor of a bequest that he did not ask for and did not expect, and next the beneficiary of an act of friendship that he did not ask for and, with part of his mind, does not want." Wheeler explains that, while understanding the urge to make one's own way in the world, Elton has been made a part of the story of the Port William membership. His choice is whether to accept that story as his own. Of most significance to understanding Wheeler's legal practice, however, is Berry's suggestion that, pulled by their friendship to Old Jack, Wheeler and Elton have left the confines of the law: "The office has faded away around them. They might as well be in a barn, or in an open field. They are meeting in the world, Wheeler thinks, striving to determine how to continue in it. Both of them are still wearing their hats and coats."[4] Wheeler begins as Old Jack's lawyer. That legal friendship, even after Old Jack's death, is a fruitful one, expanding the Port William membership, and carrying Wheeler and his new client, Elton Penn, beyond the law to the world of farm and neighborhood.

In a second story related to wills and estates, "The Wild Birds," Wheeler is a much less willing participant in the drafting of Burley Coulter's will. Burley wants to bequest his farm to his illegitimate son, Danny Branch. In helping him do so, Wheeler must again go beyond the law to serve Burley as his friend and brother and act against his (Wheeler's) own best hopes for the Coulter place and for the life of Burley. No construct as simple as legal agency can capture the complexity of Wheeler's representation of Burley.

The story Burley tells Wheeler to defend giving the farm to Danny is told not out of legal necessity but out of friendship. Burley begins: "I'm not telling you what you need to know to be my lawyer. I'm telling you what you need to know to be my friend. If a lawyer was all I wanted, I reckon I wouldn't have to hire a friend." Friendship is Burley's gift to Wheeler and, likewise, the cause of deep fear, for it demands of Wheeler a vulnerability to Burley beyond the law. Again, Berry suggests a receding of the legal context: "Whatever there may have been of lawyer and client in this conversation is long gone now, and Wheeler feels and regrets that departure, for he knows that something dark and unwieldy has impinged upon them, that they will not get past except by going through." They have entered the world of Burley's "wayward" life, a life lived in the woods and in the dark that has been filled with both sin and love.[5]

In contrast, Wheeler has served "the human homesteads and neighborhoods and the known ways that preserve them." He has committed his life to an "orderly handing down" of those homesteads via the law.[6] Burley now asks Wheeler to bless his wayward life and its good fruits in a disorderly handing on of the Coulter home place not to Burley's known heir, his nephew Nathan Coulter, but to his unknown heir, Danny Branch, who was conceived in the darkness of his unspoken love for Kate Helen Branch.

As the conversation progresses, Burley asserts his authority over Wheeler. This authority is built not on the priority of Burley's autonomous desires as Wheeler's client but rather on Burley's seniority over Wheeler in the Port William membership. Wheeler's plans for the Coulter place must "be turned loose" from the orderly world of legal ownership and succession so that Burley can "come back into the clear and show" himself. In light of Burley's authority over him, Wheeler relents to the proposed course of action. He acknowledges the provisional good to be pursued in lieu of his hope for an absolute good found via the rigidity of the law and a world without wayward sinners such as Burley. Yet relenting to draft Burley's will is not enough. Burley has made clear that their relationship is not that of client and lawyer but that of friends and maybe even brothers. Burley demands reconciliation: "'Wheeler, if we're going to get this will made out, not to mention all else we've got to do while there's breath in us, I think you've got to forgive me as if I was a brother to you.' He laughs, asserting for the last time the seniority now indisputably his, and casting it aside. 'And I reckon I've got to forgive you for taking so long to do it.'"[7] Wheeler reaches out in an embrace of forgiveness. The story is remarkable for both the authority granted to Burley by Wheeler and for the hope it displays that legal relationships might be for lawyers places of character formation.

A Legal Ethic of Care

In looking for a context to place Berry's unorthodox description of the good lawyer, those descriptions can be seen as an exemplification of the work of

Thomas Shaffer on legal ethics. Shaffer's writings are voluminous and multi-faceted; nonetheless, his theologically grounded legal ethic centers on certain essential claims regarding the work of lawyers. These claims include the priority of the church in moral discernment, the priority of Christian identity to professional identity, and the priority of service to and engagement with the client. Particularly with regard to the last claim, Shaffer's work on legal ethics suggests that legal relationships between lawyers and clients are always moral relationships. Berry displays each of these insights in his descriptions of Wheeler's legal practice.

Shaffer traces three competing strands of legal ethics that are grounded in competing understandings of the nature of legal clients. The ethic of role suggests that good lawyers do what the law requires, namely, either what their clients want (relying on "the system" to produce justice) or what the lawyers themselves believe is best (relying on an aristocratic model of lawyers as the guardians of society). The ethic of role, based in client autonomy, is the dominant legal ethic. It suggests that lawyers are obligated to do everything within the law to aid their clients regardless of the clients' proposed ends. In either version, the ethic of role assumes that lawyers are nonmoral actors in their work. A second alternative, the ethic of isolation, acknowledges that legal conversations are about moral matters but assumes that lawyers and clients are separate moral actors making moral assertions only to be accepted or rejected by the other.[8] In the ethic of isolation, clients reason on their own regarding the ends they might pursue, and lawyers see clients primarily as threats to their own morality.

Shaffer proposes a third ethic, an ethic of care, under which lawyers act as ministers to their clients in a relationship of mutuality. In other words, lawyers are motivated by service to others and acknowledge the interconnectedness of their lives and moral development with those of their clients.[9] In this context, legal conversation is moral conversation.[10] Lawyers are not mere agents for their clients. Rather, they act as companions to their clients in such a way that they discern together regarding the best ends to be pursued and the best means of pursuing those ends, including, but not limited to, the parameters set by the law.

Berry's stories display this last type of legal relationship. In drafting and probating Old Jack's will, Wheeler represents his friend in a way that exceeds the role of lawyers as the agents of their clients. He seeks not merely to fulfill Old Jack's desires; rather, he shares Old Jack's commitments and purposes for that place. Similarly, his interaction with Burley Coulter makes clear that lawyers and clients are not morally isolated from one another. Burley's demands as a client are grounded in his claim on Wheeler as his friend and brother.

Shaffer argues along these lines, suggesting that friendship changes the dynamic between lawyers and their clients by establishing a depth to the relationship that enables moral claims to be made:

> Integrity means that the lawyer has moral limits. There are things you will not ask your friend to do, and if your friend is your lawyer, there are things you will not ask your lawyer to do. In part—usually, I suppose— that is because you love her, and you perceive her character, and you want her to be and to become a good person. But also, I think, it is because you know that it would be futile to ask her. There are some things—some lawful things—she would refuse to do. Part of the value of her moral advice is that there are things she will refuse to do. This refusal is part of her character. Her character is what makes her your friend, and you her friend, in the first place.[11]

Similarly, there are things you *will* ask your friend to do that you would not ask your lawyer to do. Thus, Burley makes claims on Wheeler, such as forgiveness, that demand that he be more than a lawyer and, in fact, more than he is.[12] In doing so, clients can be viewed as gifts by which God intends graciously to discipline those in the law.[13]

A series of essential implications for a Christian construal of legal ethics flow from remaking legal relationships into legal friendships. First, legal friendships reject what Shaffer describes as "two kingdom ethics," particularly the adversarial ethic, in which the lawyer employs distinct moralities in his public and private lives.[14] Shaffer argues that this two kingdom adversarial ethic is idolatrous. It is built on the assumption that the government or the legal system will produce justice.[15] Such an assumption is self-deluded. Power does not and cannot consistently produce justice.[16] The pursuit of justice does not inhere in the adversarial system itself. Procedural justice is not the justice of the cross. Rather, justice is a complex project in which lawyers, clients, and adversaries seek a common ground on which reconciliation might be found. Therefore, it is a gift that is given to another in contrast to either a minimalist procedural account of justice or the achievement of a certain distribution of resources. For this reason, Shaffer concludes that justice is not "something people get from the government" but a gift human beings offer one another.[17]

A second implication of Shaffer's ethic of care is that it necessitates that the lawyer develop the virtue of hope. As Shaffer describes it, lawyers as ministers to their clients are required to display both compassion and hope, to walk with those who have failed, and to restore hope to those in the midst of trouble.[18] Lawyers must offer compassion to clients who have been less than they might have been; likewise, clients must offer compassion to lawyers. This issue is at the heart of the conversation between Burley and Wheeler, for Burley's irregular ways reflect his failure to make proper his marriage in fact to Kate Helen Branch and legitimate his illegitimate son. Burley calls forth Wheeler's compassion while simultaneously offering it to Wheeler for his failure to offer it freely to Burley.

Compassion, however, is always grounded in hope. It requires the provision of hope to clients and, as Berry describes it, the maintenance of hope in clients. Thus, Berry summarizes Wheeler's legal practice in the following manner: "In loyalty to his clients, or to their Maker, in whose image he has supposed them made, he has believed in their generosity, goodness, courage, and intelligence. Mere fact has never been enough for him. He has pled and reasoned, cajoled, bullied, and preached, pushing events always toward a better end than he knew they could reach, resisting always the disappointment that he knew he should expect, and when the disappointment has come, as it too often has, never settling for it in his own heart or looking upon it as a conclusion."[19] Shaffer concurs. An ethic of care entails an opening of lawyers' lives to their clients such that clients are not approached as sources of moral corruption. The gift of forgiveness demanded by Burley is a display of the hope that clients might teach lawyers how to live faithfully within the law.

Ultimately, this hope requires hope in the goodness of God, which hope is also displayed by Wheeler. As Wheeler settles another estate, that of Nathan and Hannah Coulter, with no clear heir to take over the original Feltner farm, he arranges for his own wife to receive a monetary share of that estate while giving Virgil Feltner's granddaughter, Margaret, the house and farm undivided. Margaret lives in the city, but she is Wheeler's only hope for the farm's good succession. Berry describes Wheeler's choice as follows: "Wheeler was not a great hand to depend on the future, but he would do it if he had to. 'If you know you don't know anything about the future,' he would say, 'and if you believe that with God all things are possible, then you have to think that something good may happen.' The future would be a gamble, and Wheeler, having no choice, took the gamble."[20] In this regard, Wheeler acknowledges the priority of hope over power in its various forms, including the power of the law, to achieve the good.[21]

A final implication of legal friendship as a model for good lawyering is that a variety of practices, largely at odds with the current structures of legal work, would become necessary. For example, legal friendship presupposes that lawyers have befriended their clients so as to hear the clients' stories and to understand the goods of the clients' lives. This fact requires that lawyers work in ongoing relationships with their clients, relationships that provide both lawyer and client time to know each other. Such knowledge could not be superficial. In fact, it requires a shared account of the good between lawyer and client that has developed through participation in a shared form of life. As noted above, Berry makes clear that this is exactly the type of relationship that Wheeler and Old Jack share. That relationship is premised on participation in a shared set of institutions, practices, and languages, as found in their common love of good farming.

In this regard, Berry's and Shaffer's vision of legal relationships is a challenge to some of the basic structures by which law in America is practiced. Firm practice in service to and defense of for-profit corporations, particularly large corporations with many shareholders, simply does not accommodate the development of relationships of shared goods. This conclusion fits with a basic claim present throughout Berry's writings: good work is particular. Good farming or good lawyering requires attention to detail that size and ambition thwart.[22] In contrast, for lawyers in firms, clients are always susceptible to becoming abstractions, the purveyors of questions, tasks, and work via an assembly line of handed-down projects. For this reason, the context of Wheeler's law practice as a solo practitioner or as a partner with his son is particularly significant. Wheeler is not yoked to the structures of modern legal practice in the form of the law firm.

Could Wheeler have displayed the legal friendships evident in Berry's work if he were a member of a firm? This question originally sparked the issues pursued in this essay. If Shaffer is the guide to understanding the goods of Wheeler's practice, the answer in most cases would appear to be no. Wheeler has no obligation to abstractions such as *the law*, which a firm is largely created to serve. Further, he has no obligation to the abstraction *profit*, which is more than anything the ethos of the modern law firm. Yoked unequally, Christians in the law could rarely assert the contrary legal skills that mark Wheeler's practice.[23]

Furthermore, the nature of law firm clients often undercuts the basic hopes set forth for legal friendship. A corporate client cannot be befriended.[24] No human life can be befriended, for *the client* itself is an abstraction. The lawyer serves only a board and shareholders with a profit interest. The lawyer cannot counsel such an entity on the ends it might pursue, for it serves a single end, wealth creation.[25] As Berry describes it, a corporation is, in fact, just a pile of money to which a group of people swear allegiance.[26] Such a legal abstraction is incapable of love or regret unless such love or regret can be tied to the maintenance or creation of market share. At variance with the Gospel's claim on human lives, it cannot be called to sacrifice itself.

The nature of corporations is, then, particularly worrisome for the lawyers who would serve them. As Shaffer notes, lawyers "tend to adopt the social, political, and economic opinions of those [they] serve and associate with, especially the wealthy and powerful ones." Thus, he argues that "money is the principal moral problem lawyers in the United States have."[27] This is true both because lawyers primarily serve those with wealth and because they are prone to becoming wealthy themselves. Wheeler has found a way to practice law that neither serves the rich nor has made him wealthy. This is a difficult accomplishment for a lawyer. Consistent, then, with Shaffer's suggestion cited above that lawyers' moral lives are at stake in their relationships with clients (and vice versa), lawyers who are Christians must in some instances jettison those clients who would lead them to be less than the Gospel would call them to be.[28]

The preceding paragraphs are not meant to suggest, however, the impossibility of imagining new forms of communal legal practice that would enable legal friendships to flourish. In fact, one hope in clarifying the goods of legal practice for Christians would be to spark discernment of the structures within which that practice could be pursued. Likewise, nothing here is meant to suggest that every law firm would prohibit activity subversive of the law or the production of profits. Certainly, resonances of an old professional ethic continue to be heard in many law firms today. Likewise, firms at times take actions that are, within limits, contrary to profit motives. But sporadic counterexamples do not undercut the basic arguments made herein; the concerns set forth call into question the overall ethos of modern legal practice. Finally, while I do not want to discount the practical difficulties of maintaining the finances of a firm or a small legal practice built on taking the time to befriend one's clients, I take such objections largely to be directed to the question of the cost to Christians of faithfulness within the law. There are no theological grounds for ensuring that Christian legal practice is financially lucrative or, for that matter, even self-sustaining. The church may have to subsidize lawyers if the tasks that Christians who would be lawyers are called to undertake turn out not to be profitable.

The Limits of the Lawyering in Port William

That Wheeler does not practice in the context of a law firm and does not appear to have corporate clients suggests the presence of certain limits in his practice of law. There are services he will not offer; there are tasks he will refuse; there are goods other than the law and profits that he will serve. These limits are at the heart of a faithful description of the work of Christians in the law. Accordingly, I focus next on a final story in the Port William narrative, one that displays the limits of the law in Wheeler's practice.

"Fidelity" tells the story of the death of Burley Coulter. While it is an important display of Berry's ideas regarding health, it is also important for its description of Wheeler's defense of the Port William membership. Burley, old and dying, is taken by his son, Danny Branch, and his nephew Nathan Coulter successively to the doctor and to the large university hospital in Louisville, Kentucky. Soon after doing so, Danny and Nathan realize that they have betrayed the trust that they owe to Burley, to allow him a death consistent with the life he has lived. Having realized as much, Danny awakes in the middle of the night, drives to Louisville, cuts Burley away from the tubes and machines confining him, and drives him home to Port William, where he cares for him in an old barn and prepares a grave for him.

Soon, the law, in the form of Detective Kyle Bode, comes to investigate the disappearance of Burley from the hospital. Wheeler and his son Henry, who is Danny's lawyer, gather the membership of Port William in their law office, ostensibly to be questioned by Bode. What occurs, instead, is Burley's funeral. The membership gathers and tells the story of Burley's life with them as Danny buries Burley in the woods. Wheeler's and Henry's work in this moment is guardianship. They protect the membership from the "organized world" that would seek to hold Burley hostage and condemn Danny for returning Burley to them.

Berry reiterates here that the fundamental relationship of the Catlett lawyers to their clients is friendship.[29] Further, he emphasizes that each of the

Catletts, the lawyers Wheeler and Henry and the journalist Andy (Wheeler's other son), "whatever else they were, were still farmers and still of the membership." By suggesting as much, he makes clear that their primary loyalty is to people and place, in lieu of the wider world and the law. This fact is stated starkly by Henry as Bode attempts to pressure his cooperation on the grounds of "his and Henry's brotherhood in the law":

> "Can't help you," Henry said.
> "You mean that you, a lawyer, won't cooperate with the law of the state in the solution of a crime."
> "Well, you see, it's a matter of patriotism."
> "Patriotism? You can't mean that."
> "I mean patriotism—love for your country and your neighbors. There's a difference, Mr. Bode, between the government and the country. I'm not going to cooperate with you in this case because I don't like what you represent in this case."[30]

In his conversation with Bode, Wheeler reiterates the limits of the law and, therefore, the limits of his obedience to the law:

> "Well, anyway," Detective Bode said, "all I know is that the law has been broken, and I am here to serve the law."
> "But, my dear boy, you don't eat or drink the law, or sit in the shade of it or warm yourself by it, or wear it, or have your being in it. The law exists only to serve."
> "Serve what?"
> "Why, all the many things that are above it. Love."[31]

At the end of the story, Danny returns to the membership gathered in Wheeler's office bearing no evidentiary marks of the "crime." Bode is defeated in his attempt to unearth Burley's kidnapper, having, in Berry's words, "been tempted over and over again to leave, with Wheeler, the small, clear world of the law and its explanations and to enter the larger, darker world not ordered by human reasons or subject to them."[32]

This final suggestion is particularly significant insofar as it was Burley himself who, in "The Wild Birds," drew Wheeler beyond the law into that dark world that he represents in "Fidelity." Wheeler now speaks the truth of that dark world to Bode, or at least defends it against the language and power of the ordered world. His ability to do so, however, is itself contingent on what he had learned from his client Burley. Thus, in closing the loop on this conversation, Wheeler shows that he has had his life reshaped by the good clients, including Burley, whom he has served. Yet saying it this way says too little, for Wheeler's own life is at stake in "The Wild Birds." Wheeler, like Bode, also is tempted to remain within the law. Yet Burley demands more of his friend. The arguments made by Wheeler in "Fidelity" are the proof that he is more than a lawyer, a fact that makes those arguments the most dangerous to the law.

Subversive Lawyers

What Wheeler rejects in "Fidelity" is the temptation to find his identity in the law. Shaffer argues that Christians who would be lawyers must do likewise. Christians must work in that order: as Christians who might also be lawyers. As Shaffer suggests: "Faithfulness to the tradition of Israel and of the Cross means that the lawyer stands in the community of the faithful and looks from there at the law. Faithfulness means that a lawyer imagines that she is first of all a believer and is then a lawyer."[33]

The law tempts lawyers to stake their identity in the title *lawyer,* which is a particularly tempting one because our culture places such esteem in the law.[34] In rejecting this temptation, Wheeler and Henry are not lawyers. They are friends; they are members of Port William; they are farmers. As Berry describes Wheeler, he is "in a sense not so much a lawyer as a farmer who practices law."[35] The title *lawyer* is borne by Wheeler and Henry only insofar as the law continues to serve these higher goods, and they obey the law only insofar as "law expresses love of neighbor."[36] Thus, when the law comes not in service of their neighbors, Wheeler and Henry walk outside its confines into the dark world that they have been called to serve.

The implication of the limits placed on the law and the approach to legal ethics set forth above is that Christians cannot answer definitively whether it is appropriate to be a lawyer.[37] Instead, Christians who work as lawyers awake each day and offer their work to the church and ask, Can I do this particular task today?[38] As Shaffer frames it:

> It is possible to be a Christian and a lawyer only if the question remains unsettled—so that the tentative nature of the answer is an admonition to attempt in the practice of law more than the practice itself, the conventional professionalism of it, can bear. To the extent that one determines to conduct his practice as moral conversation, his advocacy as

moral discourse, his lawyer skill as the virtue of hope, his life as an af-
firmation that justice is a gift and not a commodity one has from the
government, I think it is possible to be a Christian and a lawyer.[39]

Accordingly, he suggests that, for Christians, the law must be construed as a
sort of Canaanite idol that the people of God must be wary of at every turn
yet, nonetheless, take up and use.[40]

This means that Christian legal ethics are like all other Christian ethics.
Those who would be disciples of Jesus Christ are called to live together in a
manner that witnesses to the truth of his life, death, and resurrection. This
task requires discernment regarding the shape of Christians' life together and
in the world. Accordingly, Christians' lives are found in such communities of
discernment.[41] There is, then, no Christian legal ethic. Rather, a gathered
community is gifted with a set of memories about what sorts of activities
Christians, including those working within the law, might engage in while
living faithfully. Likewise, the community has a process set forth in Matt.
18:15–20 for discerning how to apply those memories to the particular context in which Christians in the law currently find themselves.[42]

Placing limits on the narrative of the law is highly subversive, however.
That Wheeler and Henry would, in fact, sit in the law and yet deny its su-
premacy over their loyalties is the most disturbing action that they take and
the one that most troubles Kyle Bode. Bode assumes their common cause
with him in affirming the status quo, which the law is largely built to serve.
Their rejection of the law is dangerous because it subverts the claim that the
government or the rule of law can secure peace in a world of violence.
Rejecting the idolatrous suggestion that the law offers salvation, that is, that
it is adequate to produce peace, Wheeler and Henry seek a more substantial
local peace built not on procedure but on common life and loves.[43]

Shaffer notes that, in denying the totalizing discourse of the law, Christians
are subversive of the rule of law.[44] This fact is not surprising, for the church
often serves as a rejection of the status quo that the law seeks to uphold. In
other words, in its eschatological hope, the church denies that the way things
are is the way things have to be. As John Howard Yoder notes, this claim
makes the church inherently political and often subversive: "No 'bridge' or
'translation' is needed to make the Bible a book about politics. The new order,
the new humanity, does not replace or destroy the old, but that does not
make the new order apolitical. Its very existence is subversive at the points
where the old order is repressive, and creative where the old is without vision.

The transcendence of the new consists not in its escaping the realm where the old order rules, but in its subverting and transforming that realm. It does that by virtue of its being an alternative story."[45]

In denying the law, Wheeler and Henry similarly subvert the dominant narrative of the law in a manner that suggests their hope that the world might be, at least in Port William, more than it is or, more particularly, that old men might die deaths befitting their lives among the people whom and in the place that they have loved. Further, Wheeler and Henry are subversive insofar as they use their knowledge of the law to defend the Port William membership against the powers of the existing order represented by the law. As Berry describes it:

> Wheeler started out with a clientele that he may be said to have inherited—farmers mostly, friends of his father and his father-in-law, kinsmen, kinsmen's friends, with whom he thought of himself as a lawyer as little as they thought of themselves as clients. Between them and himself the technical connection was swallowed up in friendship, in mutual regard and loyalty. Such men, like as not, would not need a dime's worth of assistance between the settling of their parents' estates and the writing of their own wills, and not again after that. Wheeler served them as their defender against the law itself, before which they were ciphers, and so felt themselves—and he could do this only as their friend.[46]

In suggesting that legal friendship is the defense of the weak against the power of the law, Berry displays Shaffer's hope that lawyers might serve as a mediating force between the discourse of the wider world and smaller communities with their own language, order, and truth.[47] And the eschatological life that the church seeks to embody is just such an alternative language, order, and truth.[48]

Shaffer notes that such mediating work between local communities and the wider world requires lawyers to be bilingual, not only in their speech, but also in their "perception of reality." In other words, the task of mediating between the wider community and the local community requires an ability to understand the vision of the wider world, translate that vision into terms that the church might understand and discern, and then return to the wider world and speak back to the powers in their own language the truth that the church has discerned "behind the wall."[49] Such work implies that, while translation and communication between those worlds are not easy, they are possible some of the time—and some of the time through the language of law.[50] Nonetheless, sometimes it is not possible. When it is, the Christian who is a lawyer may be the vehicle of the church's speech. When it is not, the Christian who is a lawyer, as Wheeler, uses his knowledge of the powers to shield the church and "the least of these" from the wider world and the law.[51] It is tricky walking between these worlds. It is particularly tricky, as Shaffer notes, in light of the power of the law itself, which so tempts those called to this task to glory in the law or their knowledge thereof. Nonetheless, this mediating work, embedded within legal friendships, might be the good work of Christians who would work in the law.

Conclusion

In the novel *Hannah Coulter*, Berry notes that, in buying a farm, Nathan Coulter "had bought a lot of work."[52] This comment is important insofar as Berry argues throughout his writings that good work is hard to find. My own experience of buying a farm, largely untended for at least a decade, has been similar. I bought a lot of work. That good work has included feeding hogs, fixing fences, raising chicks, tending gardens, praying for rain, birthing kids, mourning the lost, blessing the dead, and tending to 6:00 A.M. milkings of that four-and-one-half-year-old goat. It is good work for which I am grateful. My work in the law has always been more worrisome as to whether I might call it *good*. Yet Berry and Shaffer offer stories of the good work that lawyers might do in pursuing "the good that has been possible in this world, and, beyond that, the good that is desirable in it."

Notes

1. Shaffer largely develops his theological vision by reading stories such as those of Anthony Trollope and Harper Lee. Thus, his work is instructive as to the method as well as the content of this essay.

2. Rule 1.8(a) of the North Carolina State Bar's Revised Rules of Professional Conduct (2007) prohibits lawyers from entering into business relationships with their clients absent certain specified safeguards not present in Berry's narrative. Rule 1.2(a) suggests that a lawyer should abide by a client's decisions concerning the objectives of the representation. However, it should be noted that rule 2.1, which addresses the lawyer's role as adviser, clearly contemplates that legal advice may address moral, economic, social, and political factors relevant to a proposed course of action. Rule 1.2(d) prohibits a lawyer from assisting a client in ongoing conduct that the lawyer knows is criminal.

3. Wendell Berry, "It Wasn't Me," in *That Distant Land: The Collected Stories* (Washington, DC: Shoemaker & Hoard, 2004), 267, 271–72, 270–71.

4. Ibid., 283.

5. Wendell Berry, "The Wild Birds," in *That Distant Land*, 352, 345.

6. Ibid., 349.

7. Ibid., 351, 354, 363.

8. See, e.g., North Carolina State Bar, Revised Rules of Professional Conduct (2007), rule 1.2(b): "A lawyer's representation of a client, including representation by appointment, does not constitute an endorsement of the client's political, economic, social or moral views or activities."

9. Shaffer concurs with Berry on the foundational nature of membership to human identity: "First we are, and then we can, if we want to (and after we happen to think about it), choose to be what we are. . . . This is the human condition. We are primarily members, not choosers; we are primarily connected, not alone" (Thomas Shaffer and Mary Shaffer, *American Lawyers and Their Communities: Ethics in the Legal Profession* [Notre Dame, IN: University of Notre Dame Press, 1991], 21).

10. See Thomas Shaffer, *On Being a Christian and a Lawyer: Law for the Innocent* (Provo, UT: Brigham Young University Press, 1981), 22.

11. Thomas Shaffer, "Legal Ethics and the Good Client," *Catholic University Law Review* 36 (1986–1987): 329–30.

12. See ibid., 329.

13. See Shaffer, *On Being a Christian and a Lawyer*, 37.

14. In Shaffer's legal ethics textbook, one hero is Justice Louis Brandeis, who Shaffer suggests is a one kingdom lawyer. Shaffer relates a famous response of President Woodrow Wilson's to the suggestion that it was a pity that a man as great as Brandeis was a Jew. Wilson responded: "But he would not be Mr. Brandeis if he were not a Jew" (Thomas Shaffer, *American Legal Ethics: Text, Readings, and Discussion Topics* [New York: Matthew Bender, 1985], 253).

15. See, e.g., North Carolina State Bar, Revised Rules of Professional Conduct (2007), rule 0.1 (Preamble): "When an opposing party is well represented, a lawyer can be a zealous advocate on behalf of a client and, at the same time, assume that justice is being done." This rule is mitigated in part by rule 3.3 (Candor toward the Tribunal), which requires lawyers to not make or fail to correct a false statement or offer evidence they know to be false and to disclose to the tribunal legal authority in the controlling jurisdiction known to be directly adverse to the client's position and not disclosed by the opposing party.

16. See Shaffer, *On Being a Christian and a Lawyer*, 9.

17. Thomas Shaffer and Andrew McThenia, "For Reconciliation," *Yale Law Journal* 94 (1985): 1664–65. Expounding Plato's *Republic*, Shaffer and McThenia conclude: "Justice is not the will of the stronger; it is not efficiency in government; it

is not the reduction of violence: Justice is what we discover—you and I, Socrates said—when we walk together, listen together, and even love one another, in our curiosity about what justice is and where justice comes from" (ibid., 1665).

18. See Shaffer, *On Being a Christian and a Lawyer,* 28.

19. Berry, "The Wild Birds," 339.

20. Wendell Berry, *Hannah Coulter* (Washington, DC: Shoemaker & Hoard, 2004), 137.

21. For more on the relationship of hope to power, see Thomas Shaffer and Stanley Hauerwas, "Hope in the Life of Thomas More," *Notre Dame Lawyer* 54 (1978–1979): 572.

22. See, generally, Wendell Berry, "Out of Your Car, Off Your Horse" and "Conservation Is Good Work," both in *Sex, Economy, Freedom, and Community: Eight Essays* (New York: Pantheon, 1992), 19–26, 27–44. In making this connection, Berry makes clear that faithful living often requires imposing economic and other limits on our work.

23. Thomas Shaffer, "The Legal Ethics of the Two Kingdoms," *Valparaiso University Law Review* 17 (1983): 37: "Institutions are not redeemed—not ever, not any of them." This insight is related to Berry's claims about the value of self-employment or, more important, home employment. See, generally, Wendell Berry, "Feminism, the Body, and the Machine," in *The Art of the Commonplace,* ed. Norman Wirzba (Washington, DC: Counterpoint, 2002), 65–80. Thus, here we have another significant link between farmers and solo practitioners in the law; both are self-employed.

24. While many lawyers do befriend those who run and manage those corporations, insofar as they do so they risk developing friendships that run contrary to their legal duty as defined by professional codes of ethics, which would require them to serve the abstraction of the corporation, not the goods of its managers. See, e.g., North Carolina State Bar Revised Rules of Professional Conduct (2007), rule 1.13 (Organization as Client).

25. It is not impossible to imagine a large for-profit corporation's stockholders voting to pursue some other goal along with or even in lieu of profit. While this is theoretically and legally possible, it is, nonetheless, highly unlikely. It is perhaps more likely in a small, closely held corporation.

26. See Wendell Berry, "The Total Economy," in *Citizenship Papers* (Washington, DC: Shoemaker & Hoard, 2003), 69.

27. Thomas Shaffer, "Propter Honoris Respectum: Legal Ethics and Jurisprudence from within Religious Congregations," *Notre Dame Law Review* 76 (2001): 967, 966.

28. This comment is not meant to suggest that Christians who are lawyers might not serve those with whom they disagree, such as, e.g., the repulsive criminal defen-

dant. While a separate grounds may be articulated for serving the least of those who are marginalized in any society, my focus here is on lucrative and attractive clients, such as large corporations, that ask the lawyer to serve economic growth in lieu of the Gospel.

29. In response to Bode's question, "Is Henry Catlett your lawyer?" Danny's wife, Lyda, responds: "Henry's our friend" (Wendell Berry, "Fidelity," in *That Distant Land*, 397).

30. Ibid., 403, 410–11.

31. Ibid., 417–18. Similarly, in the story of Old Jack's will, Clara Pettit's husband suggests that the upholding of the law is a "principle," suggesting moral obligation. The banker Gladstone Pettit argues: "Wheeler, you as a lawyer and I as a banker know that this is purely a matter of law—of principle, I would say." Berry contrasts this logic to that of Wheeler, who assumed that the world "was ruled by instinctive decency" (Berry, "It Wasn't Me," 269, 268).

32. Berry, "Fidelity," 420.

33. Shaffer and Shaffer, *American Lawyers and Their Communities,* 198.

34. See Thomas Shaffer, "Maybe a Lawyer Can Be a Servant; If Not . . . ," *Texas Tech Law Review* 27 (1996): 1348.

35. Wendell Berry, *The Memory of Old Jack* (1974; reprint, Washington, DC: Counterpoint, 1999), 107. As Berry further describes Wheeler: "Farming was his passion, as the law was; in him the two really were inseparable. As a lawyer, he had served mostly farmers. His love of farming and of farming people had led him into the politics of agriculture and a lifelong effort to preserve the economy of the small farm" (Wendell Berry, *A World Lost* [Washington, DC: Counterpoint, 1996], 64). (See also Wendell Berry, "Mike," *Sewanee Review* 113 [2005]: 1–15, where Wheeler's three passions are described as lawyering, farming, and bird hunting with a good dog.) It is noteworthy that farming itself has taught Wheeler skills necessary to resist the law. He is independent in the manner of farmers, which is to say, not autonomous, but contrary. He is a man, like his son, "of contrary opinions—a man the size of a few contrary opinions" (Wendell Berry, *Remembering* [New York: North Point, 1988], 13).

36. Shaffer, "Propter Honoris Respectum," 973.

37. Shaffer, whose work is deeply influenced by that of John Howard Yoder, suggests at one point: "I wait for the day when [Yoder] will outline his own Christian ethic for lawyers" (Thomas Shaffer, "How I Changed My Mind," *Journal of Law and Religion* 10 [1993–1994]: 301 n. 21). This invitation, however, represents a misunderstanding of Yoder's claim that there is no "Christian ethic for lawyers." In this regard, the essence of Yoder's advice on the law, as set forth in Shaffer's *Moral Memoranda from John Howard Yoder,* is to avoid altogether the question, Can a Christian be a lawyer? Shaffer notes there: "The better question, John later said to me, is whether the

things a lawyer does in modern America are the things a person who proposes to follow Jesus might do" (Thomas Shaffer, *Moral Memoranda from John Howard Yoder: Conversations on Law, Ethics and the Church between a Mennonite Theologian and a Hoosier Lawyer* [Eugene, OR: Wipf & Stock, 2002], v).

38. See Shaffer and Shaffer, *American Lawyers and Their Communities*, 198.

39. Shaffer, *On Being a Lawyer and a Christian*, 32.

40. See Shaffer and Shaffer, *American Lawyers and Their Communities*, 205–7.

41. See Shaffer, "How I Changed My Mind," 297.

42. See, generally, John Howard Yoder, "The Hermeneutics of Peoplehood," in *The Priestly Kingdom: Social Ethics as Gospel* (Notre Dame, IN: Notre Dame University Press, 1984), 15–45.

43. Berry has explored this theme in essay form as well. In "Sex, Economy, Freedom, and Community," he argues for the priority of community over the public. The former, grounded in "trust, goodwill, forbearance, self-restraint, compassion, and forgiveness," "has the power—not invariably but as a rule—to enforce decency without litigation. . . . And it exercises this power not by coercion or violence but by teaching the young and by preserving stories and songs that tell (among other things) what works and what does not work in a given place" (Wendell Berry, "Sex, Economy, Freedom, and Community," in *Sex, Economy, Freedom, and Community*, 120). Therefore, he argues that justice is inadequate to community and, particularly, marriage and sexual relations, each of which depends on other practices to sustain it, not the least of which is forgiveness (ibid., 139).

In this regard, Berry works along lines consistent with the best of the Christian tradition's reflection on the limited role of litigation in the resolution of disputes within and, perhaps, outside the Christian community. See, generally, Matt. 18:15–20; 1 Cor. 6:1–10. For a book-length treatment of this issue, see my *First Be Reconciled: Challenging Christians in the Courts* (Scottdale, PA: Herald, 2009).

44. See Thomas Shaffer, "Faith Tends to Subvert Legal Order," *Fordham Law Review* 66 (1998): 1089–99.

45. John Howard Yoder, "The Bible and Civil Turmoil," in *For the Nations: Essays Public and Evangelical* (Grand Rapids, MI: Eerdmans, 1997), 84. It should be noted, however, that Yoder convinced Shaffer to change the title of his essay from "Faith Subverts Legal Order" to "Faith Tends to Subvert Legal Order." Shaffer records Yoder's comment: "It is only with a particular 'fallen' definition of what the 'order' has to be recognized as, that the only contribution for the Christian to make is subversion" (Shaffer, *Moral Memoranda*, 36).

46. Berry, "The Wild Birds," 338.

47. Shaffer, citing the work of Paul Tremblay, suggests that clients are "communities that are there for lawyers to discover and to serve" (Shaffer, "Propter Honoris Respectum," 980). With this said, it is important to note that, like *corporation* and

economy, local community can also serve as an abstraction and is not good per se. The call here is to service of the least of these as informed by the particular story of the Gospel. Lawyers who served to sustain, e.g., the racial segregation of the rural South did so in defense of local community but in contradiction to the eschatological community that is both particular and universal.

48. Arguably, it is the Christian eschatological order that Berry envisions in Port William, a community that he often describes with eschatological hopes. See, e.g., Wendell Berry, *A Place on Earth* (1983), rev. ed. (Washington, DC: Counterpoint, 2001), 72, 105, and *Hannah Coulter,* 42, 62. However, how to read Berry on this issue is a difficult question. His fiction is written with a clear sense of the value of community and often with eschatological gestures toward Port William as either heavenly or, more significantly, the New Jerusalem. However, the church and its principal practices, such as baptism and the Eucharist, make scant appearance within his fiction and do little to inform the lives of his characters.

Farming, on the other hand, *is* the constitutive practice of the membership. As noted above, Berry makes clear throughout the Port William narratives that Wheeler's life is embedded within the practice of farming. With an openness to hearing that farming can be construed sacramentally, and with Burley "preaching" to the membership at work in the fields (Berry, *Hannah Coulter,* 97), the vision of Wheeler and Henry as models for the church is by analogy in lieu of an account thereof. The farming community of Port William might also produce and sustain subversive lawyers, but it is not clear that Port William does so out of the same resources as the church.

In response, I would conjecture that Berry would point to a much more expansive vision of Christianity, perhaps one that did not need an institution such as the church to sustain it. In "Christianity and the Survival of Creation," he argues: "The most important religion in [the Bible] is unorganized and is sometimes profoundly disruptive of organization." He continues: "Religion . . . is less to be celebrated in rituals than practiced in the world" ("Christianity and the Survival of Creation," in *Sex, Economy, Freedom, and Community,* 102). While I might agree with many of Berry's arguments regarding the failures of the church, the need for its practices seems to me to be nonnegotiable. For farming to be construed sacramentally, it must have a referent. With all this said, it should be noted that Berry has acknowledged the priority of Christian practices to the survival of Christianity. See Anne Husted Burleigh, "Wendell Berry's Community," *Crisis* 18 (January 2000): 30. See also Rose Marie Berger, "Heaven in Henry County," *Sojourners* 33 (July 2004): 15: "Any religion has to have a practice. When you let it so far from practice that it just becomes a matter of talk, something bad happens."

49. Shaffer, "Maybe a Lawyer Can Be a Servant," 1353, 1354.

50. For example, Martin Luther King and the civil rights lawyers' ability to speak the truth of the black church to the broader society through the language of the law.

See, generally, the account of prophetic minority communities in Walter Brueggemann, *The Prophetic Imagination,* 2nd ed. (Minneapolis: Fortress, 2001).

51. For example, Thomas More's attempts to read Henry VIII's oath in such a way that Christians such as he himself was could faithfully affirm it. See Shaffer, *On Being a Christian and a Lawyer,* 193.

52. Berry, *Hannah Coulter,* 68.

Kyle Childress

Proper Work

Wendell Berry and the Practice of Ministry

> The virtue of our heavenly love tempers our will and makes us want no more than what we have—we thirst for this alone. . . . In His will is our peace.
> —Dante, *Paradiso*

> He was not an ambitious farmer—he did not propose to own a large acreage or to become rich—but merely a good and gifted one. . . . It was a farm of ninety-eight acres, and Tol never longed even for the two more that would have made it a hundred.
> —Wendell Berry, "Watch with Me"

This summer I'm approaching twenty years as the pastor of the Austin Heights Baptist Church, a congregation of fewer than two hundred members in East Texas, about half of whom might be present for worship on any given Sunday. At denominational meetings, and around town, I'm continually asked, "When are you going to a bigger church? Why do you stay?" Sometimes I give a long, rambling explanation, but often I respond with, "Because I read too much Wendell Berry."

I've been reading Berry since 1980 or 1981, after I discovered his essays while serving a small, rural, central Texas congregation as its brand-new college student pastor. I commuted to the church on weekends. I had never been a pastor before, and, even though I was raised in a Baptist church, it had been a much larger First Baptist Church out in west Texas. So I was looking for any insight I could get into the rural life of my congregants. At the same time, I was beginning to explore the issues of hunger, poverty, agriculture, and economics. Somewhere I found a footnote mentioning Wendell Berry. One book led me to another; it wasn't long before I was reading everything I could find of his.

I was in good company. As the veteran pastor Eugene Peterson writes: "Wendell Berry is a writer from whom I have learned much of my pastoral theology. Berry is a farmer in Kentucky. On this farm, besides plowing fields, planting crops, and working horses, he writes novels and poems and essays. The importance of place is a recurrent theme—place embraced and loved, understood and honored. Whenever Berry writes the word 'farm,' I substitute 'parish': the sentence works for me every time."[1]

But, if Berry is a farmer and not a pastor, how are we to read him as a pastoral theologian—one who has, I might add, something of an ambiguous relationship with the church? Berry and his wife, Tanya, usually attend the Port Royal Baptist Church in Port Royal, Kentucky, where she is a member and a deacon, and where their son and his family are members. Tanya also serves on the board of directors of the new Baptist Seminary of Kentucky in Lexington. The Berrys also occasionally attend the New Castle Baptist Church just a few miles down the road, where Berry was baptized as a boy, and where his membership still resides. The Berrys' daughter and her family are members there, where she is a deacon, and where one of the granddaughters is the youth minister. Berry says that he often sits on the same pew alongside his grandchildren that he sat on alongside his grandfather when he was a boy, yet his relationship with the church is sometimes like that of his fictional character Jayber Crow, who attends church but sits in the back pew.

Of Berry's poetry, his much-beloved Sabbath poems were written about Sundays, when he was as likely walking through fields, pastures, and woods as in attendance at church, which is rarely mentioned. In his fiction, the church exists on the periphery of his Port William fellowship and exhibits what Norman Wirzba calls a "disincarnate form of Christianity," a kind of gnosticism, isolated and disconnected from where the people live their lives during the week.[2] Many of us are recovering Gnostics and have served in those "disincarnate" churches, and reading Berry can serve as an effective antidote to whatever vestiges of Gnosticism might lurk in the crevices and corners of our lives.

When I was that young pastor I mentioned above, I remember running up against a particularly vicious version of Gnosticism. I was newly ordained in a church that had never had a black person inside its walls in all its 150-year history and whose members' daily racial prejudice, fear, and outright hatred never were touched by their Sunday praying, singing, and having Jesus in their hearts. Sunday was about heaven, while Monday through Saturday was where they lived. What shocked me even more was that they never saw any of it as a problem. Long before I knew the word, I was a pastor to Gnostics. That's when I discovered Berry.

I engaged Berry as a guide to good pastoral ministry by starting where he starts: with his place. Place is a beginning from which to counter disincarnate forms of the Christian faith that raise the hackles of Wendell Berry and go against the grain of biblical faith, one that is lived out in the flesh.

Berry's place is Port Royal, Henry County, Kentucky, where his family has lived and farmed since before the Civil War. He was a boy in the decade preceding World War II and saw the end of farming that used horses and mules instead of tractors. After World War II, everything rapidly moved toward mechanization and an urban, industrial economy. Berry says: "I began my life as the old times and the last of the old-time people were dying out."[3] But his father and grandfather taught him how to farm with horses and mules, and he continues the practice to this day.

After receiving his bachelor's and master's degrees in English from the University of Kentucky, he married Tanya and studied creative writing at Stanford University with Wallace Stegner. An aspiring writer, he traveled for a year in Europe, then wrote and taught in New York. Then he decided to return home and teach at his alma mater when he realized that what he knew best, and what he needed to write about, was back home in Kentucky. Most of his friends and colleagues thought he was crazy, but he bought a small, marginal farm and reclaimed it, took care of it, and farmed it using traditional farming methods.

In the more than forty years since that move, Berry has written more than forty books of fiction, poetry, essays, and biography. His first novel, *Nathan Coulter* (1960), was the beginning of a series set in and around his fictional Port William, Kentucky. It is the coming-of-age story of young Nathan in that farming community. A more recent work in the set is *Hannah Coulter*, who years later marries Nathan, becomes his widow, and reflects on what it means to be one of the members of a community of families and characters across time, many of whom are connected by blood, and all of whom are connected by the place they share.

As Berry's character Jayber Crow says: "To feel at home in a place, you have to have some prospect of staying there."[4] Just as Berry committed to staying on the farm, somewhere along the way I decided that I needed to do the same—commit to a particular congregation of people over the long haul.

I want to pastor like Berry farms. We live in what Berry calls the culture of "the one-night stand,"[5] and we clergy are often little different from the folks to whom we minister. I'm among the first to say that God sometimes calls us to move to another congregation and that sometimes, by circumstances beyond our control (economic pressures or denominational policies), we have to move. Many of us will admit that, occasionally, we move because we're climbing the denominational success ladder. But faithful staying and committing to one congregation, one community, in the world of one-night stands is a witness to the gospel of "the Word that was made flesh and dwelt among us" (John 1:14). Besides all that, good ministry takes a while.

Years ago Berry wrote: "During the last seventeen years, for example, I have been working at the restoration of a once exhausted hillside. Its scars are now healed over, though still visible, and this year it has provided abundant pasture, more than in any year since we have owned it. But to make it as good as it is now has taken seventeen years. If I had been a millionaire or if my family had been starving, it would still have taken seventeen years. It can be better than it is now, but that will take longer. For it to live fully in its own responsibility, as it did before bad use ran it down, may take hundreds of years."[6]

All pastors have church members whose lives are deeply scarred by bitterness, anger, hurt, abuse, disease, and death, not to mention the deep scarring caused by war, consumer capitalism, nationalism, and racism. These folks are scarred, in short, by sin. For the Gospel of Jesus Christ to grow and heal such worn-out, eroded lives takes patient, long-suffering, detailed work. It takes time to cultivate the habits of peacemaking, forgiveness, reconciliation, and love where violence, mistrust, and fear have long been the norms. It takes time to grow Christians.

A woman stood in my study doorway unleashing her anger on me for the umpteenth time in the seven years I had been her pastor. And I wasn't the only one who was the target of her angry outbursts, but church members as well, many of whom had known her for twenty years. Previous pastors had had the same challenge with her that I had. Over those seven years I had tried reason, confrontation, and avoidance. Nothing seemed to work. But, on that particular day, something clicked with her when, in the middle of her spewing forth, I calmly asked her why she was so angry. She stopped in midsentence, looked at me, and then, with a deep sigh, began to recount a childhood of abuse and anger. It was the conversation that turned the corner in her relationship with me as well as with the members of the congregation. She began to be more careful with what she said and how she said it, began to demonstrate the first vestiges of healing. It took seven years to get to that day, and it has taken many more years of patient, listening work for more healing to take place.

But that's not all; we pastors need more. We also need "correct discipline" along with "enough time" to farm and to pastor properly. *Propriety* is an important word to Berry. "Its value," he says, "is in its reference to the fact that we are not alone. The idea of propriety makes an issue of the fittingness of our conduct to our place or circumstances, even to our hopes. . . . We are being measured, in other words, by a standard that we did not make and cannot destroy."[7] Proper work is the practice of submitting our lives to this call and to these people in this place. It includes the pastoral practices of preaching and teaching and leading the liturgy but also the detailed, painstaking, mundane care of nurturing the people and paying attention to God working in them. Proper work is work that fits with the purpose of God in this particular place.

I recommend the following passage to every pastor-to-be:

> When one buys the farm and moves there to live, something different begins. Thoughts begin to be translated into acts. . . . It invariably turns out, I think, that one's first vision of one's place was to some extent an imposition on it. But if one's sight is clear and one stays on and works well, one's love gradually responds to the place as it really is, and one's visions gradually image possibilities that are really in it. . . . Two human possibilities of the highest order thus come within reach: what one wants can become the same as what one has, and one's knowledge can cause respect for what one knows.
>
> . . . The good worker will not suppose that good work can be made properly answerable to haste, urgency, or even emergency. . . . Seen in this way, questions about farming become inseparable from questions about propriety of scale. A farm can be too big for a farmer to husband properly or pay proper attention to. Distraction is inimical to correct discipline, and enough time is beyond reach of anyone who has too much to do. But we must go farther and see that propriety of scale is invariably associated with propriety of another kind: an understanding and acceptance of the human place in the order of Creation—a proper humility. . . . It is the properly humbled mind in its proper place that sees truly, because—to give only one reason—it sees details."[8]

Berry is describing a farmer who is considering the purchase of a piece of land. (He sounds like a pastor looking over a new church assignment or call.)

Instead of designing a blueprint for how the farm ought to be and then reworking the farm to fit the design, Berry pays attention to the particularities of the land itself and listens to others who might have wisdom about what has worked well on this place and what has not. He works patiently and humbly and lovingly. There is a kind of "hermeneutics of farming" similar to the late Mennonite theologian John Howard Yoder's "hermeneutics of peoplehood," in which one patiently and humbly listens to the sense of the congregation and the Bible and the Spirit in a particular context. For Yoder, the Bible has no isolated meaning "apart from the people reading it and the questions that they need to answer." He goes on to say that to isolate the Bible from context and the people in that context "is to do violence to the very purpose for which we have been given the Holy Scriptures."[9]

To do proper work we must acknowledge that some of what we bring to a new ministry with a congregation is an imposition on it. It can be a kind of violence. It might be the violence of forcing a particular biblical interpretation on a congregation, or the church marketing strategy that we picked up in seminary, or maybe an issue of social justice about which we are particularly impassioned. Sometimes we react to our previous congregation as we serve our present one or bring our ideal church vision and impose it on a new parish.

In my first congregation, I decided within the first few weeks that I needed to confront racism. I went at it with a hard-charging "thus sayeth the Lord." But, after lots of conflict and threats and near brawls with a few people and good counsel from some wise ones, I began to pay attention to my congregation and to what God was saying *through* them as well as to them.

I started learning how to do a kind of hermeneutics of peoplehood, sitting on front porches, and working gardens with the people, and drinking iced tea afterward while listening to their stories, including their stories of race and fear. As a result, my preaching and teaching changed. I still talked about race, but how I talked about it was different. My sermons began to grow out of the conversation between the people and the Bible and the place where we lived. I learned to listen throughout the week in order to speak for twenty minutes on Sunday morning.

The old Baptist prophet Carlyle Marney said that one time he had a couple of preacher-boys in his study telling him all the plans they had for ministry in their first congregations. "These fellows were going to bring in the kingdom with bulldozers," Marney said.

The Kingdom of God is not brought in with bulldozers. It cannot be imposed and still be the Kingdom of God, the Way of Jesus Christ. The means God uses to bring about his reign must fit with the purpose of his reign of justice, peace, harmony, and reconciliation—with God, with humanity, and with all creation. It cannot be coerced with bulldozers, tanks, or guns or with prayers ordered by the state, laws passed by Congress, or manipulations engineered by Madison Avenue. God calls us to do the work of ministry that fits with the life of the Prince of Peace, the Suffering Servant, Jesus.

Unlike the work of bulldozers, which Berry calls "a powerful generalizer" that works against the impulse "to take care of things, to pay attention to the details,"[10] "good work is always modestly scaled, for it cannot ignore either the nature of individual places or the differences between places, and it always involves a sort of religious humility, for not everything is known. Good work can only be defined in particularity, for it must be defined a little differently for every one of the places on earth."[11]

Berry's essays are peppered with biblical references and quotes, and his stories are drenched with the Bible, especially stories of paying attention to details; his knowledge of Scripture and the profound influence of the Christian tradition on literature makes his work an invaluable preaching resource. Perhaps no scriptural image is used more in his work than Jesus' parables of the lost sheep and the lost son found in Luke 15, and there is often the sense that these two parables provide a lens through which he defines and sees what community, friendship, and extended family look like. In "Making It Home," a "lost" son who has been away at war and journeys back home to his family and farm is met out in the middle of a plowed field by his father, who turns to his little brother and says: "Honey, run yonder to the house. Tell your granny to set on another plate. For we have our own that was gone and has come again."[12]

"Watch with Me" is an extended meditation on a community watching out for a lost member who has had a "spell" come over him. They watch him and try to keep him safe until he is himself again. "Thicker Than Liquor" is about a nephew seeking the one lost, drunk uncle and bringing him home. In "Are You All Right?" neighbors check on a household that is cut off from everyone else owing to rising flood waters. And the short novel *Remembering*, with its allusions to Milton and Dante, tells of a young farmer who has been "dismembered" by a farm machinery accident and a loss of a sense of self, only to be "re-membered" back into family and farm and community.[13] For Berry, the good shepherd pays attention to the details of even one lost sheep and goes looking for it until he finds it.

A veteran pastor told me "that there never has been a pastor fired for visiting too much." I spend an enormous amount of time paying attention to the details of members' lives. To put it in the language of the parable of the shepherd and the lost sheep, I'm checking on my flock. In the afternoons, I am usually out visiting with folks, for I have found that most of the good, deep-down work of cultivating disciples happens out where they live and work and spend their time, and much less often in my study, and even less in the crisis times. It is during the crisis times that people reap from what was planted and nurtured earlier during their day-to-day living.

One day I was drinking coffee with a church member when he asked if I'd go with him to look at bass fishing boats. The last thing I wanted to do was look at fishing boats, and I certainly did not have the time to spend the afternoon looking at them. Nevertheless, that's what I did. After two hours of going to various boat dealers, talking about boats and fishing, and making other small talk, he suddenly asked me how to pray. He said that he had never learned to pray, didn't know how to start, and was afraid of praying incorrectly. So we talked about prayer and then ended the afternoon by praying together. It had taken him more than two hours to get up the courage to ask me about prayer. In a normal pastoral visit in my study, we would never have gotten to it because the session would have ended after an hour. Since that afternoon, we now talk about prayer as comfortably as we talk about bass boats, and I'm aware that he's practicing prayer daily. Someday, when the crisis comes, he'll know how to pray.

Of course, it is a rare day that only one sheep is missing or in trouble. Most of the time there are eight or ten missing or sick, on top of the others I'm trying to nourish and teach and encourage. Some sheep find ways to get lost over again and over again. All of us who are decent shepherds know not only that we need some help but also that good New Testament ecclesiology says that it is the whole flock that is to take care of its members.

In Berry's stories, it is the members of the community—those who live and work and share lives—who look out for one another. As a pastor, I keep asking, "How did they get like that? From whom did they learn to share a common life, including taking care of one another in crisis?" Berry says that they learned it from a tradition, a living community-across-time. Extended families passed it along to mothers and fathers, who passed it along to their children. "Human continuity is virtually synonymous with good farming and good farming must outlast the life of any good farmer. For it to do this . . . we must have community."[14]

But communities of people who share life in this way are rare, and the sense of tradition is practically extinct. Here is where we have to move beyond Berry. In his stories, the church exists on the edge of the common life of the people as only a fading, pale reflection of the larger community. We need churches that are, instead, the very ground of community, that define, build, and embody a common life that can move beyond the walls of the church and demonstrate common living in and to the wider society. In other words, we are to do the proper work of helping congregations know that we are the body of Christ. So every Sunday in worship the scattered members of the congregation are regathered and re-membered in Christ as one body. We hear and re-hear the stories of our people across time through the reading of Scripture and participating in practices of worship spanning centuries. This work, our liturgy, then extends beyond Sunday through the rest of the week in practices of ministry and service. At the same time, this mundane, practical common life during the week helps keep our Sunday work from becoming Gnostic.

Berry provides images and stories for congregations that have little concept of what this practical common life looks like, so I encourage my congregation to read his work. His characters work together and eat together; I want the members of my congregation to eat together as often as possible. On most any weeknight, adults and families are on their way home from work, going by the grocery store to pick up something quick for supper, or stopping through a drive-through for the evening meal, and going to their individual homes for supper—even though many drive by the church on their way. We encourage people to come to the church to share their mealtime.

Beyond the good work of projects like Habitat for Humanity, I'm always on the lookout for other ways that the people of the congregation can share work. Most of them do yard and garden work, so we've decided that those who own lawnmowers and garden tillers will share them with those who need them. We also share children, children's clothes, and child care. If someone is visiting the elderly, he or she encourages others to go along, including young people who can learn how to visit and pray with others. We urge veteran Christians to develop meaningful friendships with young people and children. Even a church finance committee meeting is a place for young people to learn—not only about money matters, but also about how mature Christian people deal with such matters.

My proper work as pastor is to nourish and encourage the common life of my congregation. It's hard, sometimes tedious work and often overlooked by others. Yet it is also good and satisfying work; there can be pleasure in it. I work hard but am learning to recognize my limits and trust God for the rest. I spend more time working in the yard and garden, more time with my girls and my wife, and more time on my porch. Berry concludes the poem "The Amish Economy" with the lines:

> But now, in summer dusk, a man
> Whose hair and beard curl like spring ferns
> Sits under the yard trees, at rest,
> His smallest daughter on his lap.
> This is because he rose at dawn,
> Cared for his own, helped his neighbors,
> Worked much, spent little, kept his peace.[15]

That is the kind of pastor I want to be.

Like Berry, and like the Amish about whom he writes, this sense of pleasure and satisfaction is connected with the commitment to stay with this land, paying attention to the details of these people, coming to terms and humbly accepting our proper place with them, and learning to live within the limits of creaturely life. Berry's testimony is that love can grow from submitting to our place; gratitude springs from the grace of no longer trying to "be somebody," as he so often says, or trying to make the land into something it is not. Instead: "One's love gradually responds to the place as it really is. . . . What one wants can become the same as what one has."[16]

In a world where metaphors like *rat race, climbing the ladder,* and *dog-eat-dog* are prevalent even among ministers, loving what you do, knowing satisfaction in it, and being at peace with who you are are not small things. Indeed, it is the grace of God and a witness to the peaceable kingdom to embody such a life. Dante's *Paradiso* points to this when the poet encounters Piccarda Donatti in one of the lower circles of heaven. He says to her: "But tell me: all you souls so happy here, do you yearn for a higher post in Heaven, to see more, to become more loved by Him?" She smiles as she answers him,

"Brother, the virtue of our heavenly love tempers our will and makes us want no more than what we have—we thirst for this alone. . . . In His will is our peace."[17]

Tol Proudfoot, Berry's fictional gentle giant, good man, and fine farmer, embodies this same sense of satisfaction and peace when Berry says of him: "He was not an ambitious farmer—he did not propose to own a large acreage or to become rich—but merely a good and gifted one. . . . It was a farm of ninety-eight acres, and Tol never longed even for the two more that would have made it a hundred."[18]

Over the past forty years, Berry and his family have neither owned a large acreage nor become rich, but he has become a good and gifted farmer and has learned to live a good and gifted life as a witness to God's peaceable kingdom.

One last story: Berry tells of a cold December day when his five-year-old granddaughter, Katie, spent the day with him while he hauled a wagon load of dirt for the barn floor, unloaded it, smoothed it over, and wetted it down. For the first time, Katie drove the team. She was proud of herself, and Berry says that he was proud of her and told her so: "By the time we started back up the creek road the sun had gone over the hill and the air had turned bitter. Katie sat close to me in the wagon, and we did not say anything for a long time. I did not say anything because I was afraid that Katie was not saying anything because she was cold and tired and miserable and perhaps homesick; it was impossible to hurry much, and I was unsure how I would comfort her. But then, after a while, she said, 'Wendell, isn't it fun?'"[19]

May our work, at least from time to time, be full of such simple joy and satisfaction.

Notes

Copyright © 2005 by the *Christian Century.* "Good Work: Learning about Ministry from Wendell Berry," by Kyle Childress, is reprinted with permission in a modified version from the March 8, 2005, issue of the *Christian Century.*

1. Eugene Peterson, *Under the Unpredictable Plant: An Exploration in Vocational Holiness* (Grand Rapids, MI: Eerdmans, 1992), 131.

2. Norman Wirzba, "Placing the Soul," in *The Essential Agrarian Reader* (Washington, DC: Shoemaker & Hoard, 2003), 86.

3. Berry quoted in Kimberly K. Smith, *Wendell Berry and the Agrarian Tradition: A Common Grace* (Lawrence: University Press of Kansas, 2003), 12.

4. Wendell Berry, *Jayber Crow: The Life Story of Jayber Crow, Barber, of the Port*

William Membership, as Written by Himself: A Novel (Washington, DC: Counterpoint, 2000), 298.

5. Wendell Berry, "The Whole Horse," in *The Art of the Commonplace,* ed. Norman Wirzba (Washington, DC: Counterpoint, 2002), 236.

6. Wendell Berry, "People, Land, and Community," in *Standing by Words* (San Francisco: North Point, 1983), 71.

7. Wendell Berry, *Life Is a Miracle: An Essay against Modern Superstition* (Washington, DC: Counterpoint, 2000), 13.

8. Berry, "People, Land, and Community," 70.

9. John Howard Yoder, "The Hermeneutics of Peoplehood," in *The Royal Priesthood: Essays Ecclesiological and Ecumenical,* ed. Michael Cartwright (Grand Rapids, MI: Eerdmans, 1994), 353. Yoder was a Mennonite theologian who spent most of his adult life teaching and writing in Indiana. I wonder if Berry's study of Amish farming methods, their care for creation, their sense of community, and their theology and faith, and his resulting admiration for them, might be an influence in how his "hermeneutics of farming" and Yoder's Anabaptist "hermeneutics of peoplehood" seem so congruent?

10. Wendell Berry, "A Rescued Farm," in *The Gift of Good Land: Further Essays Cultural and Agricultural* (San Francisco: North Point, 1981), 207.

11. Wendell Berry, "Conservation Is Good Work," in *Sex, Economy, Freedom, and Community: Eight Essays* (New York: Pantheon, 1992), 35–36.

12. Wendell Berry, "Making It Home," in *That Distant Land: The Collected Stories* (Washington, DC: Shoemaker & Hoard, 2004), 236.

13. Wendell Berry, "Watch with Me," "Thicker Than Liquor," and "Are You All Right?" all in *That Distant Land,* 77–123, 145–63, and 365–71, and *Remembering* (Washington, DC: Counterpoint, 2008).

14. Berry, "People, Land, and Community," 72.

15. Wendell Berry, "The Amish Economy," in *A Timbered Choir: The Sabbath Poems, 1979–1997* (Washington, DC: Counterpoint, 1998), 190–91.

16. Berry, "People, Land, and Community," 71.

17. Dante Aligheri, *Paradiso,* canticle 3 of *The Divine Comedy,* trans. Mark Musa (New York: Penguin, 1984), 34–35 (3.70–85). Berry told me once that he could be content reading Dante for the rest of his life.

18. Wendell Berry, "Watch with Me," in *Watch with Me: And Six Other Stories of the Yet-Remembered Ptolemy Proudfoot and His Wife, Miss Minnie, Nee Quinch* (New York: Pantheon, 1994), 3.

19. Wendell Berry, "Economy and Pleasure," in *What Are People For?* (New York: North Point, 1990), 143–44.

Part 2

Holy Living

Elizabeth Bahnson

The Pill Is Like . . . DDT?

An Agrarian Perspective on Pharmaceutical Birth Control

> I am convinced . . . that no satisfactory solution can come from consider-
> ing marriage alone or agriculture alone. These are our basic connections to
> each other and to the earth, and they tend to relate analogically and to be
> reciprocally defining: our demands upon the earth are determined by our
> ways of living with one another; our regard for one another is brought to
> light in our ways of using the earth.
> —Wendell Berry, "The Body and the Earth"

I started taking the pill two months after our first son was born. It was a safety measure. After all, he was conceived while my husband and I were (incorrectly) using the natural method. I was only halfway through my master's degree program. How could I possibly graduate if I got pregnant again? So I started taking the "mini-pill" or progesterone-only-pill, which allowed me to continue breast-feeding.

I took the pill for a year and a half and didn't get pregnant, which was a relief. But, I wondered, should I be doing this? It made practical sense—I needed to finish my degree. As my husband, Fred, often reminds me, we moved to the Piedmont of North Carolina so that I could go to school, a decision that he supported but, as a native of Montana, was not entirely thrilled about. We are Christians, members of a community that has long had serious moral concerns about birth control—although our denomination does not have much to say about the matter. While the Catholic Church has an official statement against it (most notably articulated in the 1968 papal encyclical *Humanae vitae*), Protestant Christianity, at least in practice, has unofficially embraced the use of birth control. At the 1930 Lambeth Conference, the Anglican Church passed a resolution allowing the "restrict-ed" use of birth control. The Anglican Church shared some of the Catholic concerns about birth control, such as the likelihood that it would encourage promiscuity, but maintained the value of sex apart from procreation, asserting that "motive, not method, is what made birth control good or bad."[1] The conference agreed that, "in those cases where there is such a clearly felt moral obligation to limit or avoid parenthood, and where there is a morally sound reason for avoiding complete abstinence," contraceptives "may be used . . . provided that this is done in the light of the same Christian principles."[2] Where the health of the mother or the family's financial situation was pressing, contraceptives were deemed morally acceptable. However, the use of birth control was not an option if it was merely a question of convenience, selfishness, or luxury. After 1930, most other Protestant churches followed the Anglican lead.

Yet, in the largely acculturated Protestant church in America, the question of motive has become an ambiguous one. Indeed, it seems that mainline Protestants today are motivated more by the prospect of convenience than by that of welcoming the stranger or the unplanned child. How can we challenge one another's motives for using birth control when we are not held accountable for career choices or home size? At the church I attend, birth control of any kind is rarely discussed and never challenged. We are an unusually young congregation, many of whom are graduate students. On average, there are about thirty people in attendance every week, most of whom are married. There are only two children.

Farmers and Fertility

Fred and I are organic farmers. One day, we got into an argument about birth control—specifically, whether I should be taking the pill. I had been reading up on the Catholic position and was staunchly defending it. Fred was on full attack against. Suddenly I blurted, "What if it's like putting chemicals on our garden?" That stopped him in his tracks. "You're right," he said, after thinking a moment. "I guess it's kind of a 'quick-fix' to control fertility, like the 'quick-fix' fertilizers we don't use to control the fertility of our land." The argument ended there, but I couldn't get away from the thought. How could we be passionate about organic, sustainable agriculture and use hormonal birth control? If we refuse to boost our fertility in the garden using chemical fertilizers or to reduce the numbers of bugs and weeds with pesticides and herbicides, how could we justify using a chemical to control our own fertility?

While there are a lot of good arguments against using birth control, this one had a strong hold on me. I was curious: Are other female farmers asking the same question? What I found was fascinating. None of the women farmers I asked used hormonal birth control. Many of them had tried it at some point but were unhappy with the way it made them feel. Others refused to take it at all. And one friend, who had been taking the pill for years, just recently quit because she has been raising sheep for the last year. Now that she is in touch with nature's seasons and cycles of fertility, she can't justify taking a pill that tricks her body into thinking she's pregnant. I suggested to my sister, who is an organic vegetable farmer, that women who farm are more in touch with nature, including their own bodies. Perhaps that is why they complain about the side effects of the hormones. She laughed and said, "Well, I guess I am in touch with the cycles of the moon." This is because she plants by the moon. Her own cycles are connected to the lunar cycles through the soil she touches every day. It is no coincidence that these women refuse to use hormonal birth control. In every case, it was something inherent in each woman's agrarian way of life that informed her decision.

In his essay "The Body and the Earth," Wendell Berry—perhaps the preeminent agrarian thinker in America—makes a connection between human fertility and the fertility of the earth. He writes: "There is an uncanny *resemblance* between our behavior toward each other and our behavior toward the earth. Between our relation to our own sexuality and our relation to the reproductivity of the earth, for instance, the resemblance is plain and strong and apparently inescapable."[3] In this essay, I try to show how Berry makes that connection. I focus specifically on "The Body and the Earth" as it pulls together many strands of his thought and articulates well an agrarian vision of the world. Then I try to show how that vision is particularly biblical and important for the church to take seriously. Finally, I propose an agrarian perspective on birth control that might help frame the way Christians engage in this debate.

The Agrarian Vision

In "The Body and the Earth," Berry offers a sharp critique of our attitude toward the body in modern industrial society. The chief problem, as he sees it, is that we have forgotten the proper place of human beings within the order of creation. In contrast to preindustrial societies, where art and literature reveal an innate sense that humans are one small part of a much larger creation, Berry observes that, with the rise of industry, "we became less and less capable of sensing ourselves as small within Creation, partly because we thought we could comprehend it statistically, but also because we were becoming creators, ourselves, of a mechanical creation by which we felt ourselves greatly magnified" (100). Effectively thinking ourselves gods, we have created works that cut us off from the wilderness, forgetting that we are a small part of creation and dependent on the whole of creation to survive.

This forgetfulness leads to isolation because it allows us to live under the illusion that we are independent, disconnected beings who can and should pursue our individual self-interests at all costs. Thus, our relationships are increasingly determined by competition, and this isolates us—from the earth and from one another. It is this isolation, Berry argues, that is the source of the disintegration of modern society. But, for Berry, the most fundamental and damaging isolation is that of the body. Not only have we divided ourselves from others, but we are also divided within the self: "At some point we began to assume that the life of the body would be the business of grocers and medical doctors, who need take no interest in the spirit, whereas the life of the spirit would be the business of churches, which would have at best a negative interest in the body" (104). Just as modernity sets one body against another, so it sets the body against the soul. The isolated body is, thus, set against the world, pursuing its satisfaction at the expense of other bodies, of the earth, and even of its own soul. Whether we set the soul against the body or indulge the body at the expense of the soul, we are destroying both.

These divisions between body and soul and world are destructive because, Berry argues, despite our efforts to deny it, everything is connected. We are dependent creatures. Our lives and all life, human and nonhuman, are caught up in a complex system of interdependence that constitutes the whole. Berry writes: "These things that appear to be distinct are nevertheless caught in a network of mutual dependence and influence that is the substantiation of their unity. Body, soul (or mind or spirit), community, and world are all susceptible to each other's influence, and they are all conductors of each other's influence" (110). Trying to divide what is inherently connected threatens the health of the whole. It is like severing the veins of a circulatory system. We are endangering our own lives by living in denial of our connections, to others and to the earth.

As Berry sees it, this begets the disintegration of modern culture, a pattern that is at once cultural and agricultural. Culture and agriculture are dis-integrating precisely because we have divided them. We have forgotten that souls cannot thrive apart from healthy bodies, that bodies cannot thrive without healthy food, and that culture cannot thrive without healthy agriculture. Berry argues that healing is possible only by the restoration of these long-ignored connections. Body, soul, community, and world must be reconnected because the health of each is essential for the health of the whole. In a nut-shell, this is the agrarian vision of the world. It is a vision in which humans are returned to the status of creature and, thus, reconnected to everything in creation. It is a vision in which care for the earth, care for bodies, and care for souls are all bound up in each other.

From this framework, Berry considers how we might reconnect, find healing and wholeness, and overcome division. He begins by considering two core divisions in need of healing. He writes: "The divisions issuing from the division of body and soul are first sexual and then ecological. Many other divisions branch out from those, but those are the most important because they have to do with the fundamental relationships—with each other and with the earth—that we all have in common" (113). Berry brings these two relationships together in his concept of *household*. Far from our modern no-tions of home, the notion *household* suggests something more like a preindus-trial family farm or a cottage industry. It is built on the practical bond of mutual dependence and work. It is the place where a husband and wife are joined in lifework together, where they learn to enact their marriage and prac-tice their love in the midst of being bound together by necessity, not simply to each other, but also to other, similar households. But the household has been dismembered, and what was once a sexual difference—differences in particular tasks that were of equal importance for sustaining the household—became a sexual division. Just as body and soul have been divided, so have women and men, even husband and wife. Berry's critique, in this case, is a bit outdated but useful nonetheless. At the time of writing "The Body and the Earth" (the mid-1970s), he argued that, in modern industrial society, men have been cut off from their nurturing role, sent away from the home to the specialized work that is the lifeblood of the market economy, while a woman's nurture is regarded as being of little use economically. Woman is valued more for her potential buying power than for the complex discipline of housewif-ery. Berry writes: "In modern marriage, then, what was once a difference of work became a division of work. And in this division the household was destroyed as a practical bond between husband and wife. . . . It was no longer a circumstance that required, dignified, and rewarded the enactment of mutual dependence, but the site of mutual estrangement" (115). It could be argued that, in the twenty-first century, both husband and wife have been sent away from home, either to work as highly specialized, well-paid professionals or to be underpaid housekeepers and landscapers in the employ of those same professionals. Either way, households have been dismembered.

It is to the household that Berry says we must return in order to heal these divisions between men, women, and the earth. Here, he makes a vital connection. In the household, there is no sexual or ecological division. In the household, a husband and wife's work is bound to the cycles of fertility and the seasons that make human life possible: "The motive power of sexual love is thus joined directly to constructive work and is given communal and ecological value" (132). Household sex, then, is tied to the constructive work of making and sustaining one another, which is entirely dependent on the fertility of the earth. Thus, the household is the link "between human sexuality and its sources in the sexuality of Creation" (124). Our sexual relationship binds us together in the household; our household binds us to the earth. The way we treat one will invariably affect the other. This is how Berry is able to say that there is a strange "resemblance" between our relation to our sexuality and to the soil we live on.

It is at this point in his essay that Berry makes the connection between the way we treat our own fertility and the way we treat that of the earth. However, before we get into that particular discussion, we must first ask how this vision has any bearing for the church. Does Wendell Berry have anything relevant to say to Christians on this matter? In the next section of this essay, I try to show that he is not far from a biblical vision of the world. Many of the connections he makes are congruous with what the Bible tells us about humankind's relationship with soil. His critique of modern industrial capitalism is a prophetic call to righteousness—that is, right relationships with God, neighbor, and the earth.

In the Garden

We must begin with the creation account, for that is the story that tells us who we are and who God is. One of the primary functions of the creation story is to put us in our proper place in the order of creation. Central to the biblical vision is the notion that we are creatures and God alone is Creator. That essential truth should dispel any illusion we might have about ourselves as godlike. When we acknowledge ourselves as creatures, we discover ourselves connected to everything else in creation. The Old Testament scholar Ellen Davis writes: "The biblical writers . . . help us see the degree to which our relationship with God is bound up in our relationships with the other creatures whom God has made."[4] This complex relationship between God, humans, and the earth is established at the very beginning.

The two creation stories in Genesis, seen together, make clear that, while we have a share in divinity on one side, we are also connected to the fertile soil on the other. In the first creation story, humans are made in the image of God (Gen. 1:26–27). In the second, humans are made from humus; the Potter forms a human body out of clay and breathes life into it (Gen. 2:7). Thus, while humans are to rule the earth as God would (Gen. 1:26–30), representing God's interest in the world, they are also of the earth and dependent on it for life. God and the soil are the sources of human life—both at the beginning and for the rest of the story. Indeed, while humankind, as God's image on earth, has a unique place in the order of creation, the second creation story is a sober reminder of the claim that the soil finally has on us. After the disobedience in the garden, God said: "By the sweat of your face you shall eat bread until you return to the ground, for out of it you were taken; you are dust, and to dust you shall return" (Gen. 3:19 [NRSV]). In the biblical vision, Berry's dyad—body and earth—becomes a triad. God, humankind, and the soil are in relationship and—as we shall see—connected in a way that is very close to Berry's agrarian vision.

Davis argues that, while we are used to the idea that the Bible calls us to love God and neighbor, we may be surprised to discover that the Old Testament is especially interested in our relationship with soil. That relationship is first established in Eden. In the second creation story, God set the first humans in the garden to "watch and work" the land. Davis points out that these Hebrew words (*'avad* and *shamar*) are not common agricultural terms but are used more often to describe human activity toward God. When directed toward God, *'avad* means "worship" and *shamar* means "'to watch,' or 'watch over,' 'observe,' 'keep' or 'preserve.'" Humans are, thus, called into a particular kind of relationship with the soil that goes beyond "till and keep." Humans are called to serve the land, to be subservient to that on which we and all creatures depend for life. We are also called to observe the land as we would

God's commands, learning from it as well as protecting it from harm. Davis writes: "Together, these two verbs outline humanity's complex relationship with the fertile soil, a relationship that is meant to be deferential, observant, and protective. We must serve (*'avad*) the land, not worshipping it but showing it reverence as God's own creation, respecting it as one whose needs take priority over our immediate desires. We must watch it and watch over it (*shamar*) as one who has something to teach us and yet at the same time needs our vigilant care."[5] Thus, in the biblical vision, humans are members of a complex network of relationships, and the call to righteousness entails maintaining the integrity of all those relationships—to God, neighbors, and earth.

The interweaving of these relationships appears again and again throughout the Bible but is particularly vivid in the Song of Songs. In her commentary on the Song of Songs, Davis argues that, most centrally, "the Song is about repairing the damage done by the first disobedience in Eden, what Christian tradition calls 'the Fall.'" Adam and Eve's disobedience to God had the disastrous result of division: division between man and woman, humanity and nature, and humanity and God. The Song, through which we experience healing on all three levels, represents "the reversal of that primordial exile from Eden." This healing is a love story with two primary characters, a man and a woman, who speak passionately of their mutual desire. The Song shows us what pure love looks like, love as it once was in the garden. Yet the language of love that dominates the Song not only speaks of two lovers in the heat of passion but is also about the love between God and humanity (Israel in particular). Moreover, some of the most striking imagery in the Song refers to the land, which not only is the setting for the lovers' encounter but "also becomes an object of love, especially as the perfumed mountains and lush fields of Israel are at times identified with the lovely 'topography' of the woman's body."[6] In fact, the image of the woman we get in the Song looks much more like the land of Israel than a female form. This is revealing. It suggests that God loves the beautiful earth and calls us into that same kind of relationship with creation. Indeed, it calls us back into the garden to reclaim intimacy that once existed: intimacy between God and humanity, between man and woman, and between humans and the earth.

As we have seen, the church has something to learn from the agrarian vision. The Bible makes clear that we are in relationships in which the health of each affects the health of the whole. The biblical vision is like a three-sided prism through which all those relationships are displayed in myriad colors. God, humanity, and the earth are in relationship, and that relationship was once defined by pure love. Yet those relationships have been disordered since the Fall. Division has ensued. But the reality of the Fall does not mean that the connections among God and creatures no longer exist. Indeed, God, humans, and the earth are so deeply connected that disorder in one area causes disorder in another, and these relationships, using Berry's language, are still "reciprocally defining" (131). The way we treat the earth is reflective of our relationship with God, which is reflected back into our relationships with our neighbor or spouse; it is all deeply interwoven.

Sex and Soil

To return to my original question regarding birth control: Does the way we treat our own fertility relate to the way we treat the earth's fertility? In Berry's account in "The Body and the Earth," the disintegration of the household has resulted in the division of sexuality from fertility. That division, of course, is made possible by the advent of hormonal birth control. Whereas natural forms of birth control certainly existed in preindustrial societies, they were determined by what Berry calls "a cultural response to an understood practical limit." Knowing that the land can produce only so much food, most agrarian and hunter-gatherer people used some form of birth control, but it was intimacy with the land that informed their sexual practice. Modern industrial societies, however, have severed the connections between sexuality and fertility. We have also, Berry observes, done the same with the earth's fertility. We have handed it over to the "farming experts" or agribusinessmen. We have allowed the "specialists" to take over our fertility, entrusting "the immense questions that surround the coming of life into the world" (133) to those who, in return, hand us the chemicals and devices to use without restraint. We are now "free from fertility"—both our own and that of the earth—which, Berry writes, "is to short-circuit human culture at its source. It is, in effect, to remove from consciousness the two fundamental issues of human life. It permits two great powers to be regarded and used as if they were unimportant" (134).

There is danger in this "freedom," as Berry warns. As laid out in Genesis, there is a divinely ordained relationship between humans and the land that is marked by servanthood, observance, and protection. That is a stark contrast to the agricultural practices we find today on corporate farms across the world.

Rather than "watching" the land and working within its natural limits, "the dominant practices of modern industrial agriculture are based on the idea that technology has given us the power to reinvent our human relationship to the soil."[7] As we dump massive quantities of pesticides and herbicides on our genetically modified corn and soybeans, as we pump stockyards of beef and cooped-up chickens full of growth hormones, as we watch soil erode and wash into the rivers along with thousands of gallons of animal waste, we are practicing agriculture in a way that threatens the health of our relationship to God and to all our neighbors with whom we share this earth. Can the same be said about the way we treat our own fertility? That we pump our own bodies full of hormones to prevent pregnancy—thus dividing sex from fertility— is a technological achievement that skews our very sexuality.

Wendell Berry published "The Body and the Earth" when pharmaceutical contraceptives were a relatively new phenomenon. He warned that our full embrace of something about which we knew so little, and that affected so significant a part of our lives, could have dire consequences—as the technology of land use already has. It could be said that his view about our treatment of fertility was prophetic. Last summer I was in England visiting my relatives. My cousin is a geneticist, and I asked him about his latest research. He was studying the negative effects of estrogen on fish in rivers in the United Kingdom. "How does estrogen get into the water?" I asked. "The pill," he replied. Berry was right. There is, in fact, a connection between the way we treat our bodies and the way we treat the earth, and scientists are just now stumbling on this.

It is now generally accepted in the scientific community that there is a worldwide decline in amphibian populations.[8] There have been a number of reasons suggested for this: habitat depletion, infectious diseases, and environmental pollution. Recent research suggests that estrogen in the water supply is affecting the reproductive systems of amphibians. There are two forms of estrogen found in amphibian habitats, natural and synthetic. These come from human waste (hormonal birth control, hormone replacement therapy, etc.) and certain types of plants. There are also estrogen mimics that have a different chemical structure but the same effects as estrogens. These come from man-made chemicals that are used for pesticides, such as DDT, and the production of plastic. All these estrogens or estrogen mimics seem to affect amphibian reproductive systems in similar ways, which suggests that this could be one cause of population decline. It is important to note here that "amphibian populations are excellent indicators of the general health of the environment because of their position near the top of the food chain and their significant biomass in many ecosystems" and the permeability of their skin, which allows them to be more sensitive to pollutants.[9] Indeed, there *is* a connection between our attitudes toward our own fertility and that of the earth, and it is found in the creeks and streams that surround us. Our attempt to control fertility threatens the fragile ecosystems in which we live.

Over the course of writing this essay, I stopped taking the pill. I had not worked out all the reasons yet, but it seemed the right thing to do (it also saved us thirty dollars a month). One direct result has been an actual change in my own makeup. Quite literally, I find myself a happier person. I had been taking the progesterone-only pill. Progesterone is the hormone that dominates a woman's cycle after she has ovulated, approximately fourteen days prior to menstruation. As progesterone levels rise, a woman often feels slightly depressed, tired, bloated—all symptoms of PMS. By ingesting progesterone, I was daily forcing PMS down my throat. Now, as my body is returning to its natural rhythm, I find that my mood has changed, and I follow its changes throughout my monthly cycles. Estrogen, the hormone that dominates the first part of the cycle, lifts my mood. I generally feel happy, energetic, confident. After I ovulate, I can feel myself slide downward until I menstruate. The beauty for me (and for my family) is that I *understand* these feelings. Instead of getting frustrated or blaming myself for mood swings, I can see that my own body often determines how I feel. It also helps in my relationship to my husband. I can warn him, "I may be more sensitive this week." Or I can apologize, "I'm sorry I reacted that way; I think I know why I was more defensive than usual."

Early in the process of writing this essay, I contacted Norman Wirzba, then a philosophy professor at Georgetown College who is also an agrarian, a husband, and a father of four. I thought that he might have some insights on the subject of birth control and asked him to discuss my questions with his wife, Gretchen Ziegenhals—specifically, the parallels between chemicals put on a garden and chemicals put into our bodies. He replied: "My wife is concerned that women's bodies not be understood in a passive way, something like a garden upon which men can exact their wishes."[10] I agree. It is not women's bodies that we should think of as a garden. Both women and men have fertile bodies, and, when they become one flesh, their fertility is joined. It is not a singular but a plural concept—*our* fertility. But I think that the garden metaphor is still helpful here. Fred and I work the garden together. It is a mutual effort that requires both of us—he usually does the digging and planting, while I do the weeding and harvesting. We both do the cooking. But all that labor requires working together and working with nature. We have to plant cabbage and broccoli early in the spring—otherwise worms will eat it. We have to plant sweet potatoes in the heat of summer so that we can eat them over the winter. We compost our weeds and scraps and plant cover crops on our garden beds so that we will have good fertility next year. We are learning to "watch and work" the land on which God has placed us. All this helps us reimagine how we think about our own fertility. And we are learning to "watch and work" our bodies so that we do not divorce sexuality from fertility and, as Berry says in "The Body and the Earth," "pleasure from responsibility" (135).

As Christians, we are called to a particular kind of relationship with nature—the nature of the earth and that of our bodies. We are called to treat it respectfully, with holy reverence, as God's own creation. We are called to learn from it, to be amazed by it, and to work with it. And we are also called to protect it and keep it from harm. In treating the earth this way, in treating our own bodies that way, we will treat other bodies that way. This begins to approach the shalom, the peace and wholeness that God desires. Even so, we cannot plan for everything. God sends us surprises. After putting compost on my flower bed this year, a tomato plant sprouted. Instead of pulling it up, I let it grow in the middle of my perennials. To our surprise, that plant produced the first tomato of the year.

Notes

1. Jenell Williams Paris, *Making Wise Choices: Birth Control for Christians* (Grand Rapids, MI: Baker, 2003), 24.

2. 1930 Lambeth Conference of Anglican Bishops, "Resolution 15: The Life and Witness of the Christian Community—Marriage and Sex," available at http://www .lambethconference.org.

3. Wendell Berry, "The Body and the Earth," in *The Unsettling of America: Culture and Agriculture,* 3rd ed. (San Francisco: Sierra Club Books, 1977), 124. Page numbers for subsequent cites will be given parenthetically in the text.

4. Ellen Davis, *Getting Involved with God: Rediscovering the Old Testament* (Boston: Cowley, 2001), 183.

5. Ibid., 186, 192 (first quote), 193, 194 (second quote).

6. Ellen Davis, *Proverbs, Ecclesiastes, and the Song of Songs,* Westminster Bible Companion (Louisville: Westminster/John Knox, 2000), 231, 232, 233.

7. Davis, *Getting Involved with God,* 195.

8. Edmund J. Clark, David O. Norris, and Richard E. Jones, "Interactions of Gonadal Steroids and Pesticides (DDT, DDE) on Gonaduct Growth in Larval Tiger Salamanders, *Ambystoma tigrinum,*" *General and Comparative Endocrinology* 109 (1998): 94.

9. T. Rouhani Rankouhi et al., "Effects of Environmental and Natural Estrogens on Vitellogenin Production in Hepatocytes of the Brown Frog (*Rana temporaria*)," *Aquatic Toxicology* 71 (2005): 94 (quote), 97.

10. Norma Wirzba, e-mail message to author, June 17, 2006.

Fred Bahnson

The Salvation of the City

Defiant Gardens in the Great Northern Feedlot

> Farming is an altar on which only the bread and wine of truth can be placed.
> —Catherine de Hueck Doherty, *Apostolic Farming*

In these days of war, my thoughts return to Italo Calvino's *Invisible Cities,* a fantastical novel in which Marco Polo and Kublai Khan meet nightly in the Khan's palace garden for a series of fevered conversations. Marco Polo tells the Khan of all the exotic, mysterious cities within the empire. Night after night he describes each city until finally the Khan realizes that the young Venetian traveler is really speaking again and again of the same place. But these tales can only distract; the Great Khan knows that his empire is crumbling, that he himself is dying. One evening Kublai Khan confesses to Marco Polo that his empire is "rotting like a corpse in a swamp." Here is Marco Polo's response: "Yes, the empire is sick, and, what is worse, it is trying to become accustomed to its sores. This is the aim of my explorations: examining the traces of happiness still to be glimpsed, I gauge its short supply. If you want to know how much darkness there is around you, you must sharpen your eyes, peering at the faint lights in the distance."[1]

Though the rulers of the American Empire share much with Kublai Khan—for example, the desire to control the known world—they lack his wisdom in one crucial area: the ability to see that the empire is rotting. Lying, torture, preemptive war, using God as a political tool, privileging corporate welfare over the welfare of communities, mandating the pursuit of unlimited economic growth on a planet with finite resources—how long can it really last? These things can't be reduced to certain policy choices or the work of a few bad apples, as if missing weapons of mass destruction and Abu Ghraib are mere speed bumps on the road to freedom. This is simply how the empire does business, and ours is perhaps the first generation in this country's history to be able to look past the facade and see the monster behind the mask.

The empire is sick, and what is worse, it is trying to become accustomed to its sores.

Where will be found the faint lights in the distance?

Hope Grows in a Field

Adela and I are hauling water. Five-gallon buckets in each hand, we make forays down to the creek, where we dip our buckets, haul them back up the hill, then hand them off to another crew. A group of us is watering peas, potatoes, spinach, and lettuce—our first spring crops.

It's a dry March here in North Carolina's Piedmont, a tough spring to start a community garden. La Niña is upon us—which foretells a summer of drought. We don't have a well yet. I worry that we won't be able to keep hauling water through the hot summer.

Adela doesn't seem to have these concerns, and when she walks up, sets down her buckets, and smiles, my own fears vanish. We fall to talking, Adela in rapid Mexican Spanish, me in halting Gringo Spanglish. We talk about the work, the planting and watering and weeding that will need to happen before we harvest. I ask her about the years she worked in North Carolina's tobacco fields. We rest. Then we go back to work.

Though I began with the backdrop of empire, my real subject here is a garden, specifically, a community garden. I wish to articulate why the church needs community gardens, why such gardening is an act of resistance to the powers that be, and why growing food is a small but necessary witness to the Kingdom of God.

The place Adela and I watered peas is called Anathoth Community Garden. My thoughts have been shaped by this place, and it's largely the story of this particular garden and its people that I want to tell.

A year ago, when Anathoth was only an idea, I tried to write a theology of gardening. I thought that would help me voice to others why Anathoth was important and necessary. I failed. The idea was doomed before I wrote the first word because I had approached it abstractly. The story of Anathoth Community Garden had yet to begin; therefore, any theologizing prior to the story itself would fail precisely because it was prior. Theology cannot be imposed on particular stories; it can only arise out of them. This doesn't just happen magically. Theology, like gardening, requires cultivation.

Anathoth Community Garden is now a reality. The story has a beginning. I can now attempt to answer the question I'm still asked a year after the garden has begun producing food: *Why should a church involve itself in agriculture?*

Here's how our community garden works. When Adela became one of the founding members of Anathoth, she paid her five dollars for the entire year, she agreed to donate two hours of her time a week (she really works three or four), and she agreed to be put to work at whatever needs doing that day. In turn, Adela and other members receive a share of the weekly harvest—everything from arugula to Zapotec tomatoes—from April through November. Though we seek out migrant and low-income families to become members, anyone can join.

The food is grown without harmful fertilizers or chemicals. We do the work by hand, thus reclaiming the God-bestowed dignity of manual labor. Initially, the ground was plowed with a neighbor's tractor. But the permanent raised beds were built by hand, and we now do nearly all ongoing tasks—carting manure, weeding, planting—by hand as well. This privileging of hand tools over machines affords the dual pleasure of decreasing our dependence on the oil economy and providing exercise for our bodies. We prefer the scythe to the weed-whacker.[2] Energy taken from the soil in the form of vegetables is returned as compost, thus keeping the soil, in Sir Albert Howard's words, "in good heart."[3] Our goal is to make Anathoth Community Garden sustainable in the most basic sense: it will operate almost entirely on sunlight and the work of human hands.

These are the nuts and bolts of our community garden, or, rather, the roots and branches. But the invisible work, the movement of God's Spirit, that holy sap rising unseen to give life to trunk and limb—this I find harder to describe or explain.

The story of Anathoth Community Garden really begins with a murder. On a June afternoon in 2004, Bill King was closing up his shop on the corner of Mill Creek and Carr Store Road when someone walked through the door and shot him in the back of the head. Before Bill and his wife, Emma, bought the place, the little bait and tackle grocery was a haven for local crack dealers. The first thing Bill and Emma did when they arrived was to ask the dealers to leave. Parents began bringing their children to the store for ice cream; neighborhood kids rode their bikes down for a soda. When people couldn't pay, Bill would let them take food on credit. Whatever sense of safety this little farming community of Cedar Grove had enjoyed before that afternoon in June, one trigger pull had ended. A once-quiet way of life was shattered. People here were angry and afraid.

Valee Taylor, a friend of Bill's, was just plain angry. Several weeks after the murder, Valee visited Grace Hackney, the pastor of the Cedar Grove United Methodist Church (UMC), to talk about what the community should do. It's not often that a black man will set foot in a white church in Cedar Grove, but Valee and Grace had become friends after meeting one day at the post office. Valee wanted to put out a reward. Grace had another idea—a prayer vigil. Valee was persuaded. The following week, people from the community gathered in the parking lot of Bill's store, and they prayed for peace. Grace later told me that the motivation behind the vigil was to make "a statement against the domination of fear. As people of faith we are called to stand up against violence, against separation according to class, race, and other societal divisions."

Hearing Valee tell it, that afternoon was a sort of mystical experience. "The sunlight was shining down on us," he said, "the air was crisp, there was a light breeze. Here were blacks and whites together praying for peace in the
‸‸ ked about it that day, I had never understood the
God. And looking out across the parking lot—I'd

e is no bigger than a church, a post office, and a
 ̣ hundred people attended Bill's vigil. One of
᠃'s mother, Mrs. Scenobia Taylor, a fifth-genera-
᠃merican sharecroppers and daughter of Doc
᠃gest landowner in Orange County. Mrs. Taylor
᠃witnessed at the vigil. After the murder, as she
᠃n to give five acres of her land to the commu-
᠃his land would help heal the community's
᠃ ̣e give it?
᠃ce initiated a series of community conversa-
᠃ling them "Food-Faith-Farm." People came
᠃ as from the wider Cedar Grove communi-
᠃ ̣local librarian. We began by looking at some

troubling realities: Why was it that many of us had land, yet within five miles of the church there were people who didn't get enough to eat? The "rich food" of which Isaiah spoke was available only to those "with money and with price" (Isa. 55:1f [NRSV]). Couldn't some of the arable land, much of it former tobacco land that since the federal buyouts was now lying fallow, be used to grow food for people who needed it? Other questions followed: If the church's mission is to practice reconciliation, doesn't that include mending our relationship with the land, perhaps restoring some of the fertility lost from years of soil erosion? How can the *'adam* (human) care for the *'adamah* (humus); how can we "till and keep" the fertile soil to which our lives are inextricably bound (Gen. 2:7, 15)? In the midst of these questions, the idea for a community garden arose.

When Mrs. Taylor learned about the community garden idea, she knew that her dream had been prophetic. She donated the five acres to Cedar Grove UMC to act as trustee, and Anathoth Community Garden was born.

Grace invited me to get involved when the first conversations began. I live near Cedar Grove on a small subsistence farm that my wife and I work together. In May 2005, I quit my job as a writing tutor at the Duke University Divinity School, wrote grants over the summer, and by August was hired as the garden manager. I work full-time, my salary paid by donations and grants from Duke Endowment and the Valparaiso Project for Christian Practices. A continuing series of grants from the coffers of James B. Duke are funding the first three years of the garden's life.

One way to describe Anathoth is that it's a place where the fortunes of a robber baron now feed illegal immigrants and crack addicts.

The Vocation of Farming

Managing these two arable acres, which are beginning to seem more like a small farm than a garden, is the hardest job I've ever had. Nothing in my formal education prepared me for this; nor is it the livelihood I ever imagined myself making. But as tobacco–cum–turf farmer Dwight Compton once told me, you don't choose to farm—you're *chosen*. Farming or gardening is not just a job; it's a calling. A vocation.

I'm often asked why a well-educated thirty-four-year-old would take a job as the manager of a community garden. Implicit in the question are several unspoken assumptions: it's a downward move; it's a waste of a master's-level education; farming is better left to blue collars and migrants; and so on. My answer often begins as a counterquestion: "Have you ever read Wendell Berry?" Though I'm reluctant to speak of conversion experiences, I find myself reaching for that language when I describe the influence Berry's writings have had on my life. I first read Berry while at Duke Divinity School, in a Christian ethics class taught by Joel Shuman, one of the editors of this volume. In Berry's novels, essays, and poems, I saw emerging a way of life that *made sense.* Berry's agrarian world jumped off the page fully clothed and alive. Here was an antidote to the shallow consumerism in which I was mired; here was a holistic, practical vision of how to live rightly both with the land and with others. I had found a way of life I wanted to claim as my own.

In a letter to Berry (his former student), Wallace Stegner sums up my own reaction on discovering Berry's work: "Those who read you devoutly— and this letter is an indication that I am one of them—find something else in you that their world too much lacks: the value, the real physical and spiritual satisfaction, of hard human work. We respond to your pages as victims of pellagra or scurvy respond to vitamins. . . . You are a hero among those who have been wounded and offended by industrial living and yearn for a simpler and more natural and more feeling relation to the natural world."[4]

I was one of those "wounded and offended by industrial living." I grew up in southwestern Montana, a place of such beauty it makes your teeth ache. My father taught me as a boy how to visit wild places around our home in Gallatin Valley and how to leave them undisturbed by our passing. My footprint on the world then was small. But, when I moved east to attend Duke in my late twenties, I saw a larger footprint, one I had made by participating in our culture's running roughshod over creation, all in desperate hunger for *more.* Berry's agrarianism offered a way out. And so I joined that group of those Stegner mentioned, those who respond to Berry's books "as lost dogs in hope of rescue turn toward some friendly stranger."[5]

For some time afterward, my conversion remained incomplete. It was impotent because it was a conversion only from the neck up. I had no attendant practices to get my hands and feet involved. In May 2000, I graduated from Duke fully convinced that agrarianism would save us from the greed, violence, and sheer idiocy of capitalism (the idea that you can have unlimited economic growth, e.g., on a planet of finite resources), yet I hadn't the slightest knowledge of how that way of salvation was worked out. Even that idea— *agrarianism will save us*—was murky and abstract. I hadn't yet learned how one did the work necessary to sustain an agrarian way of life. I needed to see Berry's vision lived out in a particular community.

In the spring of 2002, I went to Chiapas as a "peaceworker." I lived among a group of indigenous coffee farmers whose families had been attacked by government-sponsored paramilitaries in the low-intensity war of the 1990s. This was Graham Greene country, a land where groves of crosses stood on forlorn hillsides "like trees that had been left to seed,"[6] where the Mexican government was still killing Christians, only this time under the banner of counterinsurgency instead of fascism.

Young and naive, I did little to ameliorate the situation. My "peacemaking" consisted of me spending several nights in these people's homes, eating their tortillas, drinking their sweet, weak coffee, and trying to learn to speak Tzotzil. I received far more than I gave, and what they gave me more than anything was the desire to live as they did, at least insofar as I could in my own country. Among these lovely people—Catholic pacifists who had renounced the armed path of the Zapatistas, farmers of the kind we'd call *organic*—I saw embodied the agrarian practices I now wanted to claim as my own. I returned from Chiapas determined to farm. I wrote to Berry asking if I could apprentice with him at Lane's Landing, sending along with my request some poems I'd written. Though I don't think he saw much in my poetry—"you have much to learn about making poems"—he did encourage my farming interests. He wasn't farming much now, "just some slaughter lambs," and wouldn't be able to take on an apprentice, but recommended that I should seek out a farm near where I lived in North Carolina, offering to help me locate one.

I soon found a job as a farm apprentice at Harvey Harman's place, a permaculture farm in nearby Chatham County, North Carolina. What I learned from Harvey gave me enough confidence to try my own hand at farming, if only at the subsistence level. Now, as the manager of Anathoth Community Garden, my education continues. From the vantage the garden affords, I can see the trajectory my life has taken. Its arc traces a consistency only a hand larger than mine could have writ. I guess that's what Dwight Compton meant about being chosen.

Gardening for Exiles

The year of Bill King's murder, 2004, was the year Jeremiah came up in the lectionary. It was also the year American forces tried to mop up the after-effects of the 2003 U.S. invasion of Iraq. Jeremiah knew something about invasions. At the time he was writing, the Babylonians had just sacked Jerusalem in a "shock and awe" campaign and carted off the first wave of captives. Jeremiah's people were dragged from their homes and forced to live in a strange land where they had no power and no job opportunities and didn't speak the language. Nevertheless, during the Babylonian siege, God told Jeremiah to buy a field at Anathoth. The known world was crumbling. Yet this little chunk of real estate became a symbol that God would restore Israel, that "houses and fields and vineyards shall again be bought in this land" (Jer. 32:15). Anathoth became a sign of hope in a war-torn world, a continuation of God's earlier message to the exiles already living in Babylon: "Plant gardens and eat what they produce. . . . Seek the shalom of the city where I have sent you into exile, and pray to the Lord on its behalf, for in its shalom you will find your shalom" (Jer. 29:5, 7). *Shalom* is not just the absence of violence; it is a state of well-being, of living in harmony with one's community and with the land.

Jeremiah made clear that planting gardens and seeking peace were symbiotic practices—like sowing beans with your corn or marigolds with your tomatoes—and exactly the kind of companion planting the church should be doing. How curious that Jeremiah doesn't tell the Jews to escape, or seize the reins of power, or advance the Jewish cause by getting legislation passed in Babylon's halls of power. Instead, he tells them to build houses and inhabit them, to plant gardens and eat what they produce. Marry and multiply. In other words, *settle down and flourish.* Live as if you were perfectly at home. Home is no longer a territory to be defended. Home is now whichever Babylon God happens to send you. *Shalom* doesn't begin once every last Babylonian is convinced they need to get on board. It begins with a few people planting gardens in a land at war. It begins with a field.

When we read ourselves into Jeremiah's story, we come up short. In many ways, those of us who are white, middle-class Christians aren't the exiles; we are Babylon. Real exiles—the rural poor, migrant workers, crack addicts—live all around us. How can we ourselves live in *shalom* when, within a five-mile radius of Cedar Grove, there are at least twenty families who live without indoor plumbing? North Carolina has one of the fastest-growing Latino migrant worker populations in the country. Many of these people are driven from their farms owing to the pressures of falling corn and coffee prices, thanks in large part to neoliberal economic trade policies like the North

American Free Trade Agreement that are created and enforced by our own government. Welcoming these landless exiles to grow food at Anathoth seems one way the church can seek the *shalom* of our community.

In November 2005, we broke ground, built two beds, and planted an unlikely pair of fall crops: garlic and blueberries. In spring 2006, we built more beds and planted corn, potatoes, peas, peppers, and tomatoes. The following year, we added a passive-solar greenhouse to extend the growing season, built a Celtic cross garden, and built a deck on the barn. The garden is now the host site for Volunteers for Youth, a nonprofit agency that takes young people with community service hours to fulfill and places them at work sites. On an average week, we'll host ten to fifteen of these young people on our Saturday workdays. We now have a rotating student internship program in which future pastors from Duke Divinity School serve their field placements with us, as well as a summer apprenticeship program in which young people learn how to start and manage a community garden. For the most part, the work has gone smoothly.

But not everyone is supportive. The land on which the garden sits is a mere quarter mile down Mill Creek Road from where Bill King was murdered. Further down the road from Anathoth are several known crack houses. Bill King's murderer, never apprehended, may well have set foot on Anathoth Community Garden. *Why build a garden down there where the crack dealers live?* people ask us. *What if people steal your vegetables?*

One day I called up a local chicken farmer, whom I'll call Vic, to see whether I could buy chicken manure to spread on our garden. I had never met Vic but knew that he was a former member of Cedar Grove UMC. Vic told me that they used all their manure on their tobacco fields. I thanked him anyway and was about to hang up when he said, "But even if I did have some, I wouldn't sell you any." I was blindsided by what followed. Vic proceeded to berate me, an outsider, for coming into his community "where my family has been since 1783" and "messing everything up." He said that he thought the community garden was a bad idea, that "outsiders" had taken over Cedar Grove UMC, and that, as long as "you outsiders" were doing things like starting community gardens, he'd never set foot in that church. I asked whether we could talk about this in person. Why was the community garden such a bad idea? But he only laughed bitterly and hung up.

I was tempted to laugh myself and would have had not Vic been so incensed. Against the idea of a community garden? That's like being against school lunch programs or improved health care. I had the same flummoxed reaction as I'd had when the other naysayers had argued that we shouldn't build a garden "down there." But then I began to wonder whether Vic's vitriol over what seems like a fairly innocuous thing means that maybe it's not so innocuous after all. Maybe a community garden is actually a threat to life as we know it. To acknowledge that there are people who go hungry in this community is to put some hard questions before those of us who possess the land and the means to address that hunger.

Of course, what Vic and others like him don't know yet (it's with hope, not optimism, that I add *yet*) is that the result of this barrier breaking isn't anarchy or bedlam. When strangers grow and share food together, they cease to be threatening to each other. The ones who were once abstract categories—the *poor folks,* the *rich folks,* the *black folks,* the *white folks,* the *illegal aliens*—cease to be categories and become instead the people they've always been: Larry, James, Adela, Cynthia, Vic.

The Art of Opting Out

Jeremiah teaches us that the way to get along in this world is to skirt Babylon altogether. Don't waste time fighting the empire or trying to make it a little less evil; opt out. Step around it, and go about your business. Grow your own food, for instance.

One reason you plant gardens and eat what they produce, from Jeremiah's time until now, is that you can't trust Babylon with the food supply. Since the end of World War I and the ensuing proliferation of cheap petrochemicals, we've entrusted our eating to the Babylon of the American industrial food system. This particular Babylon, like all Babylons, claimed a salvific status not granted by God. With the so-called green revolution, scientists and politicos claimed, America would be able to feed—that is, *save*—the entire world. But, in the words of James Howard Kunstler, though the green revolution boosted crop yields, it "was minimally about scientific innovation in crop genetics and mostly about dumping massive amounts of fertilizers and pesticides made out of fossil fuels onto crops, as well as employing irrigation at a fantastic scale made possible by abundant oil and gas."[7] This project has resulted in one of the most unsustainable food systems in the world, where a head of lettuce grown in the Salinas Valley in California and shipped to Washington, DC, consumes thirty-six times the fossil fuel energy in transport as it gives back in food energy.[8] But what happens when the oil runs out?

When you let Babylon grow the food you eat, you remain in its clutches. Industrialized agriculture has contributed to this country becoming one of the most obese in the world. A friend of mine in Bolivia calls the United States "the Great Northern Feedlot": we don't much care how our food is grown as long as a steady, cheap supply comes rolling down the trough.

One need not travel far into the Berry corpus to see how detrimental this industrial-eating mentality and its outworkings have been. Industrial agriculture eschews ecological knowledge in favor of what Sir Albert Howard called "the NPK mentality." At the end of the so-called Great War, the munitions factories stopped fixing atmospheric nitrogen to make bombs and began to make fertilizers. Scientists had learned that plants could be grown with only nitrogen (N), phosphorus (P), and potassium (K). The NPK mentality is a kind of reductionistic faith in these chemicals to supply everything the plant needs. But as Howard foresaw in 1943: "These chemicals and machines can do nothing to keep the soil in good heart. By their use the processes of growth can never be balanced by the processes of decay. All that they can accomplish is the transfer of the soil's capital to current account."[9] Our current food chain depends from start to finish on fossil fuels. The fertile soil in this system is no longer a living entity but rather an inert mix of sand, silt, and clay—a convenient place to prop up your crop while you feed it NPK. The results are ruinous and myriad: the dead zone in the Gulf of Mexico; topsoil disappearing faster than the earth can make it; poisoned aquifers. "Mother earth [thus] deprived of her manurial rights," Howard says, "is in revolt; the land is going on strike; the fertility of the soil is declining."[10]

We could return to the earth its "manurial rights" if we stopped relying on oil and hubris and relied instead on sunlight and local knowledge. It's how all food was grown before the advent of petrochemicals; it is how food will continue to be grown when the oil runs out. Depending on which expert is doing the predicting, that will be sometime in the next twenty to fifty years.

Another way to get around this Babylon is to buy as much of our food as we can from local farmers and to get to know their names. "Don't you find it odd," the farmer Joel Salatin asked the journalist Michael Pollan, "that people will put more work into choosing their mechanic or house contractor than they will into choosing the person who grows their food?"[11]

But perhaps the best way to opt out of industrial eating is one Jeremiah recommends, that is, trying your hand at small-scale food production. Though most of us are two or three generations removed from the land, I have a hunch that we all harbor a deep yearning to participate in the necessities of procuring food and shelter. Consider the following from Gene Logsdon, an agrarian-curmudgeon extraordinaire:

> It seems to me that the garden is the only practical way for urban socie-
> ties to come in *close* contact with the basic realities of life, and if that
> contact is not close, it is not meaningful at all. To feel the searing heat as
> well as the comforting warmth of the sun, or to endure the dry wind as
> well as the soothing breeze; to pray for rain but not too much rain; . . .
> to know that life depends on eating and being eaten; to accept the decay
> of death as the only way to achieve the resurrection of life; . . . to grow
> in personal simplicity while appreciating biological complexity, so that
> in the garden there is time to sit and think, to produce good food for the
> mind—these are all part of an education that the industrial world hun-
> gers for but cannot name.[12]

Community gardens like Anathoth can provide such close contact. There people can learn the lost art of canning or rediscover the joy of sliding their hands into garden beds the consistency of chocolate sponge cake. As Logsdon reminds us, these things are an education that the industrial world cannot provide.

I've come to exult in the resistance inherent in the act of growing food. In his book *Defiant Gardens,* Kenneth Helphand describes gardens created under the duress of war. Helphand's book contains amazing pictures of such defiant gardens: World War I soldiers on Vimy Ridge growing celery along the bottom of a communications trench; Jews growing cabbage in the Lodz ghetto; a hillside of "bonsaied" desert sage in front of the Minidoka intern-ment camp for Japanese Americans.[13] I think of Anathoth as a garden created during a war and, thus, a defiant garden. The violence isn't only in Iraq; it's right down the street at Bill King's store. It's inside us. Hauling water with Adela, planting a row of sweet potatoes with young people from Volunteers for Youth—these are small acts of protest, not just against the Great Northern Feedlot of Babylon, but also against the Babylon within our soul, the violent desire we each harbor to lord it over others.

Growing even a small portion of our own food trains us to see that food is a gift, not a commodity. "The way we eat," says Michael Pollan in *The*

Omnivore's Dilemma, "represents our most profound engagement with the natural world. Daily, our eating turns nature into culture, transforming the body of the world into our bodies and minds."[14] For Christians, the way we eat also represents—through the sharing of Christ's body and blood—our most profound engagement with each other. By sharing the Lord's Supper, we learn not just how to eat but how to share and how to receive, how to live and how to die. The orthodox theologian Alexander Schmemann puts it this way: "Centuries of secularism have failed to transform eating into something strictly utilitarian. Food is still treated with reverence. A meal is still a rite— the last 'natural sacrament' of family and friendship, of life that is more than 'eating' and 'drinking.' To eat is still something more than to maintain bodily functions. People may not understand what that 'something more' is, but they nonetheless desire to celebrate it. They are still hungry and thirsty for sacramental life."[15]

Anathoth Community Garden is, as an extension of the church, a place where those who still hunger and thirst for sacramental life can be fed. In that way, it is a school for reverence. The garden teaches us that the way we eat, what we eat, and whom we eat it with *matter.* Eating a meal of Yukon Gold potatoes and Swiss chard that you've grown with your neighbor follows organically from sharing the Lord's Supper. To think of food sacramentally is something "the industrial world hungers for but cannot name." It's up to the church to do the naming. We can renarrate for the world not only what it means to eat but also what it means to eat well. People desire to be fed; a church's community garden becomes the place to fulfill such desires even as it transforms them.

Stanley Hauerwas, a professor of theology and ethics at Duke Divinity School, recently visited Anathoth Community Garden and afterward preached at Cedar Grove UMC. In his sermon, he said of Anathoth: "A community garden—what a useless gesture." I took that as a compliment to our work, or at least an honest appraisal. Gardening will by no means change the world. Though we hope it will have some effect, that's not really why we do it; we're just trying to be faithful. A community garden won't stop the nations from wreaking havoc. It won't feed the world. How silly to waste one's time growing food when a supermarket is filled to the brim just down the road. "A garden," Berry says in his essay "The Reactor and the Garden," "is not always as comfortable as Kroger's." Yet it's exactly in the uselessness of the gesture, the smallness of it, the discomfort it causes from doing work that is physically demanding, that the garden finds its strength.[16] "It is in the willingness to accept this discomfort that we strike the most telling blow against the power plants [or Babylons] and what they represent," continues Berry. "We cannot hope to recover our freedom from such perils without discomfort."[17]

Gardening, useless though it may appear, finds a certain strength in weakness. Gardening is a "complete action," Berry says, because it's an action that is more than symbolic. It is a protest, but it goes beyond protest and proposes an answer. Community gardening can be seen as a piece of what Berry calls "the work of local culture." In an essay by that title he says: "The only true and effective 'operator's manual for spaceship earth' is not a book that any human will ever write; it is hundreds of thousands of local cultures."[18] There will be no one, overriding answer, only hundreds of thousands of answers, all worked out locally. The work of local culture is but a different twist on the same answer Jeremiah had for the Jews living in Babylon. Live locally, eat locally, "do not go cheap for power,"[19] serve God by seeking the peace of your neighbor. This is no earth-shattering revelation about how to achieve world peace or end poverty; rather, it's a matter of witness, a way of living in a place that, if practiced, might begin to resemble the Kingdom of God.

Lights in the Distance

I'm still haunted by Marco Polo's words. Where do we look for the faint lights in the distance? The lights leading us forward won't be found in the marble halls of commerce, the government, the university, or any institution, though each of those institutions may contribute. So long as the church mirrors such institutions, the lights won't be found there either. Berry's critique of the church's complicity in the violence of our national economy is no less incisive today than it was in 1992 when he wrote the essay "Christianity and the Survival of Creation." Now, as then, the church has become "willy-nilly the religion of the state and the economic status quo. . . . It has flown the flag and chanted the slogans of empire."[20]

Where I do see light, and where I do stake my claim, is in the *defiant church,* the one that prizes fealty to the Slaughtered Lamb over the gods of America, Mammon, and technological triumphalism. Defiant churches with their defiant community gardens assume a special role. They become refuges within Babylon's widening gyre, serving as both metaphor and locale for how the church lives out its mission. The answer to those who ask, *Why should churches be involved in agriculture?* is this: it's one way of seeking the salvation, the *shalom,* the welfare of the place to which it has been sent, which is nothing less than seeking the Kingdom of God.

Toward the end of *Invisible Cities,* Marco Polo says: "At times I feel your voice is reaching me from far away, while I am prisoner of a gaudy and unlivable present, where all forms of human society have reached an extreme of their cycle and there is no imagining what new forms they may assume. And I hear, from your voice, the invisible reasons which make cities live, through which perhaps, once dead, they will come to life again."[21]

The church is our Marco Polo, our guide describing myriad cities that are really one city. The voice reaching us from far away is the same one that says, *I was hungry and you gave me something to eat; love your enemies and pray for those who persecute you; feed my sheep.* In these words, we can hear the visible and invisible reasons that make dead cities live, that give life and breath to our abandoned rural areas. It is the Word that pierces and illumines the darkness.

We know that the empire is sick and, what is worse, that it is trying to become accustomed to its sores. This is the aim of the church's explorations: examining the traces of *shalom* still to be glimpsed, we gauge its short supply. To know how much darkness there is around us, we must sharpen our eyes, peering at the faint lights in the distance, the lights of the New Jerusalem of which we have already been given a glimpse.

Planting gardens and eating what they produce, seeking the *shalom* of the city—this isn't looking back to Eden; it's looking ahead to the day when "the first things have passed away" (Rev. 21:4), when the Lamb that was slaughtered will invite us all to join in that great messianic feast.

Coda

It's July now. We finally got a well, one that pumps a whopping sixty-two gallons a minute—more than enough to irrigate our two-acre garden even in severe drought. Still, I miss carrying buckets of water from the creek. There was something elemental about irrigating by hand. For one thing, it connected us to those farmers around the world who don't have electricity, who have watered their crops by hand for centuries. And the work of hauling itself, hard though it was, gave me a certain feeling of wholeness that's missing when I turn on the hydrant. Like the myriad other daily tasks here at Anathoth Community Garden, it reminded me of the simple joy of manual labor.

I remember something Adela said that day we hauled water together. On our umpteenth trip back up the hill, when my sore back muscles were crying uncle, I put down my buckets and watched Adela come toward me up the hill. I was ready to quit and said as much to her. But there were more beds to water. She wanted to keep going.

"El trabajo es bien duro, no?" I asked. "It's hard work, isn't it?"

"Si pero el trabajo es bonito." "Yes," she said, her grin pure silver, "but the work is beautiful."

Notes

Epigraph: Catherine de Hueck Doherty, *Apostolic Farming* (Combermere, ON: Madonna, 1991), 24. A condensed version of this essay appeared as Fred Bahnson, "A Garden Becomes a Protest: The Field at Anathoth," *Orion*, July/August 2007, available online at http://www.orionmagazine.org/index.php/articles/article/312.

1. Italo Calvino, *Invisible Cities* (New York: Harcourt Brace Jovanovich, 1972), 59.

2. For a description of why scythes—and hand tools in general—are morally superior to weed-whackers ("power scythes") and other machines, see Wendell Berry, "A Good Scythe," in *The Gift of Good Land: Further Essays Cultural and Agricultural* (New York: North Point, 1981), 171.

3. Sir Albert Howard, *An Agricultural Testament* (Emmaus, PA: Rodale, 1972), 19.

4. Wallace Stegner, *Where the Bluebird Sings to the Lemonade Springs: Living and Writing in the West* (New York: Random House, 1992), 212.

5. Ibid., 210.

6. Graham Greene, *The Power and the Glory* (New York: Penguin, 1990), 154.

7. James Howard Kunstler, *The Long Emergency* (New York: Grove, 2005), 7.

8. Brian Halweil, *Eat Here—Reclaiming Homegrown Pleasures in a Global Supermarket* (New York: Norton, 2004), 37.

9. Howard, *An Agricultural Testament*, 18–19.

10. Ibid., 19–20.

11. Michael Pollan, *The Omnivore's Dilemma* (New York: Penguin, 2006), 240.

12. Gene Logsdon, *The Contrary Farmer* (White River Junction, VT: Chelsea Green, 1994), 50–51.

13. Kenneth I. Helphand, *Defiant Gardens—Making Gardens in Wartime* (San Antonio: Trinity University Press, 2006).

14. Pollan, *The Omnivore's Dilemma*, 10.

15. Alexander Schmemann, *For the Life of the World* (Crestwood, NY: St. Vladimir's Seminary Press, 2004), 16.

16. For more on the benefits of physical labor, see Fred Bahnson and Richard Church, "The Work of Our Hands: Two Farmers' Reflections," *The Cresset—a Review of Literature, the Arts, and Public Affairs* 71, no. 1 (September 2007): 11–16.

17. Wendell Berry, "The Reactor and the Garden," in *The Gift of Good Land,* 169–70.

18. Wendell Berry, "The Work of Local Culture," *What Are People For?* (New York: North Point, 1999), 166.

19. Wendell Berry, "Manifesto: The Mad Farmer Liberation Front," in *Collected Poems, 1957–1982* (1985; reprint, New York: North Point, 1999), 152.

20. Wendell Berry, "Christianity and the Survival of Creation," in *Sex, Economy, Freedom, and Community* (New York: Pantheon, 1992), 114–15.

21. Calvino, *Invisible Cities,* 136.

Ellen F. Davis

"And the Land I Will Remember"

Reading the Bible through Agrarian Eyes

A Personal Preface

I am an Old Testament scholar and a native Californian—and those two aspects of my identity probably contribute in equal measure to the fact that the ecological crisis has become increasingly important as a focus of my thinking, teaching, and writing. In recent years, I have come to believe that anyone who wishes to understand the Old Testament deeply would do well to learn more about the ecological crisis—and especially about its agricultural dimensions. Conversely, Christians and Jews who wish to understand the depth dimension of the crisis would do well to ponder it in light of the Old Testament (for Jews, "the Bible"). The mutually informative relation between ecological awareness and biblical study rests on two factors. First, the ecological crisis is at root a theological crisis, a crisis in our relationship with the God who made the heavens and the earth, and the Old Testament/Hebrew Scripture is for both Jews and Christians an indispensable and authoritative witness to the nature of that relationship. Second, the Old Testament is pervasively land centered in its theological perspective. Rarely does one read through two or three successive chapters without seeing some reference to the land or to Zion, the city that is, ideologically speaking, its center, whose holiness is, in good times, the source of its fertility. There is no extensive exploration of the relationship between God and humanity (or God and the people Israel) that does not factor the land, the fertile soil, into that relationship. Overall, from an Old Testament perspective, the fertility of the land of Israel—or even of the whole earth[1]—is the best index of the health or unhealth of the covenant relationship. When humanity or Israel is disobedient, rain is withheld, thorns and briars abound, the land languishes and mourns. Conversely, "truth [or:

faithfulness] springs up from the ground" (Ps. 85:12). It is no coincidence that the most extravagant poetic images of loveliness—in the Prophets, the Psalms, and the Song of Songs—all show a land lush with growth as well as a people living in (or restored to) righteousness and full intimacy with God.

Moreover, the Old Testament is particular in its land centeredness. To paraphrase the contemporary agrarians, this literature is "placed"; the Scriptures of ancient Israel know where they come from. They reflect the narrow and precariously balanced ecological niche that is the hill country of ancient Judah and Samaria—"a strip of land between two seas," as they say, with water to the west and desert to the east. The Israelite farmers knew that they survived in that steep and semiarid land by the grace of God and their own wise practices. And it was no small part of Israelite wisdom to recognize that, unlike their neighbors—the Philistines on the fertile plain of Sharon, the Egyptians and Babylonians ranged along the banks and canals of their great rivers—they had only the slightest margin for negligence, ignorance, or error. The Bible as we have it could not have been written beside the irrigation canals of Babylon or the perennially flooding Nile, any more than it could have emerged from the vast fertile plains on the North American continent. For revelation addresses the necessities of a place as well as a people. Therefore, ancient Israel's Scripture bespeaks throughout an awareness of belonging to a place that is at once extremely fragile and infinitely precious. Fragility belongs essentially to the character of the land and may even contribute to its value. Seasonal aridity and periodic drought, a thin layer of topsoil, susceptibility to erosion—these mark the land of Canaan as a place under the immediate, particular care of God. That fragility may be a distinctive spiritual asset, rather than a liability, is implied in God's instruction to the Israelites in the wilderness: "For the land into which you are entering to take possession of it—it is not like the land of Egypt from which you have come out, where you could sow your seed and water with your foot, like a vegetable garden. The land to which you are passing over [the Jordan] to take possession is a land of mountains and valleys. By the measure of the rain from the heavens it will drink water [or: you will drink water]. It is a land which YHWH your God looks after; always the eyes of YHWH your God are on it, from the beginning of the year to the end of the year" (Deut. 11:10–12).[2]

All this is to say that as an Old Testament scholar I come naturally by my respect for land and my concern that it be "kindly used" so that it may continue to be used from generation to generation.[3] And that respect and con-

cern are compounded by the fact that I am a Californian by birth and up-
bringing. That is to say, I grew up in a lovely place—and, what is more, I grew
up attuned to its loveliness. Many of my most valued and memorable hours
were spent outside and barefoot. We were only a few miles as the seagull flies
from "the City"—San Francisco. However, we (the children at least) were
oriented to our own small island town, the water around it, and the nearby
hills, where we lived and played freely like no city child can. We found fasci-
nation in snails and slugs and tadpoles and the sea anemones that grew on the
side of the docks. In summer, we ate what we could hold of the wild plums
and blackberries, and the surplus melted into the soft asphalt; our feet carried
the purple-black stain into the fall. The roads were too narrow and the curves
too blind to give cars much freedom, so we had them mostly to ourselves, as
giant chalkboards and hopscotch grids. Thus an intense, even bodily delight
in place shaped me, and it informs the way I continue to think and feel, just
as reading the Bible slowly and carefully has shaped the way I think and feel.

Having watched drastic change take place in my native state over the five
decades of my own active observance, I am saddened. Highways run where
farms used to be. Rural areas and small towns have become suburbanized,
exurbanized, exclusivized by and for the wealthy, colonized by weekenders.
Real estate prices jump, not year by year, but month by month. Blue-collar
workers live in urban ghettos or trailer parks far from their jobs. Children
grow up and routinely move to another state where they can afford to live. As
a biblical scholar, with some awareness of how events and life patterns un-
folded in a different part of the world over centuries and millennia, I am
anxious. In the ancient Near East, "development" occurred, as did social in-
equities and environmental degradation, yet life on the land continued with
considerable continuity for most people, generation to generation. I am no
expert about land use. But as I compare the extent of environmental and social change in the premodern Middle East (in most places, up to the second
half of the twentieth century) to what I have personally witnessed in California
I would judge that the effect of our current patterns is catastrophic. In my
home state, increasingly on our continent as a whole, and around the globe,
we are on a short-term trajectory whose long-term consequences are surely
dire.

It is just because I am anxious that I read the modern agrarians: Wendell
Berry, Wes Jackson, Norman Wirzba, and others. They don't make me feel
better about our situation, but they help me make sense of it, for myself and

for my students. Their perspective seems to me deeply sane, and sane companionship is, as the sages of Proverbs knew, essential for living well—with faith and hope, if not with optimism. Reading the agrarians has changed my professional work of reading the Old Testament. I dare to think it has made my readings sharper and more concrete. If that is so, it is because the modern agrarians have helped me begin to cultivate sensibilities that were second nature to the biblical writers themselves, as members of a society that was not just agricultural but agrarian minded. In this essay, I highlight several aspects of agrarian thinking that intersect with and illumine the thought of the Bible.

Agrarian Mindedness: Value beyond Price

About fifteen years ago, early in my attempts to teach on the subject of biblical theology and land use, I was reading the shelves in the soil science section of Yale's undergraduate library—figuring that that would give me a broad and manageably (for me) shallow overview of how scientists think about land and its fertility. One title in particular caught my eye: *Meeting the Expectations of the Land.* The thought formed in my mind: "Whoever came up with that title understands how the Bible thinks about land." So I pulled it off the shelf. That collection of essays, edited by Wes Jackson, Wendell Berry, and Bruce Colman, was my first introduction to a different way of thinking about land in contemporary settings.

Two things impressed me immediately about the book. First, these authors had a sense of history. On the very first page, Jackson refers to "a systemic problem whose roots are in the roots of agriculture, at least as far back as the time thousands of years ago when patches became fields." As a biblical scholar, I tend to think that a problem that does not have a millennia-long time frame to it is not yet a serious problem. Second, in this book I heard for the first time my living contemporaries articulating a way of viewing and valuing land radically different from the "real estate mentality" that dominates virtually all public discussion and action in California: "Land cannot be possessed for very long, let alone commercialized. It will eventually claim us."[4] If I could immediately recognize Jackson's categorical statement as true, that is because it has deep resonance with the thought of the Old Testament, namely, with the central biblical conviction that the people Israel belong to their land more than the land belongs to the people. For "legally" speaking—that is, speaking on the basis of Torah—the arable land in Israel above all other places belongs to God, and the people Israel, who are themselves God's "particular possession" (*segullah;* Exod. 19:5), hold it in trust for God. Therefore, the priestly law of Leviticus, one of the most land-sensitive books of the Bible, sets severe limits on land sales: "And the land will not be sold in perpetuity, for the land is mine; yes, you [Israelites] are resident aliens with me!" (Lev. 25:23).

Agricultural land is, from a biblical perspective, literally invaluable. There is no record, biblical or inscriptional, of an Israelite voluntarily selling land on the open market[5] because—in contrast to their neighbors in Egypt and Mesopotamia—Israelites seem to have had no concept of arable land (*'adamah*) as a commodity, to be bought and sold freely. While Leviticus allows for the sale of houses within the city wall (these would have been essentially landless houses, jammed one against the other), the fertile soil cannot be handled thus, as "private property" in the modern sense. Rather, the cultural institution by which farmland is transmitted is called *naḥalah,* "hereditary portion." A piece of land is the God-given possession of a family, to be held as a trust and transmitted from generation to generation. Although the rights to land use may be sold to pay off debts, the land reverts to the original family unit every fiftieth year, the "Jubilee" (Lev. 25:30–31).

As I have already indicated, any understanding of how the ancient Israelites thought about land must begin with the recognition that they had little enough of it and most of what they had was only marginally arable. They managed to establish themselves in the steep, rocky hill country because it was the only part of the land of Canaan that nobody else wanted. They survived as farmers by becoming intimate with their land, by learning to meet its expectations and its needs, by passing on their knowledge, each generation serving as the human "seed stock" indispensable for the well-being of the next. With that small, fragile area as their population center, the early Israelites became a special breed of farmer; they became true agrarians, who practice and value "the complex accomplishment of knowledge, cultural memory, skill, self-mastery, good sense, and fundamental decency—the high and indispensable art—for which we probably can find no better name than 'good farming.'"[6]

Wendell Berry's observation about how agrarians value a *little* land captures the biblical mind-set exactly:

Agrarians value land because somewhere back in the history of their consciousness is the memory of being landless. . . . If you have no land, you have nothing: no food, no shelter, no warmth, no freedom, no life. If we remember this, we know that all economies begin to lie as soon as they assign a fixed value to land. People who have been landless know that the land is invaluable; it is worth everything. . . . Whatever the market may say, the worth of the land is what it always was: It is worth what food, clothing, shelter, and freedom are worth; it is worth what life is worth.[7]

Of course, the memory of being landless is central to the biblical story. Land deprivation is not just something that happened to somebody else, long ago. It is the essence of the "personal history" that each Israelite farmer is to recite "before YHWH": "My father was a stray Aramaean, and he went down to Egypt and sojourned there . . . , and the Egyptians treated *us* badly . . . , and *we* cried out to YHWH, . . . and he brought *us* to this place, . . . a land gushing with milk and honey. And now, look, I have brought the first-fruit of the fertile soil (*'adamah*) that you gave to *me*, YHWH . . ." (Deut. 26:5–10). The voices we hear in the Old Testament bespeak throughout an agrarian mindfulness that land—this particular land, my land, our land—is inseparable from self "before God." Land is the earnest of the covenant, the tangible sign and consequence of God's commitment to the people Israel.

"Property is a point of honor."[8] It is part of the agrarian project to redefine the notion of property, connecting it with notions of propriety: what is proper, honorable, fitting.[9] It is highly apt to that project, then, to observe that the Old Testament writers place the land within a network of relationships that are constituted and maintained through acts of mutual acknowledgment, respect, honoring; all that is implied in the Hebrew verb *zakhar*, "remember." It is what Israel "remembers" that determines whether it remains faithful to the covenant. The Mosaic commandment that stands over the Passover celebration is "*Zakhor*, Remember this day when you have come out from Egypt, from a house of slaves" (Exod. 13:3). So anyone with ears to hear knows that it is a very bad sign when, in the wilderness, the Israelites and the "riffraff in their midst" say, "We *remember* the fish that we ate in Egypt, for free . . . !" (Num. 11:5).

But surely the most redemptive act of remembering in the Bible is God's, as recorded by that green book, Leviticus, looking toward the time when the Israelites will be cast out for their rebelliousness, "into the land of their

[Babylonian] enemies." Yet even then God will honor them—not for their own sakes, but for the sake of something more enormous even than their sin: "And I will remember my covenant with Jacob, and yes, my covenant with Isaac, and yes, my covenant with Abraham I will remember—and the land I will remember" (Lev. 26:41–42). It is a remarkable statement. Can it be that God is agrarian minded, too?

In his indispensable study of Israel's land theology, Christopher Wright suggests that the covenant is properly conceived as a triangulated relationship among Israel, the land, and YHWH, "all three having the family as the basic focal point at which the conjunction of the three issued in ethical responsibilities and imperatives."[10] That sentence could almost come out of one of Berry's essays in which the claims of family, land, and human decency are shown finally to be inseparable from the claim of God on our lives. Without some comprehension of that indissoluble web of relationships, even an imperative as familiar as the Fifth Commandment is enigmatic precisely in its specificity: "Honor your father and your mother, *so that your days may be long on the fertile soil* [*'adamah*] that YHWH your God is giving you" (Exod. 20:12; cf. Deut. 5:16). Wright observes: "Because of its explicit links with the land traditions, the relationship between God and Israel was thoroughly 'earthed' in the socio-economic facts of life—shaping and being shaped by them, and at times threatened by developments in that realm."[11] He is speaking of the Iron Age, of course. But Berry and the other new agrarians might well say that the manifold crises of contemporary agriculture and industrial culture realize those threats in our own socioeconomic situation. Indeed, those crises show us what the unraveling of the web of covenant relationships looks like "on the ground."

The Primacy of the Land

A second aspect of agrarian thinking that has informed my reading of the Bible is the principle that "the land comes first," in a sense that is more than geologic.[12] The primacy of the land sets the standard for all human actions; "meeting the expectations of the land" is our first and nonnegotiable obligation. At the outset, the Bible uses poetic language to express the primacy of the land. The so-called primeval history (Gen. 1–11) gives the fundaments of a biblical anthropology, and one of those is that humans are created by God, *'adam* from *'adamah* (Gen. 2:7). Although the wordplay is captured surprisingly well by the English pun "human from humus," the Hebrew more effectively evokes a relationship that might be viewed as both genealogical and vocational. Both words are related to the word for "red" (*'edom*); in that region, red is the skin tone of both the people and the earth. *Terra rossa,* "red earth," is the geologic term for the thin but rich loam covering the hill country where the early Israelites settled. *'Adam* from *'adamah* thus evokes the specific relationship between a particular people and a particular place.

To my mind, the most suggestive expression of the primacy of the earth appears a few verses after that pun, in what is arguably the first statement about human vocation: "And YHWH God set the human being in the garden to *'avad* it and to *shamar* it" (Gen. 2:15). I leave those words untranslated for the moment because any translation dissolves the meaningful ambiguity in both verb phrases. A common translation is "to till it and to tend it," but that implies that the terms are horticultural and agricultural, and they are not. Rather, *'avad* is the ordinary verb equivalent to the English *work,* and it normally means to *work for* someone, as a servant or slave. Often, the grammatical object of the verb is a deity, YHWH or "the other gods"; it also designates service to a human master (e.g., Pharaoh). Much less frequently, *'avad* denotes *work* done *on* or *with* some material, and, in all cases but one, that material is soil (e.g., Gen. 2:5, 3:23, 4:2). In view of those nearby references to working the soil, one may certainly translate here "to work it."[13] But the wider usage of the verb suggests further that the human task is to *work for* the garden soil, to serve its needs. As all readers of Hebrew know, *'avad* is often translated "worship." While biblical religion clearly forbids divinization of the earth, one might recall that the English word *worship* originally meant to "acknowledge worth." In that sense, the Hebrew pun translates well into English.

But since the first verb can be applied to working the soil one might well overlook its inherent ambiguity, were it not for the second verb, *shamar,* which does not elsewhere refer to land care.[14] An all-purpose translation is "keep"—a flock, say, or a city; frequently the inference is "preserve, observe." Most often in the Bible, the verb is used with reference to keeping the ordinances of God: "Yes, my Sabbaths you shall keep!" (Exod. 31:13). Something that does not originate with us, something of inestimable value, is to be respected and preserved. Keeping the ordinances of God proves to be the sole condition on which Israel may retain its hold on the God-given—or, better, God-entrusted—land of Canaan. Thus Moses instructs the Israelites just on

the eve of their entry into the land: "And you shall keep [v'shamarta] his stat-
utes and his commandments which I am commanding you this day, so it may
be good for you and for your children after you, in order that you may live a
long time on the fertile soil ['adamah] that YHWH your God is giving to
you, for all time" (Deut. 4:40). This instruction to "keep" the garden could
well be seen as pointing toward the obligation to keep *torah*, the totality of
divine "teaching" that directs Israel's life in the land and with God.

So, even while the human being is still in Eden, there are limits to be
observed, standards by which the legitimacy of human actions may be judged:
"The land expects something from us. The line of succession, the true line, is
the membership of people who know it does."[15] That knowledge and the
willingness to live by it constitute for Berry and his fellow agrarians the quality that the biblical writers most often call *righteousness*. Their ability to sense
the mute expectation of the God-watched earth illumines my own understanding of this first explicit biblical statement regarding human work: "And
YHWH God set the human being in the garden to serve it and to preserve it."
"The expectations of the land" proves to be an exegetically fruitful concept,
even if not conceived with the Bible in mind.[16]

As I read it, then, both verbs, 'avad and shamar, imply the primacy and
the preciousness of the land. At the same time, there is a suggestion of its
vulnerability; anything that humans are charged to preserve they are also capable of neglecting or violating. So the two elements of the stated divine intention stand in some tension as well as in complementary relation. In order
to live, we must "work" the land, manage it, take from it. In order to "live a
long time" on it, we must limit our take; we must submit our minds, our
skills, and our strength to serving its needs. Of the tension inherent in the
biblical statement, Evan Eisenberg observes:

> There is no escaping the need to manage nature. The best we can do is
> observe the following rule: So manage nature as to minimize the need to
> manage nature. . . . We are destined to work our way across the globe,
> turning Eden into something else. And we are destined—in our better
> moments—to protect Eden against our own work. The command to
> protect puts upper limits on the scope of our work and lower limits on
> its quality. In other words, we must not try to manage too much of the
> world, but what we do manage—our cities, our factories, our farms—
> we must manage well.[17]

Working in that way requires of us humility—literally, the quality of being thoroughly "grounded," connected in mind as well as body to the humus from which human life is drawn. That fundamental recognition of the land's primacy is the motivating force and point of orientation for Wes Jackson's natural systems agriculture, which looks to "nature as measure," taking its working ideas from observation of nature's economic practices, allowing imagination and action to be limited and guided by the way the world itself *works*.[18] From an agrarian perspective, humility might be defined as letting our minds be disciplined by observation of the way the earth works—and has worked well in most places for time out of mind—and, further, disciplined by observance of its limits. That means recognizing that, along with needs and expectations, the land also has something to teach.

As a theological educator, I find one of the most appealing aspects of agrarianism to be its cheerful embrace of ignorance: "Since we're billions of times more ignorant than knowledgeable, why not go with our strong suit and have an ignorance-based worldview?"[19] Wes Jackson has long asserted that the ecological crisis is the result of "a knowledge-based worldview founded on the assumption that we can accumulate enough knowledge to bend nature pliantly and to run the world." The alternative that he and his colleagues propose is the recognition of "informed ignorance as an apt description of the human condition and the appropriate result of a good education."[20] Starting our work by recognizing our ignorance—that is an idea that echoes the thought of the biblical sages: "Rely on YHWH with your whole heart / and do not lean on your own understanding" (Prov. 3:5). As with the agrarians, the biblical writers' willingness to highlight our ignorance rests not on laziness or despair but on the confidence that there is a wisdom worked into the very fabric of things:

> YHWH by wisdom founded the earth;
> he established the heavens with understanding.
> By his knowledge the deeps were cleaved,
> and the clouds dripped dew.
> My child, do not let these depart from your eyes;
> hold onto discernment and astuteness,
> and they will be life to your soul
> and grace to your neck.

Then you will walk safely on your way,
And your foot will not stumble. (Prov. 3:19–23)

If we can look beyond our selves to see God's wise foundational work shaping our world, then we are ready to dispense with false distinctions between practical work, on the one hand, and spiritual work or religious service, on the other. For it is evident that all our activity, mental and physical, must be directed toward shaping our lives, our culture, and, indeed, the earth we manage in order to survive, in accordance with the divine wisdom manifested in natural systems. With perfect concision, Wendell Berry expresses in a few lines both an awareness of the aim and end proper for human life and the humble embrace of ignorance:

> . . . I am slowly falling
> into the fund of things. And yet to serve the earth,
> not knowing what I serve, gives a wideness
> and a delight to the air, and my days
> do not wholly pass. It is the mind's service. . . .[21]

A Humble Materialism

A third point of connection between biblical thinking and modern agrarianism is so pervasive and fundamental to both that it seems at first hardly necessary to mention, namely, their exacting concern with the *materiality* of human existence. The agrarians pose the question overtly: how can we meet our material needs, in the present and for the indefinite future, without inflicting damage? Less obviously, but with equal urgency and concreteness, the biblical writers are concerned with ordering material existence in ways that are consonant with God's will and the design of the world. (If this characteristic of biblical literature is not obvious to Christians, that is because the books that attend most carefully to the question of ordering material existence are the ones Christians are least inclined to read. Along with Proverbs, those are the second half of Exodus, Leviticus, and Deuteronomy.) So the biblical writers and the new agrarians are, in a real sense, materialists; they prefer to write in concrete and specific terms rather than in abstractions. And they are materialists of a humble sort. They do not claim that what we humans can (or, theoretically, ever could) see or touch or work on or make is exhaustive of what *is*, nor even that it constitutes the larger or more important part of what is. They simply insist, and model by example, that we "owe a certain courtesy to Reality, and that this courtesy can be enacted only by humility, reverence, propriety of scale, and good workmanship."[22]

Yet, if it sounds odd to call them *materialists* at all, that is because our society is characterized by materialism of a very different sort. In the first instance, of course, we are addicted to the acquisition and eventual disposal of vast quantities of unnecessary stuff. But we are materialistic in a second sense as well. A generation ago, E. F. Schumacher spoke of industrial society's unquestioning acceptance of the presuppositions and illusions of "materialistic scientism." Among the most powerful and probably the most dangerous of its illusions is the idea "that science can solve all problems"—although it is common experience that the efficient solution of an individual problem generates a host of new ones.[23] That sort of trust in the omnipotence of science is, of course, a kind of faith stance, albeit a wobbly one.[24] If it were held by a premodern society, we would unhesitatingly label as *magical* a kind of thinking that presumes to guarantee certain physical results yet bears such a tenuous relation to empirical reality. For, despite its ostensible grounding in science, this form of materialism is strangely oblivious to what may be the most readily observable and nonnegotiable characteristic of our material world: finitude. Those who work consciously and intelligently within material reality (as though we could work elsewhere!) are continually confronted with limits of time, space, matter, and energy. Writing some thirty years after Schumacher, Barbara Kingsolver gives an updated report on the status of the illusion: "Most of our populace and all of our leaders are participating in a mass hallucinatory fantasy in which the megatons of waste we dump in our rivers and bays are not poisoning the water, the hydrocarbons we pump into the air are not changing the climate, over-fishing is not depleting the oceans, fossil fuels will never run out, wars that kill masses of civilians are an appropriate way to keep our hands on what's left, we are not desperately overdrawn at the environmental bank, and *really*, the kids are all right."[25]

Within the first few pages of the Bible, we find a mocking exposé of an attitude very similar to our scientific materialism: the ambition and perverse confidence that led the people "on the plain of Shinar" (central Mesopotamia) to "build a tower with its head in the sky." "Let's make a name for ourselves, so we won't be scattered over the face of the earth!" (Gen. 11:4). City builders all clumped together, resisting dispersion, with their inflated imaginations in the clouds—this is a caricature of what the Israelites saw in the technologically dominant culture of their age, the great riparian civilization to the east. Beginning already in the fourth millennium B.C.E., aggressive channeling of the Tigris and the Euphrates produced an agricultural system of unprecedented productivity, which, in turn, produced a burst of population. The surplus of food and labor enabled the construction of immense walled cities—most notably, in biblical times, Nineveh and Babylon—each with a ziggurat dominating the skyline. Yet centuries of heavy irrigation exacted their environmental price, in the form of a rising water table, salinization of the soil, erosion, and silting. The Israelite caricature perhaps reflects the historical fact that, over the millennia, the cities in the lower part of the plain suffered eclipse. Gradually, and repeatedly, as the "breadbasket" for each city became unproductive, the center of power moved upstream to a less damaged region.[26] A large section of the once–Fertile Crescent remains salt fields to this day.

The Israelites, in contrast to their materially more fortunate neighbors, never had enough water or arable land to waste. Probably that is why they developed agrarian eyes and, therefore, they could see that the Babel-onians' folly lay in taking their minds off the ground, which is, for us humans, the chief and proper sphere of material concern: "The heavens are heavens for YHWH, but the earth he gave to human beings" (Ps. 115:16). The Tower of Babel story captures what may be the essence of all technologically induced disaster: the illusion that our cleverness will somehow deliver us from the need to observe the normative form of materialism that sustains life, the ambition to be exceptional—"Let's make a name for ourselves"—by pursuing an alternative "lifestyle" disconnected from the soil. In the story, God shatters that illusion with one quick divine visitation; but, in real time, it may take generations, centuries, even millennia, for the disaster to complete itself. By the grace of God, however, the biblical story may enable us to recognize ourselves in that tragic historical process somewhere short of the end. Thus, it gives us a reason and a chance to restore a humble and healthy materialism to our lives and even to our culture.

In a 1992 lecture at the Southern Baptist Theological Seminary, Berry observed: "Our predicament now, I believe, requires us to learn to read and understand the Bible in the light of the present fact of creation. This would seem to be a requirement both for Christians and for everyone concerned, but it entails a long work of true criticism—that is, of careful and judicious study."[27] As someone who engages full-time in critical biblical study, I am surprised to discover that, over the last decade, it is the agrarians who have most profoundly influenced and changed the way I read. Reading the Bible through agrarian eyes is a self-confirming activity. The more I do it, the more I see—but the singular subject is misleading, for I find that I can do this kind of reading only with my students, many of whom know more about farming and land care than I do. So they see things I do not see; thus, they deepen my insight, specifically, my exegetical insight. For what emerges from our reading is more than a general spiritual awareness of our connection with the land. Rather, we learn to read more concretely and more accurately, supporting our interpretations on the basis of what we know about ancient Israel's social structure, its geographic, topographical, and historical situation, and its theological understandings.

"*Hafokh bah vahafokh bah, hakkol bah.* Turn it over and over; everything is in it—and in it you will see [something]."[28] So the ancient rabbis spoke of the endlessly fruitful work of reading Scripture. "*Hafokh bah,* turn it over"—is it coincidence that the image is agricultural, or at least horticultural? The verb is elsewhere used for turning compost, soil in the making. Deliberate or not, the association is meaningful, for Scripture is in significant ways like the soil. Each is a rich deposit, to which time and many lives have contributed. Indeed, each is itself a living thing—a community, as the seminal ecological thinker Aldo Leopold taught us to view the soil—over which the Spirit of God hovers.[29] Each, if we attend to it with proper care, yields to us the daily bread on which all human life depends. That is why, as a Christian biblical scholar and someone who eats, I am learning to remember the land as I read.

Notes

The title of this essay is drawn from Lev. 26:42. All translations of biblical passages are my own. The essay previously appeared in Ellen Davis, *Scripture, Culture, and Agriculture: An Agrarian Reading of the Bible* (New York: Cambridge, 2009).

1. The Hebrew word '*eretz* can refer to Israel in particular or to what we would call the planet Earth, and it is not always possible to be certain whether a given biblical writer intends the wider or the narrower reference.

2. Throughout this essay, I follow the Hebrew convention of using four consonants (*YHWH*) to designate the "unpronounceable" name of God, revealed espe-

cially to Israel. Traditionally considered by Jews too sacred to be uttered, it is often rendered in English as LORD.

3. The notion of concerns and practices of "kindly use" of land being essential to securing a permanent food supply appears early and frequently in Berry's writings. See, e.g., Wendell Berry, "The Ecological Crisis as a Crisis of Agriculture," in *The Unsettling of America: Culture and Agriculture,* 3rd ed. (San Francisco: Sierra Club Books, 1977), 30, 37, and "A Good Farmer of the Old School," in *Home Economics* (New York: North Point, 1987), 160.

4. Wes Jackson, Wendell Berry, and Bruce Colman, introduction to *Meeting the Expectations of the Land: Essays in Sustainable Agriculture and Stewardship*, ed. Wes Jackson, Wendell Berry, and Bruce Colman (San Francisco: North Point, 1984), xiii, xiv.

5. See Christopher J. H. Wright, *God's People in God's Land: Family, Land, and Property in the Old Testament* (Grand Rapids, MI: Eerdmans, 1990), 56–57.

6. Wendell Berry, "The Agrarian Standard," in *The Essential Agrarian Reader: The Future of Culture, Community, and the Land,* ed. Norman Wirzba (Lexington: University Press of Kentucky, 2003), 24.

7. Ibid., 28–29.

8. G. K. Chesterton cited in Wendell Berry, "Whose Head Is the Farmer Using? Whose Head Is Using the Farmer?" in Jackson, Berry, and Colman, eds., *Meeting the Expectations of the Land,* 29.

9. "Property belongs to a family of words that . . . govern our connections with the world and with one another: property, proper, appropriate, propriety" (ibid., 30).

10. Wright, *God's People in God's Land,* 104–5.

11. Ibid., 23.

12. Writing about the possible use of biomass rather than fossil fuels by farmers, Amory B. Lovins, L. Hunter Lovins, and Marty Bender observe: "The land comes first. All operations must be based on a concern for soil fertility and long-term environmental compatibility" ("Energy and Agriculture," in Jackson, Berry, and Colman, eds., *Meeting the Expectations of the Land,* 80).

13. Although I agree with Theodore Hiebert's treatment of Gen. 2–11 in many respects, I think that, through overlooking the ambiguity of the verb *'avad,* he has overstated the case that, for J, "the land is a sovereign to be served" (*The Yahwist's Landscape: Nature and Religion in Early Israel* [New York: Oxford University Press, 1996], 157).

14. A near parallel is Isa. 27:3, where God's protection of the "vineyard" Israel is twice denoted by the verb *natsar.*

15. Wendell Berry, "It Wasn't Me," in *The Wild Birds: Six Stories of the Port William Membership* (San Francisco: North Point Books, 1986), 68.

16. Often, of course, the connection between the Bible and the writings of these authors is explicit. The title of another of Wes Jackson's books, *Altars of Unhewn Stone* (San Francisco: North Point, 1987), is one of numerous examples (cf. Exod. 20:25).

17. Evan Eisenberg, *The Ecology of Eden* (New York: Knopf, 1998), 288–89.

18. Compare Wes Jackson: "The science in support of the new-agrarian has two components. Ecologists and evolutionary biologists have wanted to understand how the world *is*. . . . For agriculturalists, how the world *works* must be of primary interest. Utilitarianism necessarily rules even though it may limit our imagination." But he goes on to say: "The nature/technology (*is/works*) dualism sponsored by Enlightenment thinking must and can come to an end. We see the possibility as we research a new agriculture at The Land Institute" ("The Agrarian Mind," in Wirzba, ed., *The Essential Agrarian Reader*, 150).

19. Bill Vitek and Wes Jackson, *The Virtues of Ignorance: Complexity, Sustainability, and the Limits of Knowledge* (Lexington: University Press of Kentucky, 2008), 1.

20. Wes Jackson, *Becoming Native to This Place* (Lexington: University Press of Kentucky, 1994), 23.

21. Wendell Berry, "Enriching the Earth," in *Collected Poems, 1957–82* (San Francisco: North Point, 1985), 110.

22. Wendell Berry, "Going to Work," in Wirzba, ed., *The Essential Agrarian Reader*, 266.

23. E. F. Schumacher, *Good Work* (New York: Harper & Row, 1979), 122–23 (quote), 98.

24. Compare the comments on the "religification and evangelizing of science" in Wendell Berry, *Life Is a Miracle: An Essay against Modern Superstition* (Washington, DC: Counterpoint, 2000), 19–21. Berry goes on to speak of "militant materialism," which is intolerant of any sort of mystery (25–29).

25. Barbara Kingsolver, foreword to Wirzba, ed., *The Essential Agrarian Reader*, xiii.

26. Daniel J. Hillel, *Out of the Earth: Civilization and the Life of the Soil* (New York: Free Press, 1991), 78–87.

27. Wendell Berry, "Christianity and the Survival of Creation," in *Sex, Economy, Freedom, and Community* (New York: Pantheon, 1992), 94–95.

28. R. Ben Bag-Bag, *Mishnah avot* 5:22.

29. Aldo Leopold, *A Sand County Almanac* (New York: Ballantine, 1970), 239–43.

Landscapes of Flesh

On Finding More Faithful Metaphors for the Body and Its Goods

A Body and a Place

As best I can remember, I was seven or maybe eight years old the first time I was there, probably accompanying my grandfather on his weekly walk to count and salt the cattle and make sure the fences were still up. For a boy that age, it was a hard-earned prize, a walk of an hour or more that demanded the negotiation of steep hills, blackberry brambles, rhododendron thickets, and a half dozen or so barbed-wire fences that seemed to have a persistent knack for tearing my clothes and leaving bloody marks on my body. My parents and grandparents called it the Old Home Place. It was the original parcel of my mother's family's farm, the narrow hollow and surrounding steep hills where my mother and her father and grandfather had been born and raised in a rambling old house that had been turned to salvage when I was still in diapers. It is the place where my ancestors are buried. It is the place I most clearly recall in connection to learning who I was, where I had come from, and what kind of things ought really to matter.

As I grew older, I often walked to the Old Place on my own, the terrain of the hike becoming as familiar to me as my own body. Sometimes I went hunting squirrels, sometimes picking berries, sometimes just for the sake of the walk, but always covering the same well-known ground. Leaving the house, I would walk northeast up the red dirt of Upper Mill Creek Road, cross the creek into the Taylor hollow, and eventually climb up the hill, past the pond at the head of the hollow where I sometimes fished for bass and bluegill. From the pasture at the top of the hill, overlooking the Elk River to the northwest, I would turn east and walk through a dense forest of beech, oak, hickory, and maple, around the southern side of a high knob, emerging from the woods on the spur ridge overlooking the original home site. Even now, from hundreds of miles away, I can see and feel the land's contours. I can hear its sounds and smell its smells: the mud and cattail around the pond and below the cisterns, the rotting leaves slowly turning to humus in the dense hardwood forests, the Hereford cattle grazing on the steep hillside pastures. I can taste the teaberry and mint leaves my grandfather gave me to chew and the pawpaws and blackberries he picked for me to eat. I can see the family cemetery on the point of the ridge, overlooking the hollow below. It is shaded by a massive old oak tree beneath which I used to sit quietly, half expecting those buried there to speak to me, telling me stories about their lives and the place we shared. I can count the graves, those of my great-great-grandparents and all the generations since, and I can almost hear their voices, carried on the wind.

All these memories and experiences are a part of me in a way that exceeds my affection for them. They have inexplicably marked my body and shaped my identity. They are the cornerstone of the history of my life and have helped make me the person I am. They have given me a sense of what it means to live well—to be healthy—as a human being. In so doing, they have shaped my entire life, including my work, first as a boy working on his grandparents' farm, then as a physical therapist, and now as a theologian, interested in each case in the human body—not just in how the body works, but also in what it is for.

Of Bodies and Bioethics

Personal reminiscing notwithstanding, this is not an essay about me. I want, rather, for it to be an essay in conversation—with the work of Wendell Berry and with the relatively young, distinctly modern discipline most usually called *bioethics*. That means that it is in some sense an essay about human bodies and the health of those bodies. As I have already suggested, there are significant connections between my story and questions about bodies and their health, but I suspect that these connections are far from self-evidently relevant to most of the people who "do" bioethics. In the current scientific and political climate, in fact, explicitly normative questions about the body and its goods are commonly regarded as matters of speculation or even superstition. Yet, as I hope to show presently, *all* questions in bioethics are ultimately, by inclusion or by exclusion, questions about the nature, destiny, and goods of the human body. I take Berry to be challenging us in this direction when he says: "The question of human limits, of the proper definition and place of human beings within the order of Creation, finally rests upon our attitude toward our biological existence, the life of the body in the world."[1] This is to say, quite simply, that bioethics is in the final analysis about what bodies are, and what they are for.

This means, as Berry goes on to acknowledge, that we cannot speak at length about the body without speaking as well about the many things our bodies do, matters as far-ranging as religion and agriculture. Indeed, he says: "While we live our bodies are moving particles of the earth, joined inextricably both to the soil and to the bodies of other living creatures. It is hardly surprising, then, that there should be some profound resemblances between our treatment of our bodies and our treatment of the earth." Our bodies are not simply contiguous but also continuous with other bodies and their places on the earth, and this means that nothing less is at stake (in understanding how properly to relate our bodies to the earth and to other creatures) than our health: "By understanding accurately his proper place in Creation, a man may be made whole."[2]

If bioethicists have succeeded in evading direct engagement with these questions, it is due in part to the problematic way the modern moral imagination has conceived the human body. Many standard approaches to bioethics take for granted what most of modern medicine seems to have assumed, which is that it is possible to make a distinction between the body and the person associated with it, that the body is in some way inhabited by that person, and that it is the private property of that person, who is free to dispose of it as he or she chooses. Philosophers know this account of the body more or less as *Cartesian,* after the seventeenth-century French philosopher and mathematician René Descartes.[3] Descartes sought to develop a philosophical method built on a foundation of absolute certainty. Consistent with the skepticism that was fashionable at the time, he engaged in a thought experiment wherein he systematically doubted everything that could to him conceivably be false. In the end, he believed, he could accept as indisputable only one thing, which was that he, as an individual person, existed as an essentially immaterial thinking thing, a *res cogitans.* His fundamental dictum is well-known today, even to nonphilosophers: *Cogito ergo sum,* "I think, therefore I am."

But, if the human subject is an immaterial thinking thing, then what is the human body? Obviously, believed Descartes, the body was something other than the active thinking subject—there was, in other words, an essential *dualism* of person and body. Descartes ultimately said that the body was a quasi-artificial, passive extension of the person, a *res extensa* that existed to be manipulated at will by the person inhabiting it. The body was, he suggested, not unlike a *machine*.[4]

Although Cartesian dualism has as a philosophical position died the death of a thousand qualifications, the metaphor of the body as machine and its associated dualism has persisted and has probably become one of the most common ways modern people think of themselves and their bodies. Intuitively, the Cartesian model has great explanatory power, and it is especially congenial to the body's rendering as an object of scientific investigation.[5] Perhaps most important, the machine metaphor is friendly to the modern sociopolitical consciousness, which purports simultaneously to privilege the autonomous will of the individual while conditionally allowing that autonomy to be restrained in the name of certain kinds of social utility.

But Are We Machines?

The machine metaphor is helpful just to the extent that it is true. In some ways, and to some extent, the human body *is* like a machine, and that metaphor has contributed a good deal toward an improved understanding of the human body. This improved understanding, in turn, has produced many medical achievements that are indisputably salutary. Yet metaphors have limits, and a failure to recognize those limits distorts our knowledge of the things to which our metaphors refer, which, in turn, distorts the ways we live in the world.[6] This is, I contend, much the case with contemporary medicine—and, thus, with contemporary bioethics. As a branch (or at least an epiphenomenon) of modern medicine, bioethics has often failed critically to account for the limits of the biomedical view of the body, which is decidedly mechanistic. And this failure has meant that bioethics has been unable to say very much about the ways in which modern medicine has, because of the limits inherent in the way it imagines the body, failed or been unable to contribute as fully as it otherwise might to genuine human flourishing.

No one has spoken as clearly and persuasively about the limits of the body-as-machine metaphor as Wendell Berry, who maintains that the machine metaphor is in many respects *unnatural*: "Of course, the body in most ways is not at all like a machine. Like all living creatures and unlike a machine, the body is not formally self-contained; its boundaries and outlines are not so exactly fixed. The body alone is not, properly speaking, a body. Divided from its sources of air, food, drink, clothing, shelter, and companionship, a body is, properly speaking, a cadaver, whereas a machine by itself, shut down or out of fuel, is still a machine." Yet we live as if these things are not the case, and our lives, including the ways we practice healing and caring for the sick, have become distorted.[7] As participants in a culture of radical individualism, we think of and treat our bodies as solitary and individual, like machines, and pay relatively little attention to the thousands of ways in which they are connected to other bodies and to our particular places in the world. We forget, ignore, or treat as irrelevant their surroundings, from which we draw life. We discount the idea that they might have purposes beyond those we individually will for them, purposes, for example, that are based on relations to bodies or landscapes that we have not chosen or perhaps even inherent in the limits imposed on us by their fragility and finitude.[8] Because of this discounting, we find ourselves immersed in a kind of ongoing and increasingly unrestricted war against limits of all kinds. Because of our ignorance of the interdependences that are fundamental to our lives as creatures, that war expands into a war against each other, against the earth, and, ultimately, against ourselves and our health.[9]

Ideally, we should be mindful of the lessons that Berry has tried to teach us, for example, that "to speak of the health of an isolated individual is a contradiction in terms" and that "the grace that is the health of creatures can only be held in common."[10] But, because our perception of what constitutes our health is partial and distorted, we fail to attend properly to the ways in which we are increasingly unhealthy members of an increasingly unhealthy creation. Medical expenditures on technologically sophisticated therapies that will benefit mainly the rich climb precipitously even as we neglect the welfare of the poor, of children, and of the earth we inhabit.[11] We spend obscene amounts of money preserving the illusion of youth or mechanically staving off the deaths of the well insured for just a few more days while infant mortality from entirely preventable causes climbs among our poorest neighbors. Our automobiles, power plants, and manufacturing facilities spew pollutants while we destroy our watersheds by lopping off the tops of mountains and dumping the remnants into adjacent valleys so that we can more cheaply get at the coal beneath the surface. We eat without thinking about what we eat or where it comes from even as we flush the poisoned topsoil on which we depend for food down rivers and into oceans that literally are being poisoned to death. It is a way of life that is good for none of us, ultimately not even for the agribusinesses and chemical companies that profit from it.

Even though we have managed largely to ignore it, the problem created by our way of life is vast.[12] The difficulties associated with trying to overcome it are bound to be legion. Yet we will not get anywhere close to a satisfying solution if we attempt to mend things quickly through massive, top-down shifts in social or economic policy. Given that the problems are so deeply entrenched as to be part of us, chances are we would simply replicate them in different ways.[13] Perhaps what we need is to change ourselves, to learn to live in the earth, to see it, and even to speak differently about it and all its inhabitants. Such an approach could begin in any number of places. But here I am interested in only one. I propose that we learn to live, see, and speak differently about our bodies. Insofar as our speech is dependent on metaphor, we need to learn to use more faithful metaphors for the human body.

Changing our speech and adopting new metaphors is no small matter, for the way we live is a function of the world we see, which is, in turn, related to the way we have been trained to speak. The philosopher Iris Murdoch has said: "I can only choose from the world I can *see,* in the moral sense of 'see' that implies that clear vision is a result of moral imagination and moral effort."[14] Murdoch understood, says Heather Widdows, that the "metaphors and pictures we use to describe the world demarcate the limits and possibilities within which we can be active in the world."[15] Moral imagination, or vision, develops only as we learn to speak in particular ways about the world; our ways of life are inseparable from our narrations of what is going on in the world.[16] We learn such narrations as members of tradition-bearing communities, which teach us to live and speak in one way rather than another.[17] Given the immensely artificial world of superhighways, supercomputers, and supermarkets in which most of us presently live, our gravitation toward the machine metaphor and its attendant dualism is not surprising. Yet there remains reason to hope that things can be different, for there continue to be among us women and men whose imaginations are fueled by what Berry says is another "expansive metaphor of farming and marriage and worship":

> All the essential relationships are comprehended in this metaphor. A farmer's relation to his land is the basic and central connection in the relation of humanity to the creation; the agricultural relation *stands* for the larger relation. Similarly, marriage is the basic and central commu-

nity tie; it begins and stands for the relation we have to family and to the larger circles of human association. And these relationships to the creation and to the human community are in turn basic to, and may stand for, our relationship to God—or to the sustaining mysteries and powers of the creation.[18]

As pregnant a claim as this one is suggests that there are other, complementary metaphors for our bodies that might help us live more faithfully. It is to the unearthing of one such metaphor that I turn next.

Searching for Metaphors: The Body as Landscape

Our search might begin quite simply by considering the ways we learn about bodies in everyday practice. We do not learn about them simply by dispassionately accumulating information about them. Rather, our learning is sensual—and sensually complex. We learn about bodies to a great extent using our own bodies, and, because of this, our learning is by nature intersubjective, meaning that the bodies we learn about have significant effects on us as learners.[19] We learn about bodies in much the same way we learn about landscapes, the particular places on earth we inhabit, which is to say we learn *as* bodies, by touch, taste, smell, and varieties of manipulations and tactile and motor observations that mark and shape both the learning body and the body learned about.

Lovers learn bodies this way, through the accumulated familiarity that comes with the recurrent intertwining of limbs and a thousand mindless caresses. Parents and children learn bodies this way as well, through myriad playful and affectionate gestures, certainly, but also through what Kathleen Norris calls the *quotidian mysteries* of everyday tasks like feeding, bathing, and dressing.[20] Athletes, whose undertakings require extraordinary levels of embodied self-knowledge, develop their skills by testing their bodies against those of their teammates and competitors, acquiring strength and flexibility, and learning to use their bodies by exploring and expanding their limits, day after day. And, lest I be accused of waxing sentimental, let me point out that students of anatomy—physicians, nurses, and physical therapists, among others—also come to learn about the body first of all by handling bodies, not just those of cadavers, but one another's as well. It is worth noting that such learning begins and always refers back to what anatomists call *landmarks*, the body's particular, readily locatable points of reference from which other features may be located and learned. Seemingly, the body is, much more than it is a machine, a *landscape,* a particular, complex place that is part of and inter-dependent with its immediate surroundings and, ultimately, all creation.

Landscapes are, first of all, *particular* places. Although the general laws of the physical and natural sciences are applicable to every landscape, those laws can never approach, let alone exhaust, all there is to be known about any given landscape. Landscapes are particular to themselves and their surround-ings and the history of their uses, and they can be known only as they are respectfully explored and inhabited. The boundaries and contours of land-scapes are not drawn arbitrarily according to the machinations of political power or economic self-interest, as on a map; rather, they emerge, often tran-siently, through the stories told by those who inhabit and use them.[21]

Landscapes are also, therefore, properly *beloved.* Knowledge of a land-scape is never separable from its habitation and use. A place may be known intimately only as it is lived on and used, yet it can be inhabited and used well only to the extent that it is loved. To love a particular place is to use it suitably and with the acknowledgment that it has an integrity and a life quite apart from what can be taken from it; to love it is, in other words, to *care* for it. "Land," says Berry, "cannot be properly cared for by people who do not know it intimately, who do not know how to care for it, who are not strongly mo-tivated to care for it, and who cannot afford to care for it."[22] This means that the question of a land's proper use and its integrity is fundamentally histori-cal, in the sense that such questions always appeal to the more basic question of the identity of the people who have long-standing connections to and af-fection for the land. To have such affection is to desire above all else the land's flourishing, its health. One cannot truly love someone or something one does not know, and such knowledge is by nature historical.[23] The misuse of land by absentee coal and timber companies, who possess nothing in the way of affec-tion for or historical knowledge of the land and its inhabitants, bears abun-dant witness to this, as anyone who has lived in or traveled through rural re-gions like my native West Virginia or my current home in the Anthracite country of northeastern Pennsylvania can attest.

To love a landscape means, finally, to understand that it is a member of creation, a part of something greater than itself. Its character and proper uses are shaped by its relation to adjacent landscapes, in the sense that landscapes are never discrete and the boundaries and transitions between them may be determined only roughly and in part. The health of upland forests and farms, for example, affects the health of local watersheds, which, in turn, affects the health of rivers and oceans and those who depend on them to live, which is to say all of us. The acknowledgment that a landscape is a member of creation is essentially a claim about how properly to relate to that landscape. Such an acknowledgment is an admission that the place in question is part of something that exists by the grace of divine agency, that it is from God and a reflection of God's being that ultimately belongs to and is destined to return to God. "The land," God reminded the Israelites, "is mine; with me you are but aliens and tenants. Throughout the land that you hold, you shall provide for the redemption of the land" (Lev. 25:23–24 [NRSV]).

The person who realizes that her beloved landscape exists as a member of the entire creation therefore understands that her place, no matter how extensive the history of its belovedness, belongs not to her but to God. She is its steward, charged for a time with its care. Berry says that this care is best understood as *usufruct,* the right of temporary possession that carries with it the assumption that whatever use is made of a place by its steward will cause it no irreparable damage.[24] One who understands her relationship to her place in this way understands that the "destruction of nature is not just bad stewardship, or stupid economics, or a betrayal of family responsibility; it is the most horrid blasphemy."[25] Love of God and love of creature are, thus, inseparable, as the writings of both Old and New Testaments consistently remind us.

Testing the Metaphor: Landscapes of Flesh

Human bodies are, as I have already said, fundamentally connected to and dependent on the earth. Beyond and because of that connectedness, moreover, bodies themselves, in their particularity, their belovedness, and their membership within creation, are metaphoric *landscapes of flesh.* In spite of their considerable similarities to one another, bodies are radically particular. Of course, it would be silly, much less unhelpful, to discount the value of statistically normative accounts of the body such as are gained from blood chemistry profiles, pediatric growth charts, and the like. Yet each body has its own particular history, and only as that history is understood and appreciated in its particularity can a given body be known and cared for properly.[26] Berry is clearly right when he explains: "The question that *must* be addressed . . . is not how to care for the planet, but how to care for each of the planet's millions of human and natural neighborhoods, each of its millions of small pieces and parcels of land, each of which is in some precious way different from all the others."[27] These human and natural neighborhoods are constituted by human bodies connected to one another and to their places, whose well-being depends on their being cared for in light of their precious differences.

To care for bodies in a way that accounts for their differences requires that those bodies are beloved. The one caring must desire the wholeness of the body cared for, not simply in the sense of returning that body to some abstract standard of health as represented by comparison to biostatistical norms, but in the sense of making possible the progress of its purposeful life in communion with particular other lives.[28] For, as Berry reminds, "no loved one is standardized": "A body, love insists, is neither a spirit nor a machine; it is not a picture, a diagram, a chart, a graph, an anatomy; it is not an explanation; it is not a law. It is precisely and uniquely what it is. It belongs to the world of love, which is a world of living creatures, natural orders and cycles, many small fragile lights in the dark."[29]

Bodies are loved properly in their particularity, certainly, but only as the love extended toward them accounts for their existence as creatures who flourish as dependent and interdependent members of God's creation. A body may be loved well only as it is loved within the creaturely boundaries of its fragility and finitude. To love it without respect to these limits is not to love it at all but to covet it for one's own purposes. The twentieth-century Protestant theologian Karl Barth maintained that human life was properly understood as a gift and a loan from God. To understand life in this way is first of all to understand its origin and continued existence as coming ultimately from God, not from itself or those who may have a stake in its continuation.[30]

And this means that a body can be properly beloved only in light of its mortality. In this respect, health is to be understood, says Karl Barth, "like life in general [as] a temporal and therefore a limited possession."[31] Illness is properly to be resisted, but also to be understood as a harbinger of mortality, which, ultimately, cannot be overcome but can be exceeded—but only by God, and only through death and resurrection (1 Cor. 15:54–57). Acknowledging this as a guiding principle is not fatalism but, as Berry says, "an indispensable form of cultural generosity. It is the one effective way a person has of acknowledging and acting upon the fact of mortality: he will die, others will live after him."[32] Love, Berry explains, "must confront death, and accept it, and learn from it. Only in confronting death can earthly love learn its true extent, its immortality. Any definition of health that is not silly must include death. The world of love includes death, suffers it, and triumphs over it. The world of efficiency is defeated by death; as death, all its instruments and procedures stop. The world of love continues, and of this grief is the proof."[33]

Modern Medicine and Landscapes of Flesh

The question of whether it is helpful to think of the body as a landscape of flesh rests on whether such thinking can foster better care of bodies, especially by those whose work is the enterprise we call *medicine*. One way the landscape metaphor might help those who care for bodies is by encouraging a sense of humility, a mindfulness of the limits of their discipline. Caring for landscapes requires a patient, intimate attention to detail for which expertise, no matter how substantial, is not a substitute. To the extent that a body is like a particular place on earth, the medical professional who seeks to care for it must understand that she is—forgive the oxymoron—a sort of invited trespasser. If she does not attend adequately to the sympathetic knowledge of those who best know and love that body, she brings to it the capacity to do considerable harm in the name of good. In a short aphoristic essay entitled "Damage," Berry tells a story that nicely illustrates this point.

The story begins with Berry's unambiguous desire to do (what he regarded as) good: "I have a steep wooded hillside that I wanted to be able to pasture occasionally, but it had no permanent water supply." He goes on to tell how he sought to improve his farm by hiring someone to dig a small pond into the hillside. Almost immediately the pond began to fill, and soon enough it was large enough to provide water for a small number of livestock. Yet, for all Berry's good intentions, not to mention his considerable knowledge of and affection for his farm, things did not unfold exactly as he had planned: "We had an extremely wet fall and winter, with the usual freezing and thawing. The ground grew heavy with water, and soft. The earthwork slumped; a large slice of the woods floor on the upper side slipped down into the pond." In reflecting on this damage, which he acknowledges having caused, Berry considers how things might have been different. "I was careful," he says, "to get expert advice": "But this only exemplifies what I already knew. No expert knows everything about every place, not even everything about any place. If one's knowledge of one's whereabouts is insufficient, if one's judgment is unsound, then expert advice is of little use."[34]

The medical stranger who comes to a body wishing to do it good—to improve it—is an expert whose knowledge and skills rightfully garner significant power and esteem. Yet, if she is truly to do it good, she must begin by acknowledging the limits of her understanding of the particular body she encounters. She must try to know it not simply as one instantiation of *a* body but as the particular, beloved body that it is. To do this, she must learn something of its aspirations and affections, its present and past connections to other bodies, and the ways in which it was, is, or has failed to be a beloved body. Most of all, she must respect its sanctity, remembering that its presence to her and, indeed, to the entire world is as a gift and loan from its creator. Only by treading lightly over the holy ground that is a landscape of flesh can she hope to count her work on its behalf as genuinely good.[35]

Treading Lightly over Landscapes of Flesh

The fact that the medical industry, like so many facets of modern North Atlantic culture, is fraught with problems does not mean that physicians and nurses no longer do the good work of caring properly for bodies. During the summer of 2002, my father's health began to fail. He was diagnosed with heart failure stemming from an aortic valve insufficiency and coronary artery disease. It soon became apparent to those of us who cared for him—my mother and my brothers and sister and me—that, unless he heeded his physicians' counsel and underwent surgery, he was not going to live long. In October of that year, he underwent a nine-hour surgical procedure during which his aortic valve was replaced and he was given five coronary artery bypasses. In spite of his weakened state and the significant damage his heart had already suffered, he recovered and after a few weeks was able to return home. For nearly a year and a half we continued to enjoy his familiar presence in our lives.

Toward the end of 2003, he began again to experience the symptoms of serious heart failure. His physicians adjusted his medications, and his symptoms grew less severe for a while, yet, over time, it became apparent to me that he was in end-stage heart failure and his best days were now behind him. One night in January 2004, I was awakened by a late telephone call from my mother. My father had gotten out of bed to go to the bathroom and had fallen, breaking his femur, the large bone in his upper leg. He had been transported by ambulance to the local hospital and then to the nearest major medical center in Charleston, some sixty miles away. Early the next morning I left to make the eight-hour drive to be with him and my family.

When I arrived in Charleston, I learned that he had, indeed, sustained a serious fracture but that his heart failure was too advanced to do the surgery necessary to repair his injury. He was being cared for in the coronary intensive care unit, and, by treating him aggressively with medications and a Swan catheter, they had made a little headway in reversing his heart failure and relieving his leg pain. But he was frail and confused and disoriented, almost to the point of psychosis, and all of us were frightened and hurt by the suffering we saw him experiencing. We took turns sitting with him, wiping his forehead, feeding him the little bit he cared to eat, talking with him when he was lucid, doing whatever we could to make him comfortable. I recall sitting at his bedside late one night as he slept restlessly, running my hand over the deformity in his thigh, and wondering how this man, on whom I had been so dependent for so long, had himself become so helplessly dependent.

His physicians were obviously deeply concerned with his condition— they kept using the word *fragile*—and it soon became apparent (to me, at least) that they wanted but were reluctant to tell us that he was not going to get better. In the midst of all this, they and the nurses who were caring for my father were amazingly kind, sympathetic, and accommodating. When we asked as a family to meet with the physicians, to give them permission, so to speak, to tell us what needed saying, they were quietly and compassionately honest about his prospects, and, when we asked that they stop treating him aggressively and move him from intensive care to a private room, they were remarkably responsive. The young intensive care physician who was the leader of this medical team was grateful for our proactive involvement. "In my position," he explained, "there's always something else to do. The problem is with knowing what *not* to do. For that, I need help, like you're giving me here."

Within minutes of being moved to a private room, my father's confusion disappeared, and he was alert and communicative. My mother asked for some time alone with him, to explain that his death was imminent, and shortly thereafter he called all six of us children into the room. In the midst of our various gestures of affection and grief, he spoke to us eloquently, almost as if he had been rehearsing for years what he was going to say. He told us of his love for us and his hopes for our future, and he admonished us as well. "The love your mother and I have given to you," he said, "has been a gift. It has been given freely, and there has been a lot of it. There's a lot of love in this room, and I want you all always to remember that it has been given, not to be hoarded, but to be spent." Soon thereafter he went to sleep, and within a few hours he was dead.

My father is dead, but he remains a significant part of the landscapes that make up my life. Recently, while I was visiting my mother, I took time to go back to the Old Place, going this time not to look about cattle or check fences or hunt squirrels but to pay my respects to my father's grave at the family cemetery. I climbed the hill and walked out the ridge until I arrived at the cemetery. I entered the gate and passed again over the familiar ground of the old graves of past generations until I came to a newer one where my father's body lay, having become yet another beloved feature of the landscape that has shaped my life. A headstone had been placed since my last visit, and I read with tearful approval the inscription beneath my father's name: "He leaves behind a legacy of love."

I am genuinely grateful for the technical expertise of the physicians and surgeons who cared for my father over the final years of his life. But I am even more grateful that, when the time came, they had the wisdom to recognize the limits of their expertise and to yield it to a higher expertise, that of love, of which their yielding was itself a form. For it is love, human and divine, that teaches us the limits that make sense of all our knowledge and skill. It is through love that we live joyfully and purposefully, even in the midst of grief, for it is love, finally, that offers the only real hope of overcoming death.

Notes

This essay was first given as one of the 2006 J. J. Thiessen Lectures at Canadian Mennonite University. That version was published as Joel James Shuman, "Baptism, Communion, and the Body: The Pedagogy of Creaturely Interdependence," in *To Live Is to Worship: Bioethics and the Body of Christ* (Winnipeg: Canadian Mennonite University Press, 2007).

1. Wendell Berry, "The Body and the Earth," in *Recollected Essays: 1965–1980* (1981; reprint, New York: North Point, 1998), 269.

2. Ibid., 270, 271.

3. For a fuller account of Descartes's method and its effect on the way that method leads us to think about the body, see my *The Body of Compassion* (Boulder, CO: Westview, 1999), 15–21.

4. Alasdair MacIntyre rightly shows that such dualisms as are the heritage of

Cartesian philosophy and contemporary reductionist materialism are but part of the same mechanistic way of regarding the body. See Alasdair MacIntyre, "Medicine Aimed at the Care of Persons Rather Than What . . . ?" in *Philosophical Medical Ethics: Its Nature and Significance,* ed. S. F. Spicker and H. T. Engelhardt (Doredrecht: Reidel, 1977), 89.

5. Here see Drew Lederer, *The Absent Body* (Chicago: University of Chicago Press, 1990). Although he is ultimately critical of Cartesian dualism, Lederer maintains that, on a strictly phenomenological basis, the lived experience of "bodily absence," especially common in modern Western culture, supports a popular version of the Cartesian position.

6. Wendell Berry, "Health as Membership," in *Another Turn of the Crank* (Washington, DC: Counterpoint, 1995), 94.

7. Ibid., 94–95 (quote), 96.

8. Wendell Berry, "Feminism, the Body and the Machine," in *What Are People For?* (New York: North Point, 1990), 190–91, and "Discipline and Hope," in *A Continuous Harmony: Essays Cultural and Agricultural* (San Diego: Harcourt Brace Jovanovich, 1972), 147.

9. Berry, "The Body and the Earth," 280–81.

10. Berry, "Health as Membership," 90; Wendell Berry, "Healing," in *What Are People For?* 9.

11. In the United States, we spend more on medicine than anywhere else in the world. This is the case in absolute terms, per capita, and as a percentage of the gross domestic product.

12. For a fascinating (and sobering) account of a possible, not too distant future created by our way of life, see James Howard Kunstler, *The Long Emergency* (New York: Globes, 2005).

13. Berry addresses this point: "That will-o'-the-wisp, the large-scale solution to a large-scale problem, which is so dear to governments, universities, and corporations, serves mostly to distract people from the small, private problems that they may, in fact, have the power to solve" (Wendell Berry, "Word and Flesh," in *What Are People For?* 198).

14. Iris Murdoch, *The Sovereignty of Good* (New York: Routledge & Kegan Paul, 1970), 37.

15. Heather Widdows, *The Moral Vision of Iris Murdoch* (London: Ashgate, 2005), 104.

16. Stanley Hauerwas, "Murdochian Muddles: Can We Get Through Them If God Does Not Exist?" in *Wilderness Wanderings* (Boulder, CO: Westview, 1997), 155–70. Hauerwas is in this essay distinguishing his work from that of Murdoch; one significant part of that distinction is that, although he learned from her the impor-

tance of vision for moral discourse, he learned from (among others) Wittgenstein that our seeing is dependent on language that we have learned as members of the particular communities that teach us to speak properly of the world (ibid., 156). For more on this point, see Samuel Wells, *Transforming Fate into Destiny: The Theological Ethics of Stanley Hauerwas* (London: Paternoster, 1998), 104. See also Brad Kallenberg, *Ethics as Grammar: Changing the Postmodern Subject* (Notre Dame, IN: University of Notre Dame Press, 2001), esp. 185–88.

17. Alasdair MacIntyre, *After Virtue* (Notre Dame, IN: University of Notre Dame Press, 1984), 204–25.

18. Berry, "Discipline and Hope," 159–60.

19. I am aware that this could well be said of *all* learning, insofar as the acquisition of knowledge is always dependent on the senses. In this case, I am using the expression *using the body* against the background of a kind of rough-and-ready practical distinction between body and mind. I do so fully aware of the irony that dualism has become so much a part of us that even its criticism evokes the use of its concepts.

20. Kathleen Norris, *The Quotidian Mysteries: Laundry, Liturgy and "Women's Work"* (New York: Paulist, 1998).

21. Here I find useful the point made by William Cavanaugh, who follows Michel de Certeau in his distinction between the ways the medieval itinerary and the modern map configure space. Itineraries, he says, "told 'spatial stories,'" while maps remove the itinerant and rationalize space as homogeneous, rendering the particular history of any given space irrelevant ("The World in a Wafer: A Geography of the Eucharist as Resistance to Globalization," *Modern Theology* 15, no. 2 [April 1999]: 183).

22. Wendell Berry, "Conservation and Local Economy," in *Sex, Economy, Freedom, and Community* (New York: Pantheon, 1993), 3.

23. Wendell Berry, "An Argument for Diversity," in *What Are People For?* 115.

24. Wendell Berry, "God and Country," in *What Are People For?* 99.

25. Wendell Berry, "Christianity and the Survival of Creation," in *Sex, Economy, Freedom, and Community,* 98.

26. In recent personal correspondence, my friend Dan Hall, who is a surgeon, suggested that well-trained surgeons, and well-trained general surgeons in particular, should learn to see the body in this way. He notes: "Perhaps more than the cognitive disciplines (internal medicine, psychiatry, etc.), surgery is absolutely about the landscapes of the flesh, and an intimate familiarity thereof—including the anatomical variations that make each gallbladder distinct at the same time it is recognizable as a gallbladder. The substance of surgical training is learning to 'see' tissue planes in much the way that you learned to see the tell of deer or the way that water moves within a landscape."

27. Wendell Berry, "Word and Flesh," 200.

28. On this point, see Karl Barth, *Church Dogmatics,* trans. A. T. Mackay et al., 5 vols. (Edinburgh: T. & T. Clark, 1961), 3, pt. 4:356–57.

29. Berry, "Health as Membership," 103.

30. Barth, *Church Dogmatics,* 3, pt. 4:327, 342.

31. Ibid., 371.

32. Berry, "Discipline and Hope," 147.

33. Berry, "Health as Membership," 105.

34. Wendell Berry, "Damage," in *What Are People For?* 5.

35. Berry, "Christianity and the Survival of Creation," 104.

Norman Wirzba

The Dark Night of the Soil
An Agrarian Approach to Mystical Life

[God] is at a total remove from every condition, movement, life, imagination, conjecture, name, discourse, thought, conception, being, rest, dwelling, unity, limit, infinity, the totality of existence. And yet, since it is the underpinning of goodness, and by merely being there is the cause of everything, to praise this divinely beneficent Providence you must turn to all of creation. It is there at the center of everything and everything has it for a destiny.
—Pseudo-Dionysius, *The Divine Names*

We are all praising, praying to
The light we are, but cannot know.
—Wendell Berry, *Sabbaths*

In "The Long-Legged House" (1969), Wendell Berry wrote that as a writer his struggle has not been to find a subject but rather to know what to do with the subject he has been entrusted with from the beginning. The subject he was referring to was Henry County, Kentucky, the region of his birth: "I was so intricately dependent on this place that I did not begin in any meaningful sense to be a writer until I began to see the place clearly and for what it was." Seeing a place clearly, Berry notes, is "an enormous labor," one that begins with the realization that we belong to a place rather than the other way around. To know that we are not the owners or possessors of the world amounts to a "startling reversal of our ordinary sense of things" and culminates, at least for Berry, in what became his governing ambition: "to be altogether at home here." The ambition to allow oneself to be entirely governed by a place, by one's belonging to thrushes and herons—this aspiration being the briefest and clearest characterization of "agrarianism"—is "a spiritual ambition, like goodness." While other creatures instinctually live in place, human beings must make the choice—informed by intelligence, propriety, and virtue—to *be* in place: "It is an ambition I cannot hope to succeed in wholly, but I have come to believe that it is the most worthy of all."[1]

It is unlikely that many would call Berry's ambition *mystical*, particularly if we go by popular characterizations of the term restricting it to obscure and esoteric teachings or exceptional, ecstatic experiences providing direct access to and awareness of the sacred. According to this common view, a mystic is someone who has extraordinary states of consciousness in which unity with the divine is achieved. As William James famously put it, a mystic has a special faculty, much like the musician has a special ear, that is open to particularly intense states of feeling reaching into depths of truth "unplumbed by the discursive intellect" and beyond the reach of institutional religious authority.[2] Mystics, in other words, are people possessed by special powers that take them out of the realm of the ordinary, out of the places of daily life and struggle, and into the holy realm of an ineffable God.

Defining Mysticism

For a number of reasons, this characterization of mysticism, though having historical precedent, needs to be challenged and corrected, particularly in a self-absorbed time like our own when creation itself is threatened by neglect, abuse, or outright destruction.[3] Rather than being a peculiar type of experience or paranormal state of consciousness, mysticism is better understood as a practical process and a way of life that is, in principle, available to everyone. Though his or her goal is an encounter with God, a mystic is someone who is particularly open and attentive to the presence of God in this life and world. What the *presence of God* means, or who the God is whom we surrender ourselves to, is, of course, not something that can be determined beforehand. Indeed, and as the witness of many mystics confirms, the God we meet on a mystical path is most often quite unlike what we expect, imagine, hope, or fear. This is why mystics speak so often of a "God beyond God."[4] In fact, given our propensity to worship the gods of our own devising or comprehension, the gods who will best sanction and further self-promoting agendas, Meister Eckhart advises the following prayer: "I pray God to rid me of God."[5]

Coming into the presence of God is always mediated by traditions, cultures, sacred scriptures, institutions, practices, and (personal and social) experiences that may or may not adequately prepare us for the task. We always start our journeys from the perspective of some place as it has been shaped by time and memory, even if the course of our journey reveals the deficiency, even falsity—because either unjust, naive, sentimental, dishonest, or unloving—of the received understanding or naming of that place. In other words, a mystical path is something like a trial in which we submit our assumptions and desires, as well as the inflated egos and the false gods of our world, to rigorous testing and questioning to determine whether we have been faithful and true to the life we have been given. Few people have the patience or depth for this testing or the courage to face up to our various forms of idolatry. This is why named mystics are relatively few in number.

The narrowing of our mystical sensitivities is also attributable to the fact that, whether we care to admit it or not, we are still too much under the modern deistic assumption that God is far removed from our world and that gaining access to this God requires some supernatural, perhaps paranormal, effort that would make us unscientific or plainly kooky. We do not see God, as the Psalmist plainly does (of the many Psalms, see esp. 65 and 104), as intimately involved in the minute and mundane movements of our being as the one who gives us life and sustains us in it. And so we go in search of a god beyond this life and this world, all the while forgetting God as the Creator underpinning the goodness in all that is. What we need to learn is that the place of God is not "somewhere else," sequestered to some special place or realm of our experience. As we develop a contemplative and mystical way of living, we will discover that God is at the center of our being, at the heart of the whole of creation as its animating, pulsating life.

It is important to be clear that mystical traditions as a whole would not be in agreement with this point. One can find in mystical writings (often influenced by Gnosticism or informed by Christian Platonism) strands of anti-materialism and otherworldliness, strands that see little or no value in being at home in our created place. In the name of detachment, for instance, we are told to be "receptive of nothing but God" (Eckhart) or to become forgetful of everything beneath us and concern ourselves with "no creature whether material or spiritual nor with their situation and doings whether good or ill."[6] But what *detachment* means and what it practically entails is a complex, not universally agreed on matter. It need not simply mean the denial or denigration of material creatures. It can be developed in terms of the denial of certain kinds of attachments that esteem self and creation falsely and do not give sufficient glory and honor to God. Think here of Thomas Merton's precise formulation: "We do not detach ourselves from things in order to attach ourselves to God, but rather we become detached *from ourselves* in order to see and use all things in and for God. . . . There is no evil in anything created by God, nor can anything of His become an obstacle to our union with Him. The obstacle is in our 'self,' that is to say in the tenacious need to maintain our separate, external, egotistic will."[7] On this view, a view that I will here develop in an agrarian way, the goal is not to become free of creation itself but instead to be freed of certain ways of being within creation, ways of perceiving, thinking, and acting that inhibit or prevent a deep encounter with creation and God.

Learning the art of detachment is not easy, especially in our time, when we have grown accustomed to the myths of self-creation and self-regulation. We find it difficult to fully appreciate that we live through our dependence on others—most directly and evidently through bodily acts of touching, eating, drinking, and breathing—and, ultimately, God. This is why we need to recover an understanding of Christian practice and discipleship as a "schooling in the ways of creatureliness," in which we learn "that courtesy to creatures in which reverence for the Creator finds expression."[8] To understand God as our Creator, as the maker of everything, is to see everything (ourselves included) in terms of their relationships to each other and *in* God. We become courteous because we fully acknowledge that who we are, even *that we are,* is a feature of our having received the gifts that others are to us. Pseudo-Dionysius, speaking of the beauty and goodness of God, put it this way: "Beauty is the cause of harmony, of sympathy, of community. Beauty unites all things and is the source of all things. . . . From it derives the existence of everything as beings, what they have in common and what differentiates them, their identicalness and differences, their similarities and dissimilarities, their sharing of opposites. . . . Hence, the harmony and the love which are formed between them but which do not obliterate identity. Hence, the innate togetherness of everything. Hence, too, the intermingling of everything, the persistence of things, the unceasing emergence of things."[9] There is, in other words, a correspondence among creatures, a mutual and created harmony and sympathy, that finds its unity and wholeness in God. If we are to come into the presence of God, we must learn to find our place in this created correspondence and live responsibly and charitably within it.

This point is of tremendous significance because it means that mystical practice requires of us that we learn to become appropriately and fully present in the places in which we move and live and that we take up our proper place as creatures within the orders of creation: "Contemplation, then, cannot properly be a prostration before a power outside us; it is a being present to ourselves *in* our world with acceptance and trust. Hence . . . the importance of attention to the praying *body;* the contemplative significance of taking time to *sense* ourselves in prayer, to perceive patiently what and where we materially are."[10] Indeed, because God, however mysteriously, is made manifest through the work of creation, we can make no claim to being present to God except insofar as we tune our living so as to be in harmony with God's life-giving presence among us. If to be alive is to be created, then to live well is to live in such a way that our own creative gestures—as witnessed in our eating, teaching, building, parenting, playing, and loving—increasingly bear witness to and honor the continuing creativity of God: "If the 'mystical' ultimately means the reception of a particular *pattern* of divine action (creative love, self-emptying incarnation), its test will be the presence or absence of something like that pattern in a human life seen as a whole, not the presence or absence of this or that phenomenon in the consciousness."[11]

This characterization of mysticism as a journey into the presence of God rather than the undergoing of exceptional states of consciousness opens new possibilities for a dialogue between Berry's ambition to be in place and the mystic's commitment to be present to creation. As I will argue, agrarian practices and sensitivities can, because of their focus on the health and vitality of embodied memberships, play a vital role in the reformulation of a contemporary mysticism that, while not in complete agreement with some traditional emphases, is firmly rooted in creation yet tuned to the life of God. As we proceed, however, we will need to be particularly mindful of the strategies that human beings have used for being in place, for what is clear is that we can be more or less successful in this effort.[12] That we can fail terribly is evident in our time as we now contemplate, for the first time in history, the near annihilation of creation's processes, memberships, and habitats. Not only are the divinely created harmony and sympathy the early church fathers talked about coming apart through our own hands, but their current dissolution also threatens to put an end to our memberships altogether.

Becoming Creatures

The sense that our destructive waywardness is attributable to a denial of our creatureliness is well understood by Berry. In "A Native Hill" (1968), he wrote: "There appears to be a law that when creatures have reached the level of consciousness, as men have, they must become conscious of the creation; they must learn how they fit into it and what its needs are and what it requires of them, or else pay a terrible penalty: the spirit of the creation will go out of them, and they will become destructive; the very earth will depart from them and go where they cannot follow."[13] It is when we make ourselves the goal of the world, as when we manipulate or redesign the earth and its creatures to satisfy self-chosen and self-enhancing aims, that the memberships of creation begin to unravel. We stifle creation by making personal pride and greed "the standard of our behavior toward the world." By failing to live patiently and with a measure of propriety, attentive and attuned to our fittedness within multiple webs of interdependence and responsibility, the beauty and good-ness of creation is destroyed:

> The world is lost in loss
> Of patience; the old curse
> Returns, and is made worse
> As newly justified.
> In hopeless fret and fuss,
> In rage at worldly plight
> Creation is defied,
> All order is unpropped,
> All light and singing stopped.[14]

In short, we are impatient and unskilled at being creatures. Our impatience is most magnified in our desire to stand alone, unencumbered by the demands and responsibilities, the limits and the possibilities that come from living within and being constituted by the many memberships of creation. On an agrarian, but also mystical, view, there is no self-standing I. What we call *I* is always already communal and relational, a creature formed and sustained through the dynamisms of soil and soul.

Understanding, let alone practicing, a patient and attentive regard for creation is anything but easy, particularly in a time of mass urbanization and readily available technology when our connections to the memberships of creation are so thin and superficial. Ours is a culture beset by biological and ecological amnesia, the mass forgetting that we are bound through our bodies to the microbial life in soils and the photosynthetic activity of plants. In the course of his writing career, Berry has spoken clearly about some of the strategies and practices we need to reconnect to our biological and cultural homes—ranging from staying in one region (saying no to upward mobility and social dislocation) and committing to a community to growing a garden and investing in a household and a local economy. What I want to do here, however, is develop the transformation of mind-set and habit that must occur if we are to fully be in the places that we are and, thus, be "altogether at home." As will become clear, what Berry has in mind is a spiritual transformation that links up in multiple ways with a mystical form of life.

Like the great spiritual masters who speak of a need for a perpetual *metanoia,* a continuous turning round of the mind and heart, in order for us to enter into communion with each other and with God, so too Berry observes that we have been infected with, and, thus, must continually treat, our developed "habit of contention—against the world, against each other, against ourselves." The breaking of this habit, this "intransigent destructiveness in us," will require a drastic change in the assumptions by which we live our lives: "It is not from ourselves that we will learn to be better than we are."[15] To correct our intransigence, we will need to become "apprentices" to creation, by learning to know the world as best we can and then cooperate in its processes.[16]

An apprenticeship is the long labor by which workers slowly and carefully learn to yield themselves to the excellences of a craft. They do not simply impose their ambitions on the work but rather let the materials (their availability and quantity), the needs of the community in which the work is performed, and the possibilities of good, safe, beautiful, and useful design determine the character and extent of the work. They must leave behind visions of profit and glory so that a genuine understanding of and appreciation for the work and the product can be achieved. The measure of the quality of our work, in other words, is not derived from what we might gain for ourselves but rather indicated in the durability and beauty of the thing made, in the health and happiness of the community in which the work is performed and the product is used, and in the long-term viability of the work itself (the work does not presuppose the degradation or destruction of the resources or workers that feed into the work). Good work—work that reflects a successful apprenticeship—will, therefore, result in healthy, flourishing habitats and dynamic, convivial communities. It does this because the workers have learned to detach from their ambition, replacing it with attachments that reflect a more sympathetic and harmonious (though not always easy) attunement to the grace at work in the world.

When we become apprentices *of creation,* we let the health of the land serve as the measure of the quality of our overall work. In a very real and practical sense, we submit ourselves to the creation and, thus, fully accept our divinely appointed vocation to "till and keep" the garden (Gen. 2:15). Berry describes the character of our submission in the following:

> Until we understand what the land is, we are at odds with everything we touch. And to come to that understanding it is necessary, even now, to leave the regions of our conquest—the cleared fields, the towns and cities, the highways—and re-enter the woods. For only there can man encounter the silence and the darkness of his own absence. Only in this silence and darkness can he recover the sense of the world's longevity, of its ability to thrive without him, of his inferiority to it and his dependence on it. Perhaps then, having heard that silence and seen that darkness, he will grow humble before the place and begin to take it in—to learn *from it* what it is. As its sounds come into his hearing, and its lights and colors come into his vision, and its odors come into his nostrils, then he may come into *its* presence as he never has before, and he will arrive in his place and will want to remain. His life will grow out of the ground like the other lives of the place, and take its place among them. He will be *with* them—neither ignorant of them, nor indifferent to them, nor against them—and so at last he will grow to be native-born. That is, he must re-enter the silence and the darkness, and be born again.[17]

There is in this language a profound sense that the mundane work of becoming a creature and making a home—what Berry also describes as our being "married" to a place[18]—is finally work of the highest spiritual order. This is why the collection of poems *The Country of Marriage* (1973) has as its epigraph a quotation from John 12:24: "Except a corn of wheat fall into the ground and die, it abideth alone." We cannot grow "out of the ground" or arrive and remain in place without a certain kind of dying to self, even a dying "into the ground," that is the mark of spiritual transformation and renewal.

Mystics have often characterized this dying as an entry into darkness because in it the self learns to shed the various forms of rationalization—the light of a natural reason—that would identify God with one element of creation or legitimate and justify the self in its ambitions.[19] The central problem with our seeking to identify or claiming to comprehend God is that, in doing so, we think that we have access to the supreme calculus that will enable us to secure and legitimate our place in the world. In other words, by claiming to identify God, we underwrite ourselves and our ambitions. In the mystical dark night, however, we gradually come to sense the hubris of our attempts to delimit or comprehend God. We give up the desire to firmly grasp, whether mentally or practically, the world for ourselves.

Entering into the Dark

In *The Ascent of Mount Carmel*, Saint John of the Cross alludes to the dark night when he says that divine truth exceeds every natural light and all human understanding. He writes: "The excessive light of faith bestowed on man is darkness for him, because a brighter light will eclipse and suppress a dimmer one. The sun so obscures all other lights that they do not seem to be lights at all when it is shining, and instead of affording vision to the eyes it overwhelms, blinds, and deprives them of vision, since its light is excessive and unproportioned to the visual faculty. Similarly the light of faith in its abundance suppresses and overwhelms that of the intellect."[20] Saint John of the Cross is drawing a contrast between a "natural way" of knowing, which is dependent on the senses, and the "way of faith," which overwhelms sight and comes to us by hearing the Word (Rom. 10:17). Of course, hearing is one of the senses too. But his point is that the object of faith is not proportionate to any sense object and, thus, is not the end product of any natural (self-chosen) desire. God cannot be seen with our eyes or comprehended in terms of the light of natural reason. Indeed, insofar as we claim to have grasped God using the various categories of the understanding, we can be sure that we have laid hold of an idol rather than God. God forever eludes all reasoning, knowing, and naming.[21]

When Berry talks about our entrance into silence and darkness, he is not simply opposing sight and hearing or natural reason and faith. His is a complex darkness that suspends and calls into question a habitual disposition to secure the world for ourselves (often through force and violence, but also through native cunning and ingenuity). He is not finally opposed to reason.

Nor does he seek its elimination. It would be better to say that he seeks to set limits to it and contextualize it within a larger pattern of human and created life formed by love. In his poem "The Design of a House" he says:

> If reason was all, reason
> would not exist—the will
> to reason accounts for it;
> it's not reason that chooses
> to live; the seed doesn't swell
> in its husk by reason, but loves
> itself, obeys light which is
> its own thought and argues the leaf
> in secret; love articulates
> the choice of life in fact; life
> chooses life because it is
> alive; what lives didn't begin dead,
> nor sun's fire commence in ember. (*CP,* 31–32)

Reasoning needs to be darkened so that the illumination of love's mysterious light can appear and shine on our living. Much as in Saint Augustine, reason is subsumed within the larger movements of love, only then truly becoming itself.[22]

In the 1980 "Sabbath Poem VI," Berry offers a meditation on precisely this theme:

> The intellect so ravenous to know
> And in its knowing hold the very light,
> Disclosing what is so and what not so,
>
> Must finally know the dark, which is its right
> And liberty; it's blind in what it sees.
> Bend down, go in by this low door, despite
>
> The thorn and briar that bar the way. (*TC,* 30)

Our problem is not the intellect itself but rather our ravenous nature and our desire to reduce all creation to a utilitarian or market-driven end. What Berry opposes is the sort of scientism epitomized by modernity's ambition to take control of the world by force and with the aid of technologies that mask our fragility and dependence on others.[23] Through scientific and economic reductionism, the intellect has become blind. Though it looks, it no longer sees truly since it has lost the imagination to see the sanctity of created things or the vast and indescribably complex memberships of which they and we are but one part.[24] Our naming of things is superficial and not detailed enough, which means that, in our engagement with them, we readily violate their integrity and wholeness.

And so we are instructed to "bend down." Our bending, as the thorns and briars make plain, is hardly a straightforward or smooth effort since it must fully come to terms with the harvest of human sinfulness. As Berry continues: "Greed and sloth / did bad work that this thicket now conceals" (*TC*, 30). Human sinfulness is not an abstraction. It is made manifest in soil washed into the sea, in watersheds poisoned by the use of synthetic fertilizers and pesticides, in mountaintops blown up and then removed for their coal, and in rural communities destroyed and emptied out by the world of finance. When we bend down, what we are, in fact, doing is signifying a humble disposition that is prepared to learn from creation and is willing to be taught by it in the ways of interdependent living. To bend, like a servant, is to give up the hubristic assumption that we can live well alone and through the forceful imposition of our will on the world.[25]

It is extremely difficult to argue the case for humility in our time. We resist recommendations to service and fidelity because we see in them the potential for abuse or outright humiliation. The paradox, however, is that it is precisely the quest for self-assertion that has culminated in the degradation of creation. The evidence is clear that our desire to control the world and to engage it on our terms has led to its ruination. We are in need of a better way, a way that is more faithful and true to the biblical mandate to serve and keep creation. Since hubris has done so much harm, we need to rehabilitate the practice of humility.

> O bent by fear and sorrow, now bend down,
> Leave word and argument, be dark and still,
> And come into the joy of healing shade.
> Rest from your work. Be still and dark until
> You grow as unopposing, unafraid

As the young trees, without thought or belief;
Until the shadow Sabbath light has made
Shudders, breaks open, shines in every leaf. (*TC,* 31)

Before we can enter into the "joy of healing shade," we will first need to become dark and still ourselves. What does this mean?

In various places Berry speaks of our "serving the dark." Often what he
has in mind is the practice of tilling the soil. There is in this tilling much more
than simply the preparation of a seedbed for a crop. If we remember that the
word *culture* in Middle English usage referred not to the refinements of civilization but to a cultivated piece of land, then it becomes clear that our tilling
is, ultimately, about the preparation and formation of people so that they can
live worthily and sustainably in a particular place.[26] As Berry likes to say, there
is no culture without *agri*culture. This is because the tending of plants and the
husbanding of animals are the ideal training ground for the moral and spiritual virtues that would make for a good and beautiful home (*and* a faithful
mystic). True farmers and gardeners have tamed the ego by making the care
of another their first priority. They have submitted their plans and designed
their economies in such a way as to contribute to processes of fertility and
growth. They have brought personal desire into alignment with the needs,
potential, and limits of another in its particular place.

To be in alignment with creation is a complex effort that requires us to let
go of our own personal ambitions so that we can see clearly the creation before us and, thus, enter into the presence of God. The first thing we need to
do is give up otherworldly aspirations. In "The Wild Geese," Berry said:

And we pray, not
for new earth or heaven, but to be
quiet in heart, and in eye
clear. What we need is here. (*CP,* 156)

Far from denying the idea of heaven, Berry is asking us to give up the dreams
of wish fulfillment—how much of our imagery of heaven is precisely the end
result of a personal dream?—and instead see the presence of God already in
our midst.[27] In fact, the desire for heaven is, in many instances, a disguised,
Gnostic form of disdain for creation, a desire to be rid of and to escape created, bodily life and its limits.[28]

The Mystery of God and Humanity

If what we need is here within creation, this does not mean that the presence of God will suddenly become obvious to us. As we have already seen, though God is in all things and underpins them as their animating source and destiny, at the same time we must admit that God is not to be reduced to or identified with anything in creation. God is everywhere *and* nowhere at the same time. God is transcendent, as Thomas Carlson helpfully puts it, "through his incomprehensible immanence."[29] The realization of the incomprehensibility of God, however, leads to the further realization that we too, as made in the image of God, are also finally incomprehensible to ourselves. Moreover, creation as a whole must finally also be incomprehensible since it is the concrete manifestation of God's groundless yet abiding love, a divine love that is, as Eckhart said, "without why."[30] From our point of view, we simply do not understand why creation is what it is and why it moves in ways that result in such beauty but also unspeakable suffering and pain. And so, as we immerse ourselves deeply into creation, as we "bend down," as Berry suggests, we are met on all sides by the darkness of incomprehension.

Divine incomprehensibility and human incomprehensibility yield a most important result, namely, the truth of human ignorance. This is no merely provisional or temporary ignorance (that will, thus, be overcome someday) but an essential part of who we are. In his most recent collection of essays, Berry has stressed the cultural necessity of acknowledged ignorance as an antidote to the arrogant and destructive "corporate mind" that thinks it can foresee and plan a better world according to its own devising.[31] What an industrial, merely economic mind forgets is that we cannot comprehend the orders of creation because ignorance of various forms—inherent, historical, moral, and scientific as well as that which follows from character weakness, false confidence, fear, laziness, and for-profit/for-power motivations—reflects a limited, even damaged mind. Even if we were to become fully human and realize every created capacity, we would still be faced with the incomprehensibility of divine, sustaining love:

> The mind that comes to rest is tended
> In ways that it cannot intend:
> Is borne, preserved, and comprehended
> By what it cannot comprehend.

Your Sabbath, Lord, thus keeps us by
Your will, not ours. And it is fit
Our only choice should be to die
Into that rest, or out of it. (*TC,* 7)

This point needs special emphasis because of what it can teach us about human "dominion" over creation (Gen. 1:26). For centuries, people have assumed that, even though we are creatures, we are, nonetheless, special because God has put us over all other living and nonliving things. Among some early church fathers like Gregory of Nyssa and John Scotus Erigena, there was the view that God creates creatures "in" humanity and that humanity contains within itself all creatures. The logic behind this view was that, if we are made in the image of God, then we transcend all creatures by means of our knowledge of them (as reflected in our freedom over them and our naming of them). For Erigena, it made little sense to say that we have dominion over creatures if we did not have the concept of them in our minds. Insofar as the human mind shares in the divine mind in its ability to see, hear, scrutinize, and possess a hold over creatures, it must contain within itself the substance of all created things. Human dominion, as Gregory argued, must, therefore, take shape in our control of creation through technological means. But this leads to a curious result: "The subject who cannot know its own nature at the same time relates to creation through an all-inclusive vision of comprehension and dominion."[32] We should wonder about claims to "all-inclusive" dominion, particularly if we take seriously the threefold incomprehensibility of God, creation, and humanity. If we are serious about living faithfully and attentively with our creatureliness, then we will need to chasten the desire for complete control.

How should we think incomprehensibility and dominion together, particularly when we know that ignorant arrogance matched with great power leads to ever greater destruction? We need to start by acknowledging that the admission of systemic ignorance is at the same time a call for restraint and humility. Those committed to taking up a divine pattern of life in this world must move beyond a ravenous and rapacious intellect and into the wider movements of love. Love is not a sloppy willfulness but a disciplined and attentive regard for another. Christians believe this because they have in mind the ministries of healing, feeding, forgiving, and reconciling as concretely and practically revealed in the life of Jesus Christ. The freedom that marks our creatureliness and that makes possible our dominion reaches its most authentic pitch in the love shown by Christ. The Christian's freedom is always freedom "in Christ," which means that the dispositions that guided his life—what I earlier referred to as the pattern of God's continuing activity among us—must also guide our own. Whatever technological ambitions we might have must be restrained and contextualized by this pattern.

This conclusion is of the highest significance because it means that the transcendence that we enjoy over creation by virtue of our freedom and reasoning capacities is turned back to creation in the form of a loving *descent* (bending down) that commits to be with its members in their need and pain.[33] This is what Christ's ministry teaches: that to truly and fully be ourselves we must give ourselves away. Paul summed this up beautifully in his account of the kenotic, self-emptying mind of Christ, "who, though he was in the form of God, did not regard equality with God as something to be exploited, but emptied himself, taking the form of a slave, being born in human likeness. And being found in human form, he humbled himself and became obedient to the point of death—even death on a cross" (Phil. 2:6–8). This giving away of self, this loving abandon, is the definitive expression of the divine life. Indeed, this is precisely what created life is: a perpetual, incomprehensible giving away: "God's utterance lovingly gives life; gives all life, all unfading freshness; gives only life, and peace, and love, and beauty, harmony and joy. And the life God gives is nothing other, nothing less, than God's own self. Life is God, given."[34]

If mystics are those who seek to take up the divine pattern of life within their own, then the giving away of one's life will become a defining feature of mystical practice. According to Berry, we have a concrete model to learn from: the soil's fertility. In the growing and the dying of things, and in their regeneration through processes of decomposition and recomposition, we see, even as we do not fully understand, the miracle of continuing life. As we contribute to the processes of fertility and growth—practically speaking, by consuming food and energy in just, sustainable manners and by committing to the strengthening of local communities—we enrich creation and so participate, however inadequately, in God's continuing creative work. Speaking of sowing clover and grass, Berry says in "Enriching the Earth":

All this serves the dark. I am slowly falling
into the fund of things. And yet to serve the earth,

not knowing what I serve, gives a wideness
and a delight to the air, and my days
do not wholly pass. It is the mind's service,
for when the will fails so do the hands
and one lives at the expense of life.
After death, willing or not, the body serves,
entering the earth. And so what was heaviest
and most mute is at last raised up into song. (*CP,* 110)

Resurrection and Soil

To appreciate this view, we need to understand that soil is a marvel. It is not something we can make. All that we can do, besides destroy it, is cooperate with the dark processes at work within it—die into it—recognizing that, in the midst of this darkness, life is made out of death. Berry admits that, when talking about soil, it is hard to avoid the language of religion:

> The most exemplary nature is that of the topsoil. It is very Christ-like in its passivity and beneficence, and in the penetrating energy that issues out of its peaceableness. It increases by experience, by the passage of seasons over it, growth rising out of it and returning to it, not by ambition or aggressiveness. It is enriched by all things that die and enter into it. It keeps the past, not as history or as memory, but as richness, new possibility. Its fertility is always building up out of death into promise. Death is the bridge or tunnel by which its past enters its future.[35]

Life continually dies into the soil and emerges as new life. And so it makes some sense to refer to soil as a site of resurrection. Here, we apprehend something of the hospitable character of the divine life that is forever creating room for others to be and to flourish, but then also to die and make room for yet more life.[36] Divine hospitality finds its analogue in the soil: "Hospitality is the fundamental virtue of the soil. It makes room. It shares. It neutralizes poisons. And so it heals. This is what the soil teaches: If you want to be re-membered, give yourself away."[37] The remembrance that William Bryant Logan is talking about is not simply of the mental sort but the re-membering where we fully join into the life of posterity through our bodies, into the memberships of creation. Through our surrender to the land and to community we gain an entrance into the mysterious presence of God in creation. The supreme passivity and submission of the body to creation, seen first in our need to eat and drink but then also in our dying into the earth at burial, is the constant, concrete reminder and tutor in the ways of spiritual submission. We enter into the dark ground with our bodies and our spirits and, thereby, anticipate the miracle of new life:[38]

> Let the world bring on me
> the sleep of darkness without stars, so I may know
> my little light taken from me into the seed
> of the beginning and the end, so I may bow
> to mystery, and take my stand on the earth,
> like a tree in a field, passing without haste
> or regret toward what will be, my life
> a patient willing descent into the grass. (*CP,* 114)

When Berry characterizes human life as "a patient willing descent" and models personal growth after a young tree that is "unopposing and unafraid . . . without thought or belief" (*TC,* 31), he is describing a way of living that has detachment at its core. By *detachment,* we can now see, he means not a flight or an escape from the world but our full immersion into creation, our giving ourselves to others so that they can more fully be. Detachment is a form of engagement marked by conviviality and celebration rather than contention and needless destruction. Put more precisely, since we are always already (through the passivity of our bodies) within creation as one of its members, what Berry is recommending is a way of being present to one another in which we see and welcome things for what they are rather than what we want or wish them to be. This is a way of being marked by the letting be of things, what Meister Eckhart described as our "releasement" into things and into God "without restraint."[39] Detachment, in other words, makes it possible for us to fully be with others since we no longer receive or engage them in terms of the agendas or idols we carry through life. In this respect, Berry is in agreement with the definition of *wisdom* offered by Maximus Confessor: "Wisdom consists in seeing every object in accordance with its true nature, with perfect interior freedom."[40]

When we enter the mystical path, what we are really trying to do, more than have some special apparition of God, is come to see (however imperfectly) the world as God sees it. We resist this form of seeing because it means that we must give up points of view that establish and legitimate our standing in the world. We resist detachment because it makes us vulnerable to the contingency, suffering, mystery, and unpredictability that creation itself is. We prefer not to serve the soil, or enter into the dark "ground" that is creation's life and death, because it entails our submission to the unknown and incomprehensible.[41] Berry's work, however, stands as a reminder to the damage done to the countless bodies and memberships of creation that ensues from our failure to "serve the dark." It also shines as a witness to another way, a way that might yet lead us into the "blessed conviviality" ("To Sit and Look at Light-Filled Leaves" [*TC*, 8]) of creation that marked the first Sabbath day.

Can we be at peace with one another and with God and so be "altogether at home" in creation? Can we finally become the courteous creatures God intends for us to be? Berry offers no simple or painless solutions. What he recommends is love's labor, a labor informed by virtues of modesty, attention, fidelity, humility, thrift, propriety, generosity, mercy, and gratitude. What we need to learn to do as much as possible—and for this we will need the help and guidance of spiritual traditions, the insights of ecology, the support of a community, and the memory of good work—is how to get ourselves and our ambition out of the way so that the incomprehensible, gracious givingness of God (what Berry sometimes calls *Sabbath light*) can shine throughout creation and in us.

If a mystical path is one in which the traveler learns to submit to God, then it is the virtue of agrarian life to show us that our submission is authentic only as we commit ourselves to the health and vitality of creation, for it is here that God's ways, however mysteriously, are being worked out. It is here, in the soil beneath our feet and among countless created neighborhoods rather than in some faraway celestial place, that God meets us in work and grace that exceeds our comprehension and our wrongdoing:

> For we are fallen like the trees, our peace
> Broken, and so we must
> Love where we cannot trust,
> Trust where we cannot know,
> And must await the way-ward coming grace
> That joins living and dead,
> Taking us where we would not go—Into the boundless dark.
> When what was made has been unmade
> The Maker comes to his work. (*TC*, 74)

Notes

This essay previously appeared as Norman Wirzba, "The Dark Night of the Soil," *Christianity and Literature* 56, no. 2 (Winter 2007): 253–74. Reprinted by permission.

1. Wendell Berry, "The Long-Legged House," in *The Long-Legged House* (1969; reprint, Washington, DC: Shoemaker & Hoard, 2004), 141, 150.

2. William James, *The Varieties of Religious Experience* (New York: New American Library, 1958), 293 (see generally lectures 16–17, which were the 1901–2 Gifford Lectures).

3. An excellent place to begin, one that submits James's version to sustained analysis and critique, is Nicholas Lash's *Easter in Ordinary: Reflections on Human Experience and the Knowledge of God* (Notre Dame, IN: University of Notre Dame Press, 1988). In preparing these general remarks on mysticism, I have also benefited greatly from Bernard McGinn's magisterial, multivolume history of Western Christian mysticism, *The Presence of God: A History of Western Christian Mysticism*, esp. vol. 1, *The Foundations of Mysticism: Origins to the Fifth Century* (New York: Crossroad, 1991).

4. Olivier Clément, *The Roots of Christian Mysticism: Texts from the Patristic Era with Commentary* (New York: New City, 1993), 26–35.

5. Meister Eckhart quoted in Reiner Schürmann, *Wandering Joy: Meister Eckhart's Mystical Philosophy* (Great Barrington, MA: Lindisfarne, 2001), 209.

6. *Meister Eckhart: From Whom God Hid Nothing: Sermons, Writings, and Sayings*, ed. David O'Neal (Boston: Shambhala, 1996), 108; *The Cloud of Unknowing* V (New York: Doubleday, 1973), 53.

7. Thomas Merton, *New Seeds of Contemplation* (New York: New Directions, 1961), 21.

8. Nicholas Lash, "Creation, Courtesy and Contemplation," in *The Beginning and the End of "Religion"* (Cambridge: Cambridge University Press, 1996), 173.

9. Pseudo-Dionysius, *The Divine Names*, in *The Complete Works* (Mahwah, NJ: Paulist, 1987), 77–78 (4.7). Basil the Great speaks similarly in *Homelia hexameron* (2.2): "God has united the entire world, which is composed of many different parts, by the law of indissoluble friendship, in communion and harmony, so that the most distant things seem to be joined together by one and the same sympathy" (available at http://www.ccel.org/ccel/schaff/npnf208.txt).

10. Rowan Williams, "On Being Creatures," in *On Christian Theology* (Oxford: Blackwell, 2000), 76. I would add that we must be present not only to ourselves in the world but also *to others* since it is through them that we live.

11. Rowan Williams, *Teresa of Avila* (Harrisburg, PA: Morehouse, 1991), 145–46.

12. For an agrarian-inspired examination of the problems and prospects of living in place, see Wes Jackson, *Becoming Native to This Place* (Washington, DC: Counterpoint, 1994).

13. Wendell Berry, "A Native Hill," in *The Long-Legged House,* 193.

14. Wendell Berry, "Six Days of Work Are Spent," in *A Timbered Choir: The Sabbath Poems, 1979–1997* (Washington, DC: Counterpoint, 1998), 29. Page numbers for subsequent citations from *Timbered Choir* (hereafter *TC*) are given parenthetically in the text.

15. Berry, "A Native Hill," 210.

16. "It is the creation that has attracted me, its perfect interfusion of life and design. I have made myself its follower and apprentice" (ibid., 201).

17. Ibid., 207.

18. "The way I go is / marriage to this place, / grace beyond chance, / love's braided dance / covering the world" (Wendell Berry, "In Rain" [1982], in *Collected Poems, 1957–1982* [San Francisco: North Point, 1985], 268). Page numbers for subsequent citations from the *Collected Poems* (hereafter *CP*) are given parenthetically in the text.

19. Here we should note that a philosophical/theological definition of *idolatry* is one in which the idol is not simply a fabricated object but the fulfillment of a human gaze or desire. Idols are, thus, the full extension of the self and its aspiration. They are mirrors to (and, thus, a confirmation of) the self rather than an opening to the divine (as an icon is supposed to be). For a development of these themes, see the recent work of Jean-Luc Marion, including *God without Being: Hors-Texte,* trans. Thomas A. Carlson (Chicago: University of Chicago Press, 1991), esp. chaps. 1–2.

20. Saint John of the Cross, *The Ascent of Mount Carmel,* in *The Collected Works of St. John of the Cross,* trans. Kieran Kavanaugh, O.C.D., and Otilio Rodriguez, O.C.D. (Washington, DC: ICS, 1979), 110 (2.3).

21. Pseudo-Dionysius reminds us that it is even improper to stay with the image of darkness: "There is no speaking of it, nor name nor knowledge of it. Darkness and light, error and truth—it is none of these. It is beyond assertion and denial" (*The Mystical Theology,* in *The Complete Works,* 141 [bk. 5]). In this essay, however, I will continue to use the metaphor of darkness as a way of describing our "unknowing" in the service of a more faithful and true life.

22. Augustine writes in his *Homilies on the Psalms* that we become fully conscious of God only insofar as love grows in us because God is love: "Before you had the experience [of love], you used to think you could speak of God. You begin to have the experience, and there you experience that you cannot say what you experience" (quoted in McGinn, *The Foundations of Mysticism,* 241). True intellect is humbled or, as Berry would say, is "bent down" (see the discussion of "Sabbath Poem VI" that follows in the text) because it has been overwhelmed by love and, thus, rendered speechless.

23. Here, Berry joins hands with other "traditionalist" critics of modernity like Ananda Coomaraswamy, Kathleen Raine, and Philip Sherrard. In a tribute to

Kathleen Raine, he describes the nihilism of modernity as the desecration of humanity, once thought to be made in the image of God, but now reduced to being little more than a "higher" animal. With this desecration came "the implied permission to be more bewildered, violent, self-deluded, destructive, and self-destructive than any of the animals" (Wendell Berry, "Against the Nihil of the Age," *Temenos Academy Review*, no. 7 [2004]: 82).

24. Think here of Augustine, who describes how, in turning our backs to the divine light that sustains all things and is the sense of their truth, we darken our minds and bring destruction to one another and the world (*Confessions*, 4.30).

25. Berry observes that even our best attempts to heal are not without damage and pain: "An art that heals and protects its subject is a geography of scars" (Wendell Berry, "Damage," in *What Are People For?* [New York: North Point, 1990], 7). In the short text "Damage," Berry reflects on his effort to repair the destruction caused by his desire to have a pond midway up a slope in one of his fields.

26. For a helpful discussion of the original link between culture and land and the gradual eclipse of land in the name of civilization, see Jonathan Bate, *The Song of the Earth* (Cambridge, MA: Harvard University Press, 2000), chap. 1.

27. Berry notes that his primary aim in life is not to get into heaven: "Though heaven is certainly more important than the earth if all they say about it is true, it is still morally incidental to it and dependent on it, and I can only imagine it and desire it in terms of what I know of the earth. And so my questions do not aspire beyond the earth. They aspire *toward* it and *into* it. Perhaps they aspire *through* it" ("A Native Hill," 200).

28. I have developed this theme in "Placing the Soul: An Agrarian Philosophical Principle," in *The Essential Agrarian Reader: The Future of Culture, Community, and the Land,* ed. Norman Wirzba (Lexington: University Press of Kentucky, 2003).

29. Thomas A. Carlson, "Locating the Mystical Subject," in *Mystics: Presence and Aporia,* ed. Michael Kessler and Christian Sheppard (Chicago: University of Chicago Press, 2003), 213. As Carlson points out, according to Erigena, an invisible, incomprehensible God realizes himself in creation, thus turning it into a dark theophany manifesting this divine, inaccessible incomprehensibility.

30. Meister Eckhart, Sermon 81, "I Have Chosen You," available at http://www.geocities.com/athens/acropolis/5164/EckSermlxxxi.htm.

31. Wendell Berry, *The Way of Ignorance: And Other Essays* (Shoemaker & Hoard, 2005).

32. Carlson, "Locating the Mystical Subject," 221.

33. The desire to ascend "beyond places and times" (ibid., 219), so much in evidence in strands of Western spirituality and modern technology, must, therefore, be counteracted by a self-emptying descent into the heart of creation. Only then will we,

as Berry suggests, "grow out of the ground like the other lives of the place" ("A Native Hill," 207).

34. Nicholas Lash, *Believing Three Ways in the One God: A Reading of the Apostles' Creed* (Notre Dame, IN: University of Notre Dame Press, 1992), 104.

35. Berry, "A Native Hill," 204.

36. John of Damascus referred to the divine act of creation as the "making room" within the divine life so that what is not divine can emerge. For a development of this theme, see my *The Paradise of God: Renewing Religion in an Ecological Age* (New York: Oxford University Press, 2003), introduction and chap. 1.

37. William Bryant Logan, *Dirt: The Ecstatic Skin of the Earth* (New York: Riverhead, 1995), 19.

38. Again, it is agrarian imagery, imagery that has become foreign to most people only in recent times, that conveys the sense of this submission best. By working with the soil, the farmer or gardener "enters into death / yearly, and comes back rejoicing. He has seen the light lie down / in the dung heap, and rise again in the corn" ("The Man Born to Farming," in *CP*, 103). Compare: "The seed is in the ground. / Now may we rest in hope / While darkness does its work" ("The Seed Is in the Ground," in *TC*, 131).

39. See the treatment of this theme in Schürmann, *Wandering Joy*, 9–18, 182–209; and Eckhart's sermon "Blessed Are the Poor" (O'Neal, ed., *Meister Eckhart*, 210–15). Berry refers to "the last labor of the heart" as the ability "to learn to lie still, / one with the earth / again, and let the world go" ("Awake at Night," in *CP*, 128).

40. Maximus Confessor, *Centuries on Charity*, 2.64, quoted in Clément, *The Roots of Christian Mysticism*, 223.

41. For an excellent discussion of the "mysticism of the ground," see Bernard McGinn, *The Harvest of Mysticism in Medieval Germany (1300–1500)*, vol. 4 of *The Presence of God* (New York: Crossroad, 2005), 83–93. *Grund* (ground or foundation), as it was employed by mystics, was intimately associated with *Abgrund* (abyss).

Part 3

Imagination

D. Brent Laytham

"The Membership Includes the Dead"

Wendell Berry's Port William Membership as *Communio Sanctorum*

Christians who recite the Apostles' Creed profess, among other things, belief in "the communion of saints." Exactly what this profession means isn't always clear, either to the Christians themselves or to the wider world. As a Christian, I have developed a greater understanding of and appreciation for the *communio sanctorum* by getting to know the membership of Port William in the fiction of Wendell Berry. This is because, as Hannah Coulter says in Berry's recent novel, "the membership includes the dead."[1]

Any reader of Berry's fiction will know that its focus is a group of Port William farmers and townspeople so intimately related that they call themselves "the membership." Though the members attribute this name to one of their own, Burley Coulter, it has older, theologically more explicit roots in Paul's description of the church as one body with many members (see 1 Cor. 12). Not surprisingly, the membership's life together manifests many of the characteristics Paul names as attributes of the body of Christ, including profound and tangible ties between the living and the dead. Thus, both the membership of Port William and the membership of Christ's church are, and know that they are, a community that extends through time in spite of death.

When Christians have thought about this real relationship with brothers and sisters both living and dead, they have typically used the name *communion of saints*. Berry sticks with the term *membership*, but it often seems like he is gesturing toward the same reality. I will investigate that resemblance, guided by the conviction that Berry's membership has much to teach Christians about how to understand and embody our conviction that we belong to the communion of saints.

The essay will describe four key dimensions that constitute the membership, each one able to enrich or enlighten Christian understanding of the communion of saints. First, Berry's membership is placed on common ground. Though this emphasis on locality might seem inimical to a Christian sense of membership in a global church, we will see that it actually serves to correct a Gnosticizing tendency in modern theology. Berry can help the church recover the centrality of place for the *communio sanctorum*. Second, in Berry's fiction, membership is given rather than earned. Though most of his members prove themselves worthy of their belonging, they do not work their way into the fellowship; belonging always comes as a gift. Here, Berry helps Christians see the communion of saints as a fruit of God's giving and a society of mutual aid rather than as an exclusive club for especially gifted Christians. Third, Berry's members are held together by powerful bonds that run deeper than affection and intention. It is their common life of shared place and labor and love that binds them together. This raises for Christians the question of whether they presently share a common life powerful enough to bind them together with all the saints. Finally, Berry's members see themselves as living in the midst of those who have died yet remain somehow alive. The visions that come to Jayber Crow, Hannah Coulter, and Andy Catlett of being "surrounded by such a great cloud of witnesses" (Heb. 12:1) offer consolation and sustain hope. Learning to rest confidently in such visions, while also striving hopefully toward the resurrection of the body and the renewal of all things, is not just their work but that of every saint within Christ's *communio*. Berry's fiction can help orient us to our proper work of hope.

Placed

Wendell Berry has rightly complained that contemporary Christianity "is not *earthy* enough."[2] One gospel song, titled "This World Is Not My Home," puts the exclamation point on Berry's claim. Each verse and refrain concludes: "And I can't feel at home in this world anymore." Songs like this turn our minds away from the Christian conviction that God has made all things well, and our hearts away from the given place of our lives. Unfortunately, this song represents an all too common tendency among Christians: they think and feel that they are homeless, or they believe in a heaven that competes with—and calls them away from—this earth.

Technically, such a view is called *Gnosticism*. More colloquially, we might call it *homeless faith* or *dis-placed discipleship*. Though judged a heresy in

Christianity's second century, Gnosticism has continued to dog the church ever since, weaving itself into our convictions, including our understanding of the communion of saints. A Gnosticized understanding of the *communio sanctorum* diminishes or even negates the significance of place by affirming an invisible, "spiritual" relationship of all Christians every*when* and every*where*. As one recent study put it, the communion of saints "transcends all boundaries and limitations of time and space."[3] Apparently, place does not matter at all.

Unlike a Gnosticized *communio sanctorum,* Berry's membership is placed. It is the membership *of Port William,* not the membership of anywhere or of nowhere. The common ground the members share is the very foundation on which membership rests. We see this clearly in *The Memory of Old Jack,* when Mat and Margaret Feltner go to Cincinnati to visit Nettie Banion, their former pensioner. The visit is exceedingly awkward, even though these are people who care deeply for one another: "Nettie was glad to see them, but quiet, uncertain, strange to them suddenly, *no longer held to them by any common ground.*"[4] Of course, in Berry's fiction, common ground does not automatically create community, but you cannot have real community without it.

Commenting on this visit many years later, Hannah Coulter says that Nettie was "not at home there, and not to be at home again in this world." The only place she could have been at home "would have had to be in Port William" because "the Banions belonged to the Feltner place by the same history as the Feltners. . . . *The two families belonged to each other.*"[5] Note the direction of belonging in Hannah's claim: because they belonged to the place, they belonged to one another. This is a regular theme in Berry's fiction: the members belong to their farms as much as their farms belong to them. Old Jack is the quintessential embodiment of this: he cares for his land "not because it belonged to him so much as because, by the expenditure of history and work, he belonged to it."[6]

These farmers have their roots sunk so deeply in the earth that not even the hope of heaven can displace them. Several of them say they want to be buried under a tree or in a field on their own farm rather than in the church cemetery. Their point is not to reject Christian belief in eternal fellowship with God but to express their profound sense that such fellowship includes and requires place. In "That Distant Land," Andy Catlett narrates Mat Feltner's death, which came on the second day of harvesting tobacco in a patch of heartbreakingly long rows. Each time a worker finished a row, Burley Coulter would sing: "Oh, pilgrim, have you seen that distant land?"[7] It might appear that, by singing a song about going to heaven as encouragement to "go down the row," Burley was disparaging Christian hope and trivializing Christian faith. But, given the context, in which Andy has emphasized that they continually kept the dying Mat in their minds while harvesting the tobacco, it is better to hear in Burley's singing a double valence: the song orients them to their heavenly hope in and through the land rather than apart from it.

Hannah Coulter includes a key chapter titled "Our Place," the plural possessive pronoun already suggesting the way we can belong to one another only in a particular place. For Hannah, love of a particular place marries heaven and earth: "And it is by the place we've got, and our love for it and our keeping of it, that this world is joined to Heaven." She makes this claim over against the modern American dis-ease that continually looks for a better place while overlooking or despising one's present place. But her point also speaks directly to the older Gnostic dis-ease with the placedness of our lives. For as Hannah sees it: "Love in this world doesn't come out of thin air. It is not something thought up. Like ourselves, it grows out of the ground. It has a body and a place."[8] Because Hannah's many loves were grown on this soil and patterned by working this place, love for the place is not in competition with love for her family. Instead, continuing to love the place keeps her connected with those, now gone, whom she has loved there and connects her too with the God whose love creates all things.

Andy Catlett, who like Berry left home for some years to pursue a writing career, tells us at the end of *A World Lost* that he has come to find his happiness in the joining of place and saints: "Slowly I have learned that *my true home is not just this place but is also that company of immortals* with whom I have lived here day by day. I live in their love, and I know something of the cost."[9] For both Andy Catlett and Hannah Coulter, the palpability of place is intrinsically connected to the presence of members both living and dead. Berry renders this most poignantly in the final chapter of *Remembering,* where Andy Catlett returns—both physically and psychically—to the place that is his home: "His own place becomes palpable to him [as he drives toward Port William]. Those he loves, living and dead, are no longer mere thoughts or memories, but presences, approachable and near." The presence that Andy experiences is not merely a matter of thought and memory; it is a real presence: "Now they are coming to him again, those who have brought him here and who remain—not in memory, but near to memory, in the place itself and in his flesh, ready always to be remembered—so that the place, the present life of it, resonates within time and within times, as it could not do if time were all that it is living in."[10] Clearly, Andy, whose life is now shaped by homecoming rather than leave-taking, could never sing "this world is not my home." But he could sing "for all the saints who from their labors rest" because their long labor of love remains present in this place. In Wendell Berry's membership, the communion of saints is placed on common ground.

Modern Christians would do well to learn from Berry the significance of a placed membership because fellowship abstracted from the common ground of a shared place is not real relation. Learning again the significance of placed "presences, approachable and near," will not require us to invent new strategies. But it will require us to learn again the significance of things we are already doing and, perhaps, to recover older Christian practices that were more attentive to place. Specifically, I believe that Christians may recover their place among "that company of immortals" by greater attentiveness to Holy Communion and by a recovery of the ancient practice of venerating relics.

Whether they call it *Holy Communion, the Lord's Supper, Eucharist,* or *Mass,* all Christians know that this meal is placed. Christians must come together around the table if they are going to share it with one another. Communion can't be done by telephone, Internet, or television; it requires common ground. It also creates common ground by uniting us with Christ, with one another, and with all God's saints. This claim sounds at first like Communion is an activity that abstracts us from our particular place and time into some idea of universal fellowship. Instead, according to William Cavanaugh, in Communion "one becomes more united to the whole the more tied one becomes to the local."[11] Because each Communion table is concretely placed in space and time, it becomes the place where we realize— not just mentally but actually—a fellowship that transcends spatial and temporal limitations. So Communion becomes a place—indeed, becomes *the* place—where the *communio sanctorum* is most fully realized. As such, Protestant Christians would do well to practice it more frequently, and all Christians should practice it more knowingly.

We should also try to recover one of the earliest Christian expressions of the *communio sanctorum*—the practice of venerating relics. A relic was some part of the physical remains of a dead saint that was treasured by a congregation. The first known practice of treasuring relics is told in the second-century *Martyrdom of Polycarp.* The church of Smyrna retrieved the burned bones of the martyred Polycarp in order to bury them in a place where, in succeeding years, they gathered annually to remember his "birthday" (i.e., the anniversary of his death). Their practice of an annual worship feast at the site of burial brought together story and soil in a way that profoundly "placed" them as a congregation. At its best, such a practice of integrating relics into the church's worship life brought together the story of a faithful life with the soil on which that life was lived and sustained the connection between the living community and the deceased member. Unfortunately, in the later Middle Ages, relics became a real problem, partly because of superstitious beliefs about their miraculous power, but more fundamentally because they were being sold and stolen. This dislocated them from their proper place, meaning that the story a relic embodied became divorced from the soil on which that story had been lived. Such abuses do not undercut the fundamental value of a placed practice of relics, however, any more than binge eating undercuts the goodness of a bowl of fresh blueberries. Contemporary Christians would do well to seek ways to recover some form of treasuring relics, whether in the form of a church cemetery, columbarium, memory garden, or something else. Whatever form our renewed practice of relics takes, the point would be to restore the connection between story and soil, to recover the common ground that binds us in a living membership with those who have died in Christ.

Neither relics nor Communion can automatically bring us to say with Andy Catlett that "my true home is not just this place but is also that company of immortals with whom I have lived here day by day." But, practiced with proper attention to the way they place us on common ground with one another and with Christ, they might help us learn what Berry's membership already knows: our profound need for a beloved place.

"Altogether Given"

The entire third part of the Apostles' Creed names what we are given in Christ. From "the Holy Spirit" now outpoured to "the life everlasting" now anticipated, all is gift, and all is given. Though Christians know this, we frequently fail to live it. We think and speak and live this third article, not as a gift from God that we are receiving, but as a given—a factual reality that we recognize and recite to God. The difference is whether the given is excessive gift or objective fact, whether it claims our gratitude and obligation or just our assent.

That difference is especially evident in the way we believe in the communion of saints. We should say "I believe in the communion of saints," not just to assert that this fellowship of the faithful exists, but to claim our share in this gift and to name our indebtedness for it. For Protestants (like me), this can be difficult. The heritage of the Reformation leaves us worried that any recognition of the *communio sanctorum* as God's gift, as grace in action, will compete with and detract from the saving grace of Jesus. Of course it doesn't, any more than recognizing the good creation as God's gift could eclipse Christ as God's full self-giving (see John 1:1–3). But our suspicion lingers, leaving us uncertain what good the communion of saints might be or do. So we name it in the creed as mere given rather than given gift.

Catholics can also distort the gift character of the *communio sanctorum,* though for different reasons. They have retained the early Christian sense that the holy lives of particular saints are gifts God gives the church. Moreover, they have nurtured an awareness of present relation to individual saints who, though they have died, are alive in Christ. This present relation allows Catholics (and Protestants too) to ask one of the faithful departed to continue to give us the gift of his or her prayer. But herein lies the danger, for, when we concentrate on what this or that saint might do for us, several problems too easily follow. First, we lose the larger sense of the *communio sanctorum* as a fellowship, a belonging to one another in Christ. Second, we lose the early Christians' sense that the *communio* is the gift of mutual aid, or giving and receiving in both directions. Finally, we risk transforming the *communio sanctorum* from gift acknowledged into reality understood, with the temptation to develop technologies for using and exploiting that reality. When my family had difficulty selling our house, a neighbor advised us that, if we would bury a statue of Saint Joseph upside down in the yard, it would sell immediately. Such an outlook epitomizes through caricature the loss of real communion with the saints. The given is no longer gift, but . . .

In his fiction, Berry illuminates the way membership is given as a gift. The novels *Jayber Crow* and *Hannah Coulter* narrate how their protagonists are given the gift of belonging to the membership of Port William. But the most poignant accounts of membership as gift are found in two short stories about Elton and Mary Penn. The first, "A Jonquil for Mary Penn," tells how they began their marriage on a rented farm in the Cotman Ridge neighborhood. There they were given tutelage in the arts of housewifery and husbandry, learning the economy of farming through the shared work, wisdom, and laughter of their neighbors. Disowned by her parents for marrying Elton,

Mary learns to think of herself as belonging here through the mutual sharing of the neighborhood and especially of her five female neighbors. Her sense of belonging thus comes as an unexpected, unasked gift, eliciting in her a holy gratitude. One fall day "she had stood on the highest point and had seen the six smokes of the six houses rising straight up into the wide downfalling light. . . . It was like watching the rising up of prayers or some less acknowledged communication between Earth and Heaven."[12]

Berry is telling us that membership is a belonging that is given through shared place, shared labor, and shared love. That belonging is itself a gift, apart from any benefits that it might produce. Yet it clearly produces benefits that are economic (Mary describes it as "a wonderful provisioning"), emotional ("Oh, I'm wonderful"), and educative ("She came knowing little, barely enough to begin, and they taught her much").[13] Berry's narrated description of the membership is remarkably similar to the claim of Pope Leo XIII that "the communion of saints is nothing else but a mutual sharing in help, satisfaction, prayer and other good works."[14] Berry's fictional membership can help us recover that clear sense that the communion of saints is a gift given for sharing good work and mutual satisfaction. We are given both belonging and benefit in integral relation.

If Mary Penn embodies the way the gift of membership naturally evokes our gratitude, Elton epitomizes the way we resist receiving what is given. From the time he left home at age fourteen, Elton had been fiercely independent. When Jack Beechum tries to leave his farm to Elton and Mary, an incident narrated in the novel *The Memory of Old Jack* and the short story "It Wasn't Me," we see Elton's "longing for independence" collide head-on with his *indebtedness for belonging*. His struggle "between gratitude and resentment," played out in conversation with Wheeler Catlett, provides us insight into the economy of membership and instructs us on the obligations of belonging.[15]

In order to fulfill Old Jack Beechum's dying wish, Wheeler helps Elton buy the Beechum farm at auction. Old Jack chose the Penns because, as his tenants, they had proven faithful both to the farm and to him. "He thought you were worthy," Wheeler explains. Others think so too. Later that year, when the male membership gathers in the tobacco-stripping room that once was Jack's but now is Elton's, Burley Coulter assesses Elton in the words of Old Jack: "By God, son, you're a good one!"[16] Wheeler tells Jack's daughter:

"Clara, I don't know anybody more worthy to walk in your daddy's tracks than Elton Penn."[17] Indeed, Elton is worthy and gifted.

But "It Wasn't Me" is not primarily a story of how good people get what they deserve, of how the gifted will finally win out. Instead, it contrasts the economy of price, where value is calculated and merit rewarded, with an economy of gift, where there is a giving and receiving that is "not accountable." It invites us to realize, along with Elton, that life and love and membership are "goods and services that we didn't make, that can't exist at all except as gifts." In the end, the best things we want and need are given to us, not earned or deserved. This is a difficult discovery for Elton, who tells Wheeler: "I want to make it on my own. I don't want a soul to thank." In response, Wheeler helps Elton see that belonging is not earned but given. Wheeler tells Elton: "You have it because I've given it to you. . . . I gave it to you because it was given to me." Here given precedes giving. Berry's members recognize that they stand in a succession of gift that "has been here since the evening and the morning were the third day."[18]

Thus, in the course of the story, Elton comes to see that, though he may have bought a farm, he is being given a belonging. "It Wasn't Me" is a story of election into membership (and Berry uses the theological term *election*).[19] Its outcome matters, not just to the Penns, but to all the saints of the Port William membership. As Wheeler explains it: "What has happened has been desirable to a lot of people we never knew, who lived before us."[20] His point is not unlike that of the author of Hebrews, who tells in chapter 11 of all the faithful saints who, nonetheless, "would not, apart from us, be made perfect" (Heb. 11:40). This suggests finally that membership in the communion of saints is not just given *to* us but also meant to be given *through* us to others.

Elton's acceptance of membership as a given gift may help us negotiate one of the most difficult aspects of some theologies of the communion of saints—the notion that some of the saints may have earned their place. Though, technically, all Christians believe that we are saved because of what Jesus Christ has done, some Christians have believed that some of the saints are so holy that they are in a different category than the rest of us. One way that idea has played itself out is the belief that the holy saints go directly to heaven when they die while the rest of us wait in purgatory. Another way is the idea of a treasury of merit. This is the notion that these holy saints have been so worthy that they have extra good works that they don't need but that we do. If appropriately requested, their excess can be credited to our deficit in the economy of salvation. Either way, these understandings of the communion of saints separate the "good ones" from all the rest of us in inappropriate ways.

"It Wasn't Me" drives home the point that belonging to this membership is a gift that is not earned. Though worthy, Elton and Mary Penn become part of the membership just like everyone else: by receiving what is given. Likewise, though we are indebted for being given membership in the communion of saints, "it's *not* payable" and "it's not accountable"[21]—neither by us regular folk nor by the most holy ones in our midst. With Elton Penn, we can learn to renounce independence and embrace election, trying neither to earn our entrance nor to deserve our inclusion but instead to continually live in the economy of the gift. With Mary Penn, we can learn the joy of recognizing our belonging to this fellowship. For, finally, all is gift, *given to us* by God through those who have gone before us, and *given through us* by God to those we welcome in God's name.

Bound

In a culture of isolated individuals, Christians regularly sing their connection to one another in songs like "Blessed Be the Tie That Binds." According to the doctrine of the communion of saints, the central tie that binds the saints together is Jesus Christ. In Berry's fiction, the members are bound together by place, work, and love. Hannah Coulter names the first two when telling how she came to be a member of Port William: "I had my *place* and my *work* among them. They let me belong."[22] Having already considered place as the binding ground of community, let us take up work as its binding activity.

Work is the most obvious bond of the membership. Work is so central in Port William that Hannah Coulter can say: "Our life and our work were not the same thing maybe, but they were close." It is not just that they are all people who do the same thing for a living—in this case farming. Rather, it is that their way of farming requires them to work together, a shared activity that not only requires them to be present with one another but also binds them to one another. Hannah describes the membership as "a whole company of people [who], at different times, in different combinations, might be at work on our place, or we might be at work on theirs." The membership is not just an idea of belonging to one another but belonging embodied in and through shared work. It was while working together that Burley Coulter "would preach the membership," that is, proclaim to the members the identity and significance of the Port William membership.[23]

This central role of shared work in binding the membership together is especially evident, as Hannah narrates, "during the tobacco harvest, when we would all be together."[24] Andy Catlett describes the tobacco cutting itself as "a sort of ritual of remembrance, too, when we speak of other years and remember younger selves and the absent and the dead—all those we have, as we say, 'gone down the row with.'"[25] Here, the sharing in work binds together not just those alive and present but those members who have died.

In this way, Berry's membership resembles the early Christian sense of the communion of saints, which Michael Perham describes as characterized by such a strong "sense of belonging to each other" that not even death could break the fellowship. Perham emphasizes that this was easier because "those who had died were those whom they had known and honoured and loved in this life. The communion of saints meant fellowship not with distant figures of previous centuries and cultures but with contemporaries who had died for the faith and in the faith."[26] In short, the early church's understanding of the communion of saints was strongly rooted in a common life of shared activity.

Without love, however, place and work are insufficient to bind together a genuine community. Love is the third—and most important—bond of the membership. Berry's members love their farms and their farming; they are "farmers by calling and *by devotion*."[27] Because of this, they also love one another. Burley Coulter, credited with coining the term *membership,* exemplifies this bond of love through the changes of his life. In his younger, wayward days, he was a member because "the people who cared about him and were troubled by him" continued to want him to belong. That is, the love of others made and retained his membership. "Later, he was a member because *he* wanted to be," caring about and caring for the membership.[28] That care—both as affection and as action—constitutes Burley's love for "the daylit membership of kin and friends and households."[29]

The love that binds the membership is not something that they produce, however; it is something in which they participate. When Jayber Crow has a vision in the Port William church of "all the people gathered there who had ever been there," he says: "I seemed to love them all with a love that was mine merely because it included me."[30] Hannah Coulter helps us see that this surrounding, including love is God's love. She calls it *the room of love:* "The room of love is the love that holds us all, and it is not ours. It goes back before we were born. It goes all the way back. It is Heaven's. Or it is Heaven, and we are in it only by willingness. By whose love, Andy Catlett, do we love this world and ourselves and one another? Do you think we invented it ourselves? I ask with confidence, for I know you know we didn't."[31] Hannah's rhetorical question to Andy reminds readers that love for the dead is sustained by the practice of remembering. Here, Berry helps Protestant Christians see that the Catholic practice of venerating saints might best be understood as a practice of loving memory, a re-membering that that is "a form of love."[32]

Hannah Coulter brings together work and love and remembering when she reflects on what it means to do chores today that she first learned from and did with her Grandmam: "It is hard to say what it means to be at work and thinking of a person you loved and love still who did that same work before you and who taught you to do it. It is a comfort ever and always, like hearing the rhyme come when you are singing a song."[33]

Through shared labor and love, Berry's membership is bound together in ways tangible enough to bring awareness, comfort, and direction. Is there a correlate binding in the communion of saints? Do we adequately know, feel, and perform the bonds that constitute us as members of one another? The obvious correlate to the work of farming is our sharing in the labor of liturgy, the common work of worship that enacts and enables our love of God, eliciting at the same time our love of one another. The problem is that few Christians now experience their lives as structured by and bound to worship in anything like the degree to which Berry's membership find their lives shaped by farming. The love and labor of farming binds the membership together because it makes them who they are. Modern Christians, on the other hand, have identities authored by other labors and other loves, which leaves us, if not unbound, then at least imagining that we are connected by our decisions and affections rather than by our common life. In reciting the Apostles' Creed, we confess ourselves bound to the communion of saints, but, generally, we do this against appearances and experiences. Yet, occasionally, singing an old and favorite hymn, or praying an ancient prayer, we may experience the rhyme that Hannah Coulter names: us doing now in the same place what those we loved did here before us and taught us to do. Perhaps the most obvious "rhyme" of our Christian labor and love is the practice of baptism, as we now bind new members with the same words and action that bound us (and every Christian) to Christ and, thus, to one another.

The Hereafter in the Here

The *communio sanctorum* lives in hope, which means that it "bears the faith conviction that death is not the end of the 'communion of saints'; it extends beyond this age."[34] The creed suggests this by immediately mentioning three dimensions of the Christ future toward which we go: "the forgiveness of sins, the resurrection of the body, and the life everlasting."

Do we find analogous hope and faith orienting the lives of Berry's members? Yes, though it is not always easy to perceive. There is a certain ambivalence in the way members talk about final things. On the one hand, they often sing songs about heaven or life after death. For example, "Watch with Me" ends with the bedraggled neighbors singing "O the land of cloudless day," and Jayber Crow tells us that he "loved to hear them sing 'The Unclouded Day' and 'Sweet By and By.'"[35] On the other hand, as Burley Coulter puts it in a letter to his nephew Nathan, the members' "knack is for the Here" far more than it is "a knack for the Hereafter." Burley goes on to say: "And surely the talk of a reunion in Heaven is thin comfort to people who need each other here as much as we do. I ain't saying I don't believe there's a Heaven. I surely do hope there is. That surely would pay off a lot of mortgages. But I do say it ain't easy to believe. And even while I hope for it, I've got to admit I'd rather go to Port William."[36] While Burley's theme here is how little comfort talk of heaven provides in the immediate circumstance of a loved one's death, his "I'd rather go to Port William" suggests that the primary orientation of the membership is not heaven but home. More important, Burley seems to suggest that death is the end of real fellowship between the living and the dead.

Yet if we read Berry carefully—listening to Jayber Crow, Hannah Coulter, and Andy Catlett—we find that they hope in heaven and know that even now the membership includes "lives dead, living, yet to be."[37] Toward the end of his story, Jayber reminds us that it has been "a book about Heaven," though it almost turned "out to be a book about Hell." What has made it finally about heaven is forgiving love. Jayber tells how he has forgiven others—some of this forgiving easy, some "that was harder and took longer." But, while he can forgive others, the question lingers whether and how he can be forgiven: "There is Hell enough, maybe, just in the knowledge of what you might call the leftovers of my life: things I might once have done that are now undoable, old wrongs, responsibilities unmet, ineradicable failures." That same question holds for each member and for the membership as a whole: Will there finally be enough forgiveness to make things right? In a sense, the answer has already been given to Jayber in two visions. In the first, napping in the back of the church building, he has a vision of the church gathered in and by an including love. In the second, sitting in the quiet of the cemetery after a day of cleaning graves and remembering the dead, he sees "the community as it never has been and never will be gathered in this world of time. . . . I saw them all as somehow perfected, beyond time, by one another's love, compassion, and forgiveness as it is said we may be perfected by grace."[38] In these visions, and in his life story, Jayber shares his hope that even now we live in a surrounding love that will finally make all things well.

Hannah Coulter's story is of learning to live without expectation, though not without hope: "Love, after all, 'hopeth all things.' But maybe you must learn, and it is hard learning, not to hope out loud." Not surprisingly, then, Hannah doesn't often explicitly articulate her Christian hope. She does aver: "Some day there will be a new heaven and a new earth and a new Port William coming down from heaven." She does speak of being "buried up on the hill at Port William beside Nathan, to wait for the Resurrection with him and the others." Yet her orientation is primarily not to a hoped-for future but to the presence—even now—of eternity in time. In "telling over this story," she brings into mind "the whole membership, living and dead." Her mind itself "has started to become, it is close to being, the room of love where the absent are present, the dead are alive, time is eternal, and all the creatures prosperous."[39]

The fullest expressions of hope in relation to the *communio sanctorum* come from Andy Catlett. On the final page of *A World Lost*, Andy names the members who have died. He then asks: "But how can I deny that *in my belief they are risen?*" He goes on to imagine them "waking, dazed, into a shadowless light in which they know themselves altogether for the first time." This light is true and beautiful, and "in it they are loved completely, even as they have been, and so are changed into what they could not have been but what, if they could have imagined it, they would have wished to be." In this passage, a member confesses belief in forgiveness, resurrection, and eternal life. Indeed, Andy's imagination of risen life includes both final judgment and a purgatory of sorts. The light in which the risen find themselves "is merciless until they can accept its mercy; by it they are at once condemned and redeemed. It is Hell until it is Heaven. Seeing themselves in that light, if they are willing, they see how far they have failed the only justice of loving one another; it punishes them by their own judgment."[40] This is not far from Catholic theology's view of purgatory as when the dead "experience as a burning anguish their own lovelessness when faced with God's love. Thereby they will be cleansed 'as through fire' (1 Cor. 3:15) by means of the infinite love of God that embraces and heals them."[41]

For Andy, and I think for Berry too, it is crucial to notice that the tense of resurrection faith is not future but present: not "they will rise," but "they are risen." Resurrection is not so much a still future reality toward which the membership goes as a present reality for those who have died, a reality that permeates our present if we have eyes to see it. The description of the vision that concludes *Remembering* makes this clear. In the vision, Andy Catlett sees "Port William and its countryside as he never saw or dreamed them." He sees the dead membership alive, beautiful, ripe, at peace. His resurrection vision is not of what will be but of what is: "He sees that they are the dead, and they are alive." It is not what we will see at the coming of Christ and the general resurrection of the dead but what we can see now if we have eyes to see it: "He has come into the presence of these living *by a change of sight*." What Andy perceives is the presence of eternity in time: "He has entered the eternal place in which we live in time."[42]

In Jayber, Hannah, and Andy—Berry's most theologically aware characters—we see that the Port William membership does not reject the hereafter in favor of the here but rather knows and celebrates the hereafter in the here. Their awareness of eternity's presence in time is conditioned by memory and place and love. But it is an awareness of a reality that does not depend on memory, is not produced by longing, and is not confined to the mind. It is a real communion, very much like the early Christian understanding of the *communio sanctorum* as N. T. Wright describes it: "The church on earth believed itself privileged to enjoy an intimate fellowship with those who had gone on ahead. . . . Christians here are to be conscious of their communion with the redeemed in heaven, who have already experienced the fullness of the glory of Christ."[43]

Berry's profound vision of the membership of Port William offers the Christian church an opportunity to rediscover the meaning and significance of its own identity as *communio sanctorum*. Through the many stories that finally constitute their one story, these members remind us that we are given belonging, placed on common ground, bound together by the work of worship, and, thus, live each day in the company of immortals.

Notes

1. Wendell Berry, *Hannah Coulter* (Washington, DC: Shoemaker & Hoard, 2004), 94.

2. Wendell Berry, "The Gift of Good Land," in *The Gift of Good Land: Further Essays Cultural and Agricultural* (New York: North Point, 1981), 267.

3. Bilateral Working Group of the German National Bishops' Conference and the Church Leadership of the United Evangelical Lutheran Church of Germany, *Communio Sanctorum: The Church as the Communion of Saints*, trans. Mark W. Jeske, Michael Root, and Daniel R. Smith (Collegeville, MN: Liturgical, 2004), 2.

4. Wendell Berry, *The Memory of Old Jack* (San Diego: Harcourt Brace Jovanovich, 1974), 13 (emphasis added).

5. Berry, *Hannah Coulter*, 95 (emphasis added).

6. Berry, *Memory of Old Jack*, 164.

7. Wendell Berry, "That Distant Land," in *That Distant Land: The Collected Stories* (2004; reprint, Washington, DC: Shoemaker & Hoard, 2005), 317.

8. Berry, *Hannah Coulter*, 83, 88.

9. Wendell Berry, *A World Lost*, in *Three Short Novels: Nathan Coulter, Remembering, A World Lost* (Washington, DC: Counterpoint, 2002), 326 (emphasis added).

10. Wendell Berry, *Remembering*, in ibid., 216.

11. William Cavanaugh, *Theopolitical Imagination* (London: T. & T. Clark, 2002), 115. What Cavanaugh notes about Communion is simply a sacramental specification of a more general phenomenon on which Berry commented: "When I have thought of the welfare of the earth, the problems of its health and preservation, the care of its life, I have had this place before me, the part representing the whole more vividly and accurately, making clearer and more pressing demands, than any *idea* of the whole" (Wendell Berry, "A Native Hill," excerpted in *The Art of the Commonplace*, ed. Norman Wirzba [Washington, DC: Counterpoint, 2002], 5).

12. Wendell Berry, "A Jonquil for Mary Penn," in *That Distant Land*, 205.

13. Ibid., 205, 209, 201.

14. *Mirae caritas* (May 28, 1902) and *Acta sanctae sedis* 34:649, both quoted in vol. 4 of *The New Catholic Encyclopedia*, 2nd ed. (Detroit: Thompson/Gale, 2003), s.v. "Communion of Saints."

15. Wendell Berry, "It Wasn't Me," in *That Distant Land*, 282, 283.

16. Berry, *Memory of Old Jack*, 217, 222.

17. Berry, "It Wasn't Me," 270.

18. Ibid., 287, 288, 283, 287, 282.

19. Ibid., 272.

20. Ibid., 287.

21. Ibid., 287.

22. Berry, *Hannah Coulter*, 41 (emphasis added).

23. Ibid., 89, 93, 97.

24. Ibid., 93.

25. Berry, "That Distant Land," 313–14. Something similar would happen when Mat Feltner cleaned the cemetery each year (see Wendell Berry, *Jayber Crow: The Life Story of Jayber Crow, Barber, of the Port William Membership, as Written by Himself: A Novel* [Washington, DC: Counterpoint, 2000], chap. 19).

26. Michael Perham, *The Communion of Saints* (London: SPCK, 1980), 11–12, 11.

27. Wendell Berry, "Fidelity," in *That Distant Land*, 397 (emphasis added).

28. Berry, *Hannah Coulter*, 96.

29. Wendell Berry, "The Wild Birds," in *That Distant Land*, 348.

30. Berry, *Jayber Crow*, 164, 165.

31. Berry, *Hannah Coulter*, 158–59.

32. This idea can be traced in Bilateral Working Group, *Communio Sanctorum*, 81.

33. Berry, *Hannah Coulter*, 107.

34. Bilateral Working Group, *Communio Sanctorum*, 70.

35. Wendell Berry, "Watch with Me," in *That Distant Land*, 121, and *Jayber Crow*, 163.

36. Wendell Berry, *A Place on Earth* (1983), rev. ed. (Washington, DC: Counterpoint, 2001), 104, 105.

37. Berry, "The Wild Birds," in *That Distant Land*, 363.

38. Berry, *Jayber Crow*, 354, 355, 355, 164–65 (first vision), 205.

39. Berry, *Hannah Coulter*, 146, 43, 180, 158, 158.

40. Berry, *A World Lost*, 326 (emphasis added, first quote).

41. Bilateral Working Group, *Communio Sanctorum*, 76.

42. Berry, *Remembering*, 221, 221, 221 (emphasis added), 220.

43. N. T. Wright, *For All the Saints? Remembering the Christian Departed* (Harrisburg, PA: Morehouse, 2003), 16. I have sometimes wondered whether Berry so emphasizes this present relationship with those who are dead yet live that he underplays the future tense and bodily focus of Christian hope. Exploring that question would require another essay.

Philip A. Muntzel

Embedded Hopefulness

Wendell Berry and Saint Thomas Aquinas on Christian Hope

> Such hope is not an expression of the insufficiency of the present in comparison with the sufficiency of a hoped for future; it is rather an expression of the plenitude of the present, a present alive with the sense of the possible.
> —Milton Mayeroff, *On Caring*

Introduction: Christian Hope and Its Misrepresentation

Christian belief calls for a distinctive kind of hope, one directed toward the enrichment that God's love does and will provide. Christian hope is an expression of the confidence that God's love is powerful enough to make that enrichment possible. To state this compactly, Christians hope for God and in God. Such hope can enhance life, sustain it in the face of unavoidable tragedy, and foster the courage to face the many challenges life presents.

I have no doubt that this hope, with its twofold relation to God's enriching and empowering love, has found expression in the lives of countless believers. But I also believe that Christian pastors, teachers, and theologians have sometimes failed this hope. The failure I have in mind is one of misrepresentation, a failure adequately to articulate its features and its reach and scope. Without a tedious catalog, let me briefly suggest some of those failures.

One misrepresentation would be that of subordination, if not neglect. I have in mind here the way hope has become something of a stepchild in the way the triad of Pauline Christian traits—faith, hope, and love—has been used to shape pastoral and theological concerns. To cite just one historical example, the Reformation-Counterreformation debates over the doctrine of justification stressed faith or love, with hope receiving minimal attention.

190

Another misrepresentation is a serious narrowing of its scope. Scripture envisions a heavenly new creation, which includes a new earth, but the voices of homilists have often restricted hope to a concern for the salvation of individuals. The miraculous, world-transcending dimension of Christian hope has spawned more problems than simply the issue of hope's scope and reach. Pastors and theologians have sometimes played off that transcendent dimension against worldly involvement. Much as this essay's epigraph from Mayeroff captures the contrast between hopes that play off a rich future against an impoverished present, Christians have sometimes presented the hope for a transcending end-time as an escape from the everyday. And, in reaction to such a distractive presentation of the eschatological dimension of Christian hope, Christian activists have often reduced its reach to one of worldly transformation. Recently, Christian futurists, trying to preserve the transcendent dimension of Christian hope while keeping its social relevance alive, have treated it as a revolutionary dynamic, constantly disrupting the present. This is a different way of letting the discontinuities override possible continuities between present hopefulness and an imagined, boundless future.

It would be presumptuous to claim that Wendell Berry offers an antidote to all the misrepresentations of the twofold way that Christian hope relates to God and to the complexities of relating hope to this life and not merely the life to come. But it is my contention that his treatment is profoundly relevant to addressing the pastoral and theological quandaries and misrepresentations that attend any presentation of Christian hope. For one reason, he is a profound student of love, the wellspring of Christian hope. Second, he is insistent that proximate, localized relationships are the critical arena for imagining and discussing Christian invocations of God's mysterious fullness. In this essay, I refer to this feature of his treatment of hope as its *embedded* character.

To indicate the relevance of Berry's treatment of Christian hope I provide two discussions. First, after making some observations about hope in general and Christian hope in particular, I offer a detailed display of his embedded approach to hopefulness. I discuss the way natural, social, and spiritual dynamics contribute to his perspective. The second discussion offers a brief comparison of his approach to the treatment of Christian hope provided by Thomas Aquinas. The convergence and divergence I see between these different Christian voices should indicate that Berry can offer a corrective to an authoritative treatment of the Christian virtue of hope.

Clarifications: Christian Hope and General Features of Hoping

As I noted, Christian hope rests on some very specific claims about God. Yet the twofold relation of Christian hope to God and the classical association of Christian hope with virtues needs clarification. A brief look at the general features of hoping may help.[1]

All hopes express a desire for some good. But this general feature helps us to understand a specific hope only when we discover the specificity of the good in question and the importance with which that good is held. Ephemeral goods ground tepid, transient hopes, whereas vital goods spawn profoundly intense hopes. One might think that very specific goods would fall into the ephemeral category, but that could mislead. It is true that some hopes for general goods are of such basic, wide-ranging importance that we do not sense the need to spell out the object of such a hope. For example, if one states that a person has "lost hope," we generally mean that she has lost the hope of finding meaning and fulfillment. In such cases, the spelling out of the object of hope is unnecessary. But very specifically targeted hopes can also address vital, wide-ranging goods. Such is the case with Christian hope for God. Christians believe that it is important to specify that their hope is for the God who promises abundant life, yet that specifically targeted hope is properly understood to be for a good that is of fundamental, life-transforming importance.

Hopes relate to more than desired goods. Hopes, unlike wishes (which can entertain the fanciful or idle), express desire for goods we believe we may possibly realize. This belief rests on the existence of some power or agency deemed to have strength to achieve the good. The powers or agencies themselves can be diverse—natural powers of healing, those of human skills, and so forth—and the strength they possess can range from the weak to the overwhelming. Thus, hopes vary, not only with regard to the importance of the good they target, but also in the degree of confidence they exhibit. So one can generalize that all hopes exhibit a double reference; they are both *for* some targeted good and invested *in* some power of the possible. What is unique about Christian hope is that the target and the agency of the possible overlap. It is God who provides both the goodness and the power to make Christian hope both profound and confident. I like the way the theologian Julian Hartt compactly captures this overlap. He observes: "Christian hope is properly transcendental when one apprehends in faith the end toward which the whole creation is being moved as the very thing in which one's own being is to be, is being perfected. . . . Christian hope thereby relates the actualities of self, society and cosmos to an unseen reality."[2]

Hartt observes what Berry will note in his view of "membership": one cannot separate one's own goodness from the whole goodness that God embraces. And he captures the overlapping double reference to God by noting that God is the "unseen reality" that both perfects and moves the seen reality in which one participates.

An additional feature of hoping that illuminates the unique character of Christian hope is its persistence. Some hopes not only have a durable, persisting presence in a person's affections and attitudes but also persist in a manner that shapes the very identity of that person. In such cases, we refer to the persons as *hopeful*. Of course, persons can be hopeful in an episodic way, being hopeful about a range of specific projects and events. Yet some persons have a stance toward life as such that can be designated as *hopeful*. We distinguish such a person from one who is typically despairing or presumptuous. Christian hope belongs in this class of hopes. Saint Thomas Aquinas treats faith, hope, and love as qualities having this persisting character. Thus, he and his fellow scholastics referred to these persisting qualities as *virtues*, comparable to the moral qualities that persist to mark a person's moral character. I use the term *hopefulness* to suggest this virtue-like quality, an affective disposition so rooted in a person's psychology that it becomes a basic, persisting part of her identity. I believe that this is the kind of hope that Wendell Berry sees as appropriate to the reciprocities we experience and engage.

Berry's Embedded Hopefulness: Hope Cycling into and toward God's Love

I begin my discussion of Berry's embedded hopefulness with a caution. My aim is to show how his account counters possible misrepresentations of Christian hope, and to do that it is imperative that I show how he embeds hopefulness in God's love. Yet his account of such a love-shaped hope is sometimes difficult to discern precisely because it is embedded. He refuses to isolate our experience of hope in and for God from our more tangible experiences of loving relationships. Berry apprehends reality as a dynamic complexity in which various part-whole relationships exhibit a mutual reciprocity. As he states it: "Each part is connected to every other part." And those connections spawn effects that move "backward and forward, up and down, round and round, compounding and branching as they go." His account of hopefulness is one in which the enabling and enriching love of God moves in a "spherical network" of "concentricities."[3]

This suggests that Berry wants to avoid any hierarchy of importance where only the last cycle, which explicitly invokes the divine, is *the* religious or spiritual component. Just to illustrate, in referring to "that Heaven of which we have heard," he describes memories of his mother's patient, forgiving love.[4] Just so, as we peel back some of the layers of Berry's embedded account of hopefulness, we must remember that each layer has its own integrity even as it cycles into larger relationships.

Hopefulness in the Cycle of Nature

Berry portrays nature as a place of hopefulness. Nature provides a horizon of goodness even as its resident powers enable us confidently to attend to its promise. He will not use my abstraction of *nature* to make this point. He explores the sexual and medical dimensions of being physical. Woodlands and flowing rivers are also prominent in his explorations of the natural world. His pronounced attention to agricultural life exhibits the goodness and enabling power of natural reality.

The agronomist Sir Albert Howard provides Berry with a metaphor for showing the dependence of farming on the goods and powers of the natural world. Howard refers to nature as the *wheel of life,* and Berry employs this metaphor to insist that farming must remain attentive to the particular cycles and limits of nature if the practice of farming is to yield nature's goods over the long haul.[5] Berry also speaks frequently of wilderness. Clearly, one significance of wilderness follows Howard's suggestion. The rhythms of wilderness provide a cycle of limits and possible goods that are practically important for good farming. But, if the "wheel of life" is to inform our farming, it must be attended to in a sustained, attentive way. If nature's wheel is not engaged in this disciplined way, the possible goods are exploited or abused. Thus, nature can yield despairing or presumptuous responses without this discipline. What, then, does Berry mean by a *disciplined practice*?

Nature, social life, and our religious relation to mysterious wholeness offer both the goods and the powers that can yield a virtue-like hopefulness.

But Berry is no romantic who believes that we easily recognize and nurture the possible goods in these intersecting reciprocities. We can tragically ignore or confound the possible goodness in these relationships. Moreover, he is not a promethean who believes that, out of their own inherent rationality and power, humans can wrest possible goodness from the neutral dynamics of reality. Rather, disciplined practices become the mediators by which possible goodness is recognized and brought to fruition in our experience. But Berry does not convey the critical role of disciplined practices in an abstract way. He not only displays the role of practices by describing such practices as farming, marriage, and poetry but also lets a morally compelling account of the practice of marriage become his paradigm for discussing any particular disciplined practice. So let us return to the example of farming and see how its marriage-like qualities can disclose the enrichments and possibilities that ground hopefulness.

Berry farms some marginal, sloping land. But he is committed to making that farm flourish, attentive to and appreciative of the good gifts that land can yield. So fidelity and humble, attentive knowing inform the way he engages the land. He decides that a dam bulldozed carefully into one of his hillsides would contribute to the land. But the thoughtful pond-building project fails. He misread the limits of the land, and the broken dam damages or wounds the land. There was no presumption in his pond building. He was attentive in his attempt; still, his knowledge was inadequate. Having failed the land, he finds that the possibility of capitulating to those limits looms large.[6] But Berry does not despair; his fidelity to the land and his trust that there are powers in nature to heal the wounds he has inflicted sustain his relationship to that land. The hope is difficult because the temptations to presumption and despair remain. But nature's goodness and enabling capacity sustain his marriage-like farming, and his marriage-like farming enables those possible goods to reemerge.

Berry's sensitivity to the need for morally attuned practices in order for the goods of nature to be experienced and protected explains some of his agricultural critiques. Industrial agriculture ignores the limits that must be observed if the goods and enabling powers of nature are to be respected. Embedded hopefulness is schooled by the real but limited powers operative in nature and the real but limited goodness that nature provides. Industrial agriculture is fueled by presumptive practices and becomes destructive of the land and the communities that nourish marriage-like farming. His critique of scientism has the same backdrop. Berry is not opposed to science. He knows that generalized knowing of nature needs to be gathered, stored, and utilized. But the scientific method can be used to destroy other forms of wisdom that are born of communal traditions of wisdom and care. Faithful attentiveness is required to experience nature's healing goods and to respect its resilient but limited powers. Scientific appeals to value neutrality can obscure the practices required to see nature as a place of hope.[7]

I conclude this examination of how Berry sees the dynamics of nature related to the goods and possibilities that nurture hopefulness by returning to the theme of wilderness. I indicate above that Berry sees more than nature's practical guidance in wilderness. It is also a venue for mediating a sense of the mysterious holiness of existence. The Sabbath poems are a good illustration of this. Berry certainly cherishes the value of good work that is nurtured by the discipline of farming, but these poems express his recognition that we also need a retreat from the practical. Wilderness can offer such a sense of the transcendent. That is one reason why he insists that the Bible is an "outdoor book"; it calls attention to a holiness that is not isolated from any of our natural or social engagements.[8] Wilderness can lift the imagination to a sense of enriching possibilities that temporal conditions and social commitments preclude. A good illustration is the way Jayber Crow and Mattie Chatham expand the horizons of their loving relationship by sharing the mystery yielded by a patch of wilderness, tellingly named the *Nest Egg*.[9]

To summarize, nature is dynamic. Its rhythms harbor guidance to the good gifts of land. Our disciplined attentiveness to those rhythms makes nature itself a place of hopefulness. But nature points beyond itself because it is also the place of God. Nature, like intimate love, harbors the miraculous to yield a greater, more unbounded hopefulness.

Hopefulness and the Cycle of Social Life

There is significant symmetry between the way the goods and powers of nature require appropriate disciplines to foster hopefulness and the way social relationships depend on disciplines to provide a pathway to hopefulness. I will touch briefly on Berry's treatment of social life and temporality, provide an illustration where Berry's sensitivity to tragedy and death is evident, and close with the way social relationships can evoke a sense of the holy. My aim is, in parallel to the previous section, to show how social relationships can be places of hopefulness even as they shape the Christian imagination to sense a greater whole for their loving.

A recent writer has argued that we face a sharp choice with regard to experiencing time. No one, he claims, can avoid sensing the past as utterly gone. Our only choice is to regard the present either as a means to an unbounded field of improvement or a brief moment of meaningful defiance of an inexorable, arbitrary future.[10] Berry would reject this manner of describing our temporality. It is not a matter of choosing between a stark optimism or pessimism; rather, it is the way we handle our "littleness" in the midst of the great sweep of natural and historical powers. On the one hand, we can capitulate to our smallness and give in to despair, becoming either passive subjects to the flow of time or defiant, destructive rebels. On the other hand, we can engage in the opposite but equally untenable ignoring of our limited but real "authorship," in which case we become presumptuous. Berry suggests that there is another path. We can accept our partiality as part of a larger whole that graces us. In such a case, the person "sees the truth, recognizes his true heir, honors his forebears and his heritage, and gives blessings to his successors. He embodies the passing of human time, living and dying within the limits of grief and joy."[11]

This pathway of hopefulness differs from the alternatives of optimism and pessimism. Berry refuses to let our partiality be turned into an isolated individualism. Just as we are part of the wheel of natural life, so are we parts of a social wheel—connected in limited but real ways to the past and the future. Just as disciplined practices enable us to respect nature's cycling as a template for receiving limited but real gifts, so do disciplines that honor our heritage and our faithful relations to unknown future generations foster a hopefulness that guards our limited powers of authorship from squandering stances of presumption or despair.

Berry's sensitivity to limits does not yield to hopelessness. Yet he refuses to offer an account of hopefulness that is blind to the fragility of our lives. There is no better way to illustrate this sensitivity than to show how some of his characters deal with tragedy, defeat, and death.

Berry's story of Ernest Finley and Ida Chopp illustrates the way marriage can sustain hopefulness in the face of tragic death. But it also illustrates how a hope can be illusory and lead to a tragic retreat from social bonds. Ernest is one of the interesting bachelors who populate Berry's fiction.[12] The tragedy in Ernest's case is that he cannot overcome a grievous loss to his wholeness.

Crippled by war, Ernest returns with a wound that is more than physical. As Berry puts it, he is "defeated" by his lameness. There is no destructive lashing out against this defeat, nor does he presumptuously ignore his limitation. But he lets the wound direct his life, and he builds a realm of social possibility that gives in to that wound. Ernest builds his life around his considerable skill as a carpenter. But his life is like his little carpentry shop, built to accommodate his lameness. To be sure, he attains a social "membership"—he is a cherished family member and respected craftsman. But his work does not carry him into deep exchanges of friendship or marriage or flow beyond itself to build its own, fuller place. In a revealing description, Berry notes that he "perfects his silence."[13]

Ida Chopp is also wounded. Violence, in the form of a natural disaster, has killed her only child and driven away her husband, Gideon, in a grief-stricken attempt to escape his wound. Ida does not let her wounds prevail. Marriage and shared work have opened her to a life of enriching possibility. In resuming her daily chores and daily visits to an empty mailbox, she maintains a fidelity to those goods that shape her hopefulness. Even though her world is damaged, she refuses to despair. To recall Berry's parameters of social life, she lives hopefully "within the limits of grief and joy."

Ernest's and Ida's lives intersect when community leaders assign Ernest to help repair the flood-damaged buildings on the Chopp homestead. Exposed to Ida's appeal, industry, and hospitality, Ernest allows himself to imagine their relationship becoming a marriage of mutual love and shared nurturing of a place. He knows deep down that Ida's fidelity makes his hope illusory, but his need for intimacy and wider membership is too powerful to resist. At the same time, this false hope has revealed the shortcomings of his previous social connections. Berry describes Ernest as "caught" between a restricted world and an illusory world. When that visited mailbox finally rewards Ida with a letter from Gideon, Ernest sees no alternative to his two, failed social worlds. As Gabriel Marcel, the philosopher of hope and despair, would say, he saw his future as all "plugged up."[14] Ernest's suicide is tragic, and I think we can even describe it as a case of social despair. But I do not think Berry would call it a case of complete despair. The manner of Ernest's suicide affirms his bodily connection to the earth, and Berry, who refuses to let our imaginations finalize death, sees the ground as "the body's bride."[15] Ernest Finley affirms a possible goodness in serving the earth with his death, but that death also signals

Berry's sensitivity to the power of wounds, the ones we inflict and the ones we suffer.

Gabriel Marcel suggests that hopefulness emerges only when we have been genuinely tempted to despair.[16] I am not sure that Berry would concur, but he is certainly attentive to the way partialities can beckon us beyond their boundaries. He insists that we acknowledge and respect limits even as he cautions us to not let those limits trap our lives and imaginations. We noted this in the case of wilderness. Wilderness offers its own beauty and power, but it can also transport us into the enrichment and power of holiness. The same is true of our social relationships of faithful love. A mother's love can be a venue for the transcendent. Hannah Coulter will look back on her marriage with Nathan, dwelling on the losses, difficulties, and joys that marked it. Then she declares: "This love would be one of the acts of the greater love that holds and cherishes all the world."[17] Social life offers its own gifts, which empower and enrich. We can hope in and for our own loves. Yet those loves call us into holy mystery. Or as Berry states it:

> Nothing
> is given that is not
> Taken, and nothing taken
> That was not first gift.
> The gift is balanced by
> its total loss, and yet,
> And yet the light breaks in,
> Heaven seizing its moments
> That are at once its own
> and yours.[18]

Hopefulness and the God-World Cycle

The reference to a *God-world cycle* is another abstraction open to misinterpretation. It is simply meant to convey the way Berry holds God's transcendence and presence in a dynamic interaction with the interactions that define the world. I have illustrated his refusal to let God's transcendence lead to a dualism that isolates God from the dynamics of nature and social life. In an insightful study, the theologian P. Travis Kroeker describes Berry's Christian thought as "sacramental" and "radically incarnational."[19] Those theological categories are helpful as long as they capture the part-whole dynamic used to portray a divine reality at once present and transcendent. Wary of both abstractions and theological labels, Berry describes himself as a "bottom up" religious thinker and elaborates on that approach by noting: "To preserve our places and to be at home in them, it is necessary to fill them with imagination. To imagine as well as see what is in them. . . . To see them with the imagination as belonging to the Creation. . . . In that imagining, perhaps we may begin to see it in its sacredness, as unimaginable gift, as mystery—as it was, is, and ever shall be, world without end."[20]

In exploring Berry's explicitly religious imagination, it is imperative to keep in mind his sustained critique of a dualism that would shut down the role he ascribes to the Christian imagination. Berry will let things stand on their own, but never divorced from imagining them as gifts and possibilities of the holy. Christian hopefulness is directed toward and invested in God's love. If I am going to claim Berry's account of hopefulness as Christian, I must show that it is rooted in an understanding of God's love. An evocation of divine love raises the question of what theologians call *eschatology*, a consideration of the *last things* or, more helpfully, the consummation of all things. In recalling Julian Hartt's summary account of Christian hope, I suggested that God's perfecting culminates in an end, a finality. I have noted Berry's penchant for the eschatological reference to the heavenly, which raises the question of whether his insistence on the inextricable relationship between the earthly and the heavenly leaves him with a compromised eschatology.[21] Stated more simply, does Berry tie God's consummating mystery too closely to his grasp of the worldly? I believe my answers will foster the conclusion that he provides us with a Christian view of hopefulness that is invested in the enabling and enriching love of God and, further, a view that does not compromise God's consummating work.

An exploration of Berry's imaginative vision of the holy must first acknowledge his refusal to reference only Christian sources. Berry ranges widely over religious and nonreligious sources to explain the integrated reciprocities he portrays. Chinese, Islamic, and especially Buddhist allusions dot his works. But this openness does not result in some amorphous spirituality or hydra-headed religious eclecticism. He firmly embraces the Christianity he was "born to."[22] This serious engagement with his inherited religious place surfaces in many ways. Christian poets like Dante, Milton, and Herbert are important resources for Berry's Christian imagination. But one is most struck by his rich knowledge and use of the Bible. One repeated reference, for example, is to a passage in the book of Job (34:14–15) in which the dependence of the world's existence on the presence of God's spirit is professed. But I find the most telling scriptural resource for his Christian vision to be the Gospel of John. He tells us quite forcefully: "I take literally the statement in the Gospel of John that God loves the world. I believe that the world was created and approved by love, that it subsists, coheres and endures by love. I believe that divine love, incarnate and indwelling in the world, summons the world toward wholeness, which ultimately is reconciliation and atonement."[23] This biblically based theology of divine love helps explain some of the "embedded" or "interpenetrating" connections I have indicated. Wilderness can transport a human love to a level of mystery because that mystery is affirmed to express divine love. Nature can be imagined as a realm of gift giving because it expresses and coheres in a greater economy of love. And his mother's love and Hannah Coulter's love can be designated as *heavenly* because they both express and beckon toward that greater love. Berry's character Hannah makes utterly clear that her worldly love opens her to God's love. She states that the mystery of God's presence creates a "room of love" where the "absent are present, the dead are alive, time is eternal and all the creatures prosperous."[24]

Berry will describe himself as a "marginal" Christian. I think this may be due to the fact that he resists so strongly the dualistic Protestantism in which he was raised.[25] But I would resist the view that his theology of love is marginal. The love at the center of this theology makes Christian hopefulness viable, for it is God's love that enriches, and it is God's love that opens the possibility of that enrichment under the conditions of limitation or under conditions of unbounded fullness. Berry's God-world cycle is a reciprocal movement of love and, therefore, a cycle that fosters hopefulness.

I turn now to the theological issue of Berry's eschatology. I suspect that way of putting the problem makes it sound very academic, something for armchair Christian thinkers to debate. But the implications for Christian belief and practice are real. Pastoral conversations at bedsides and funeral sermons are not armchair matters. Does divine love actually shatter the finality of death, or is eschatological language only a collection of metaphors that remind us of a life well lived? More to the point, does Berry so fear dualism and so insist on world-God connectedness that a consummation beyond all limits is untenable for him? To start, it must be clear that Berry has serious reservations about how the final consummation is sometimes portrayed. He remarks that some of his boyhood exposures to views of the end-time were "bloodcurdling."[26] Such alienating eschatological views may explain his sympathy for the way his fellow Kentuckian artist Harlan Hubbard could quite literally declare of the local woodlands: "This is Heaven."[27] But it would be a mistake to put Berry's references to heaven on the same level as Hubbard's. The numerous ways in which Berry invokes heaven, including those I have noted and others unmentioned—like Jayber Crow's reference to the book about his life being a book "about Heaven"—are more subtle.[28] He is making a point about knowledge and imagination. He is not denying the possible existence of some consummating, boundless blessedness. Nor is he really endorsing Hubbard's willingness to collapse the unseen into the seen. He is making his often-repeated religious point that life cannot be understood without the larger horizon of divine love and that, without experience of woodlands, gifts of the land, intimate love, and a mother's patience, we cannot make sense of a love that surpasses seen reality. In technical terms, he is making a point about religious epistemology. He states, for example, that he refuses to let his religious imagination carry him "beyond" what he knows about the earth, but in the next breath he insists that his religious imagination must go "through" the earth.[29]

Berry affirms: "Beyond reach of thought / Let imagination figure your hope."[30] He realizes that the full reach of God's love goes beyond thought to depend on an imagination figured by our experience of tangible love. At the same time, it would be presumptuous to finalize our experiences of love and isolate them from a transcendent implication. The Christian philosopher Paul Ricouer makes the same point. Commenting on the Christian use of eschatological language, he suggests that such language follows the "law of superabundance." That is, it addresses the unreachable fullness of God's working by denying or removing any restriction or contradiction we know from our experience of abundance. So, in effect, we move from known abundance to the unknowable abundance by removing all negativities.[31] Berry's funding of the Christian imagination follows a similar pattern. There is no collapse of the transcendent into the worldly, nor is there any presumptuous finalizing of the worldly.

My exploration of the interwoven strands of Berry's spherical network of reciprocities is now complete. Each strand is relevant to understanding his view of Christian hopefulness. But the interweaving of the strands into his

Christian convictions about God's love is the core. That divine love is enriching and beckoning of a greater enrichment. But that love is also empowering. It opens possibilities even in the face of our known limits. It is a compelling view of Christian hope in and for God. Its worth will be even more visible if we compare it to an authoritative theological account of the virtue of Christian hope.

Saint Thomas Aquinas: A Transcendent but Narrowed Hope in and for God

In many ways, this is a curious juxtaposition. I do not know of any direct dependence of Berry's on the medieval giant of Scholastic theology. Berry does write on the great chain of being, an intellectual tradition that shaped Thomas and the Thomistic tradition. But that does not build a bridge between their projects. Perhaps no Christian projects are more disparate: a contemporary Christian artist and critic intent on shaping the Christian imagination in relation to very concrete relationships, and a medieval Christian intellectual attempting to combine scriptural insights, Augustinian theology, and a freshly discovered ancient philosophy into an instructional instrument. Different projects indeed.

Yet each is a serious Christian, and each is trying to make sense of how critical Christian traits should be understood and connected. It can be instructive to juxtapose disparate Christian voices whose projects overlap, particularly when one, like Thomas, has founded a long and respected way of approaching and articulating the features of Christian hope.

The convergence I discuss centers on the twofold reference of Christian hope to God's love. Berry is not particularly interested in the analytic maneuvers involved in showing that double reference. He simply employs it, showing how God's love enables and summons even as it provides foretastes of its enriching wholeness. Thomas, however, is a theologian for whom analytic distinctions are a critical stock in trade. What is interesting in the case of Thomas is that he initially did not see the need for or the importance of featuring this double reference. But he does develop it, to some extent against the grain of his own systematic tendencies.

Initially, Thomas features one reference to God. His initial work treats Christian hope as a hope for God. This is understandable. He adopts a general approach that shows all reality in a profound arc of returning movement.

All reality is on an unfolding journey of return to God. Couple this vision with a philosophical method that explained movement and behavior in terms of fulfillment of a built-in, defining purpose, and one can understand why his treatment of discrete topics is so end oriented, so teleological. To illustrate, the three theological virtues are understood as sequential, ever developing stages in a trajectory culminating in ultimate blessedness. It is no surprise that he first treats hope exclusively in terms of the desire for the ultimate good that God provides. To be sure, that goodness is also qualified as difficult, future, and possible. But the stress remains on God as the appropriate target of our longing for our own good. There is no special spelling out of what enables that movement toward God. God's attractive desirability (as the generous Good) is deemed sufficient.[32]

Thomas's later discussions of Christian hope indicate a decided shift. God is no longer just the singular, yet-to-be-realized end of hope. He is also the enabling power on whom the believer relies, the helper to whom the believer adheres. It is clear that it was not an easy shift to make, as is evidenced by the shifting technical vocabulary for presenting God as both present helper and yet-to-be-realized good. In one comment, Thomas simply states that Christian hope has "two objects," a significant remark for a systematic thinker who has stressed the singularity of ends. In that same treatise, he designates one object as "formal" and the other as "material."[33] He shifts his terminology to the arena of causation in his most famous work, calling God's blessedness the "final cause" and God's help the "efficient cause."[34] Some commentators might find this shifting categorization troublesome, but I think that it simply evidences a significant change that he would not forgo simply on the grounds that it was awkward to describe. Thomas does not explain why he makes this shift, but I find Bernard Lonergan's suggestion persuasive. Lonergan notes that Thomas became increasingly sensitive to the charge of semi-Pelagianism, a charge that believers were not portrayed as sufficiently dependent on God's present and operative grace.[35] There is a bit more to state about how Thomas uses Aristotle's views on friendship to introduce this second reference to God, but the point here is clear. Thomas is willing to alter a systematic tendency and method in order to make a more important theological point. Berry and Thomas converge on the important Christian stance that its hope must display a twofold character, confidence in the power of God's love to open possibilities and the enriching quality of that same love.

The approaches diverge on the important issue of how the self relates its own good to the full goodness that God's love encompasses. Thomas relates Christian hope to a regard for one's own good that is separate from regard for the goodness of others. And the help from God that grounds the confidence in possibility that is expressed in Christian hope is also narrowly focused on the subject of hope. To put it in Berry's terminology, Thomas lets the partiality of Christian hopefulness be understood apart from the wholeness in which that partiality participates.

This narrowing of the concern that informs Christian hope stems from an effort to give a completing primacy to the Christian virtue of love, of *caritas*. Faith begins an abiding stance because it opens the believer to the truth of God's goodness. Since faith grasps the fullness of that goodness, it never departs from the relationship of believer with God. But the virtue of hope is presented in a gateway role. The subject of hope sees that divine goodness solely through the lens of self-fulfillment. And the divine help that opens the possibility of self-flourishing is portrayed in terms of a form of secondary friendship, a friendship that Aristotle portrayed as solely based on the mutual seeking of self-advantage. Given this narrowed focus on the self and its limited function of moving the believer into the higher relationship of full love with God, the virtue of hope dissipates and disappears once the virtue of love with and for God is realized. The blessed can maintain hope for others, but that hopefulness would arise from the virtue of love, not the now unnecessary virtue of hope.[36]

There is nothing amiss in the aim to highlight the primacy of God's encompassing love. The misrepresentation of Christian hope arises because hopefulness is not fully integrated with the form of that love. If Berry and Hartt are correct that the believer must grasp his or her goodness in terms of a love that is and will make all things flourish, then a separation of self and other distorts the goodness that God offers. Nor can God's gracious, enabling love be grasped as focused on one's own well-being in a narrowing way that ignores the plenitude of that grace. Logically, one cannot hope for what has been realized, but, if the self is connected to a larger wholeness, as Berry instructs us, then one's own goodness is forever bound up with the time-bound and time-transcending flourishing of the whole creation.

The separation of the individual's goodness from a grasp of the larger reality of social and natural dynamics is not typical of Thomas.[37] Yet his integration of hopefulness with God's empowering and enriching love perpetuates a misrepresentation of Christian hope.

The importance of Berry's embedded treatment of Christian hopefulness is visible in the corrective it provides. For Berry, the place of God is a place of hopefulness because the place of God is a place of love. God's love empowers a plenitude of possibility, and God's love draws our partiality into the healing, flourishing mystery of wholeness. Berry's treatment of Christian hopefulness is an abiding contribution to the shaping of the Christian imagination and to Christian reflection on that virtue.

Notes

1. For a more complete analysis of hoping, see my "Hope and the Moral Life: A Study in Theological Ethics" (Ph.D. diss., Yale University, 1984), chap. 1.

2. Julian Hartt, "Concerning Faith and Hope," in *Theological Method and Imagination* (New York: Seabury, 1977), 105.

3. Wendell Berry, "The Body and the Earth," in *The Unsettling of America: Culture and Agriculture,* 3rd ed. (San Francisco: Sierra Club Books, 1977), 110. See also Mindy Weinreb, "A Question a Day: A Written Conversation with Wendell Berry," in *Wendell Berry: American Author Series,* ed. Paul Merchant (Lewiston, ID: Confluence, 1991), 29; and Morris Allen Grubbs, ed., *Conversations with Wendell Berry* (Jackson: University Press of Mississippi, 2007), 43–44.

4. Wendell Berry, "To My Mother," in *The Selected Poems of Wendell Berry* (New York: Counterpoint, 1998), 161.

5. For one such reference to Sir Albert Howard, see Wendell Berry, "Discipline and Hope," in *A Continuous Harmony: Essays Cultural and Agricultural* (San Diego: Harcourt Brace Jovanovich, 1972), 97.

6. Despair is a common theme in Berry's art and reflection. See, e.g., Wendell Berry, "A Poem of Difficult Hope," in *What Are People For?* (New York: North Point, 1990), 58–63.

7. For Berry's critique of scientism, see his "Discipline and Hope," 93–105. For his critical response to the reductionistic materialism of E. O. Wilson, see Wendell Berry, *Life Is a Miracle: An Essay against Modern Superstition* (Washington, DC: Counterpoint, 2000).

8. Wendell Berry, "Christianity and the Survival of Creation," in *Sex, Economy, Freedom, and Community* (New York: Pantheon, 1992), 103.

9. Wendell Berry, *Jayber Crow: The Life Story of Jayber Crow, Barber, of the Port William Membership, as Written by Himself: A Novel* (Washington, DC: Counterpoint, 2000), 349–50.

10. Joshua Dienstag, *Pessimism: Philosophy, Ethic, Spirit* (Princeton, NJ: Princeton University Press, 2006), 17.

11. Berry, "The Body and the Earth," 99.

12. Each of these cases, whether it be Ernest, Burley Coulter, or Jayber Crow, allows Berry to explore the way marriage and its disciplined nurturing of love does or does not become part of a life.

13. Wendell Berry, *A Place on Earth* (1983), rev. ed. (Washington, DC: Counterpoint, 2001), 36. For critical segments of the Ernest and Ida stories, see chaps. 9 and 11.

14. Gabriel Marcel, *Homo Viator* (New York: Harper & Row, 1962), 36.

15. Wendell Berry, "The Clear Days," in *Selected Poems*, 96. For poems that also stress that the body can serve the earth, see Wendell Berry, "Testament," in ibid., 93–95, and "Enriching the Earth," in *Collected Poems, 1957–1982* (San Francisco: North Point, 1985), 110.

16. Marcel, *Homo Viator*, 36.

17. Wendell Berry, *Hannah Coulter* (Washington, DC: Shoemaker & Hoard, 2004), 68.

18. Wendell Berry, "Sabbaths 1998, VI," in *Given: New Poems* (Washington, DC: Shoemaker & Hoard, 2005), 61.

19. P. Travis Kroeker, "Sexuality and the Sacramental Imagination: It All Turns on Affection," in *Wendell Berry: Life and Work*, ed. Jason Peters (Lexington: University Press of Kentucky, 2007), 120, 135.

20. Wendell Berry, "Notes: Unspecializing Poetry," in *Standing by Words* (San Francisco: North Point, 1983), 90–91. See also Grubbs, ed., *Conversations with Wendell Berry*, 139.

21. For one of Berry's explicit "interpenetrations" of the heavenly and the worldly, see Grubbs, ed., *Conversations with Wendell Berry*, 140.

22. Berry, "Christianity and the Survival of Creation," 95–96.

23. Wendell Berry, "Health as Membership," in *Another Turn of the Crank* (Washington, DC: Counterpoint, 1995), 89.

24. Berry, *Hannah Coulter*, 158.

25. Grubbs, ed., *Conversations with Wendell Berry*, 192.

26. Ibid., 57.

27. Wendell Berry, *Harlan Hubbard: Life and Work* (Lexington: University Press of Kentucky, 1990), 37–44.

28. Berry, *Jayber Crow*, 351.

29. Wendell Berry, "A Native Hill," in *The Long-Legged House* (1969; reprint, Washington, DC: Shoemaker & Hoard, 2000), 200.

30. Berry, "Testament," 94.

31. Paul Ricouer, "Hope and the Structure of Philosophical Systems," *Philosophy and Christian Theology: Proceedings of the Year 1970 of the American Catholic Theological Association* 44 (1970): 207–82.

32. Thomas, *Commentum in quator libros sententiarum Magistri Petri Lombardi* (Parma [American reprint]: Musguria, 1948), bk. 3, distinction 26.

33. Thomas, "Quaestio disputata, de spe," in *Quaestiones disputatae II,* ed. P. Bazzi et al., 8th rev. ed. (Rome: Marietta, 1949), art., ad 7.

34. Thomas, *Summa theologica,* 2nd English Dominican ed. (New York: Benziger, 1947), IIa, IIae, questions 17 and 18.

35. Bernard Lonergan, S.J., *Grace and Freedom* (New York: Herder & Herder, 1971), 60–61.

36. Thomas, *Summa theologica,* IIa, IIae, question 18.2.

37. Students of Thomas have recognized this incongruity. For the view that Thomas's view of the virtue as transient requires revision, see Karl Rahner, "A Theology of Hope," in *A Rahner Reader,* ed. Gerald A. McCool (New York: Seabury, 1975), 224–39. For the argument that Thomas generally overcomes any opposition between love of self and love of others, see Thomas Osborne, *Love of Self and Love of God in Thirteenth-Century Ethics* (Notre Dame, IN: University of Notre Dame Press, 2005), chap. 3.

Scott Williams

Alien Landscapes
Christianity and Inevitable Violence

One of the nice things about war, at least from the American perspective, is that it offers a comfortable sense that violence is localized and that its locale is *over there*. This secret comfort usually comes with a sense that the violence is also inevitable, which means that it is doubly important to keep over there, where it is engaged in by foreigners and people in uniforms. So much of the initially enthusiastic Christian response to the current war in Iraq seemed to rest on those assumptions. But there are good reasons for Christians to question both these descriptions of the violence we meet in the world. Most violence is, in fact, neither so neatly localizable nor so comfortingly inevitable. I want to explore the possibility of alternatives to that neatness and that comfort by holding up for examination a case of violence that is much harder to look at, precisely *because* of its ubiquity and its apparent inevitability as a component in the lives of those of us who don't wear uniforms. That example is electricity—and, more specifically, the radically extractive method of producing electricity-generating coal known as *mountaintop removal,* in which the tops of mountains are simply sheared off in order to expose coal deposits beneath.

Violence in Appalachia

In the summers of 1920 and 1921, southern West Virginia was the scene of some of the most historically significant and at the same time largely unremembered domestic unrest in U.S. history. I myself was raised in West Virginia and first learned the particulars of it only as a nearly grown man in a movie theater during a showing of *Matewan,* John Sayles's cinematic vision of the seminal events of what would later be called the *mine wars.* The Battle of

Matewan, between union coal miners and Baldwin-Felts private detectives who had been hired in this particular case to evict union miners from company housing, resulted in the death of several men, including the mayor of the town of Matewan, and made a folk hero of the police chief, Sid Hatfield (yes, he was one of *those* Hatfields). Hatfield was later indicted on murder charges in nearby McDowell County and shot, as they say, in cold blood by company detectives on the McDowell courthouse steps. This, in combination with the imprisonment by the Logan County sheriff of some union organizers, led to the climax of this particular mine war at the Battle of Blair Mountain. There, union miners had a full-scale engagement with the military of the U.S. government, having disregarded an ultimatum from President Warren G. Harding to return to their homes.

One would think that such a momentous event as an armed insurrection would have been on prominent display in the required West Virginia history class that we all took as eighth graders here. It was not. This is not to say that I had no idea that strange and violent things had taken place in the process of taking, for example, my coal-mining grandfather from abject poverty to relative prosperity over a period of fifty years or so. There were, I was told, occasions when it was necessary for him and others to travel to work armed with rifles. There was another in which he himself had beaten a mine foreman to within an inch of his life for admonishing my one-armed great-grandfather over the speed (or lack thereof) with which he loaded his coal. And there was yet another, decades later, in which that same foreman showed up on my grandfather's front porch seeking his forgiveness for years of workplace abuse.

These stories—both the larger story of the United Mine Workers of America and the more personal ones involving my grandfather—were and in a certain sense still are stories that seemed to take place on another planet. They seem alien, not only because of the nakedness and the nearness of their violence, but also because most of us have very little real experience with the kind of poverty that might lead to such violence. But, more than that, I think that the stories seem alien because most of us would rather not face the history of violence that makes our current consumption of electricity possible. Light-switch tripping is, in a certain sense, underwritten by the sorts of violence that I've related only in skeletal form here, which is only another way of saying that electricity runs on coal and that, to a certain extent, coal runs on bygone violence. The violence of the mine wars, the violence of previous schemes to deprive Appalachians of the mineral rights to their lands (an injustice that has never been meaningfully put right), the violence of workplace injustice and the struggle to right it even after the unions had been established for several decades are all what we might call the *constitutive violences* of the coal and electric power industries.

I've described these constitutive violences as *bygone,* and there is a certain sense in which that is true. They happened before most of us were born. The original subjects of the outrageous injustices of early coal mining are for the most part dead. There is, of course, another sense in which the violences are ongoing. The fact that West Virginians tend to benefit so very little in real terms from coal is one set of examples of this. Given the richness of the natural resources in places like West Virginia and the dramatic need for those resources outside the state, one might expect that public universities in such places would rival the Ivy League. They do not. One might further expect that the last thing such places would require is state-funded taxing of the poor and unwise in the form of gambling to subsidize the state budget. But, strangely, they do. So there is a sense in which coal continues, in my view, to do violence to the place from which it is extracted. But to make that point in this way is to invite more controversy than one might want. Some might take issue with my accounting of what benefits ought to accrue to the denizens of such places in view of our capitalist political economy. Others, wiser in my estimation than the first group, would point out that there could be great harm done to West Virginians, Kentuckians, and Montanans (to name only a few examples) in having them become subnational versions of the United Arab Emirates. Such a situation would improve them financially, but, taken alone, that form of improvement tends not to produce any other improvements.

The other problem is that this sort of violence remains hidden because it is clothed in relative prosperity. The violence is no longer *naked* in the way it was ninety or one hundred years ago and is, therefore, more difficult to talk about. People in Appalachia and elsewhere really are and have been fed, clothed, and sheltered well by their work in the coal mines. That is why we don't talk about Blair Mountain in the eighth grade. The fact that this is meager recompense is easy to hide in the face of having such necessities met. So the violence of coal has been, up until very recently, difficult to describe, even for the people who have inherited it in Appalachia.

I say *up until very recently* because, in the past several years, the violence has once again become naked. The landscape has once again become alien in a way that those who observe it cannot fail to recognize. Just as the story of Blair Mountain shocks us into the knowledge of past violence, so mountaintop-removal methods of coal extraction make our experience of our own landscape interplanetary. Mountaintop removal is a relatively new process for gaining access to coal seams using so-called drag line equipment. This is a process in which, as one might expect, mountaintops are simply sliced off in what can be described only as a kind of radical terraforming. This reshaping of the landscape is made all the more jarring by the concomitant process of valley filling. Again, the practice is well named. When one cuts off the top of a mountain to reach a coal seam and has removed the coal, there's a great deal of former mountain stuff left over. This is disposed of by depositing it in former streambeds, thus filling in what had been a valley. It's hard to imagine more intensive rearrangements of local mountain landscapes than the kind that mountaintop-removal coal extraction entails.

But it would be a mistake, and an intellectually dishonest one, to regard that rearrangement as somehow self-evidently evil. Landscapes are certainly wonderful things to look at, but it seems an open question whether the preservation of a scenic vista should stand in the way of any use of the land, even if that use radically transforms it. One of the things that has to be resisted, it seems to me, is the knee-jerk impulse to keep things in the natural world exactly the way they are in order to continue looking at them. There's a kind of eco-pornographic vision going on in that kind of reaction that, rather than regarding the natural world as the site of an interaction that produces mutual benefits (say, in the way that farming does or used to), views the natural world (as though we could regard it as *another* world) as something simply to be viewed, an image or object that can be regarded without having to undergo the risk of real relationship with it. Now, the kind of interaction that mountaintop removal entails might seem so destructive and radically transformative of the land as to fail as an example of a mutually beneficial relationship between human beings and the so-called natural world. It certainly seems that way to me, but it's a controversial point.

Far less controversial is the idea that such landscapes cannot be attacked in such a way without doing violence to things other than the landscape itself. One simply cannot remove the top of a mountain and fill in a nearby streambed without disrupting *other things*. Those other things are, invariably, human communities. Consider the following assessment of that disruption: "The impact of mountaintop removal on nearby communities is devastating. Dynamite blasts needed to splinter rock strata are so strong they crack the foundations and walls of houses. Mining dries up an average of 100 wells a year and contaminates water in others. In many coalfield communities, the purity and availability of drinking water are keen concerns. Blasting and shearing mountains have added to the damage done to underground aquifers by deep mines."[1]

It's hard to imagine a more fundamental devastation for a community to absorb than one that attacks its ability to have shelter and to drink safely. To refer to such devastation as an *environmental* problem is, in a certain sense, to miss the point. It isn't an attack on something *around* human beings—their environs. It is an attack on the human beings themselves and involves them at the level of their livelihood just as surely as the early labor wars did. It is in this sense, as well as the more literal one of landscape destruction, that the strange violence of electricity production has once again become undeniable in its visibility and in its power to alienate human beings from their own landscapes by making them simply uninhabitable. Some*one* has violence done to them when we trip light switches and *always has*. Only inattention can any longer keep that violence invisible.

Christianity and Inevitable Violence

Now that's a depressing story if one takes it seriously. It's even more depressing if that seriousness is honest in admitting that each of us is implicated in it. Most of us use lots of electricity, even those who know about its violence, and the truth is that most of us don't know how to stop doing so. What's worse is that this business with electricity is only one example of a kind of violence that makes our lives as they are currently shaped possible. We seem to have a similar problem with oil, paper, national security, and corn. Our lives are constructed in such a way that we can't imagine them without a great many things that seem impossible to procure without supporting all kinds of violence that we would normally deplore. The deplorability becomes even more intense (one hopes) when the "we" in question is "we Christian ministers and laypeople." This raises the question of how we narrate such violence in light of the life and teaching of Jesus of Nazareth. In other words, how do we who claim to understand the world through the cross of Christ and hope to have our lives shaped by anticipation of Christ's Kingdom account for the fact that so many (apparently fundamental) components of our lives are dependent on the kinds of violence that Christ refused? Or, put more simply, how do we respond to the apparent inevitability of the violence in our lives? I'd like to think about that question with the help of a writer who has spent considerable time wrestling with it and others similar in kind, Wendell Berry.

One might almost say that Berry takes such a question as the engine for his whole authorship. Certainly, if you began to read Berry, as I did, with "Why I Am Not Going to Buy a Computer" and its companion piece, "Feminism, the Body and the Machine," you will have seen its importance in understanding not only his work but also a great deal of modern life and its neglected dependencies. "Why I Am Not Going to Buy a Computer" begins modestly enough with the following description of Berry's own situation: "Like almost everyone else, I am hooked to the energy corporations, which I do not admire. I hope to become less hooked to them. In my work, I try to be as little hooked to them as possible. As a farmer, I do almost all of my work with horses. As a writer, I work with a pencil or a pen and a piece of paper."[2]

Berry goes on to narrate for his readers the pressure to deepen his connection to the energy corporations by beginning to employ a computer. He claims that "a number of people" have tried to convince him of the usefulness of such a switch (one might imagine that this is the same "number of people" who now want very badly for us all to have cellular phones). What follows that is a list of "standards for technological innovation" that Berry thinks should be applied to any contemplated improvement in our daily tool set. They are as modest as his description of his own life, beginning with, "The new tool should be cheaper than the one it replaces," and ending (perhaps a trifle less modestly) with, "It should not replace or disrupt anything good that already exists, and this includes family and community relationships."[3]

Several things can be learned from Berry's way of handling the practical problem of a computer, it seems to me. The first of them is its confessional nature. Berry begins by admitting that he is implicated in the problem he's trying to solve, granting that there isn't any place of electricity-free purity for him to stand any longer. There isn't, in a sense we've perhaps already rehearsed well enough, any getting out of the problem of coal and electricity. We're hooked to it, to use Berry's phrase, in a way that can seem inevitable. If that were true—if our connection to electricity were, indeed, inevitable—there would be little point in moving to the second essential component of Berry's response to the computer—the articulation of a hope that things might be different.

The hope of becoming less hooked to the energy corporations is, to most of us, only a fool's hope, or at least a hope that is clearly and determinedly defied by present circumstances, so powerful is our connection to electric current. But Berry hopes this hope anyway, which is already an astonishing act. Even the publication of his essay implicated him all the more in the kinds of violence he hopes to avoid, one would think. Yet it turns out not to be an utterly foolish hope inasmuch as he tells us what he can do to begin to make that hope shape his own life. Write with pen. Farm with horse. Edit and correct writing with spouse's help. Do what you can when and where the opportunity presents itself even if it's small (which it will not always be). These are practical responses to a common problem and are no less practical and no less *respons*ible in not entirely solving the problem they address. This is, at least in part, the meaning of having a hope about something.

Finally, Berry recognizes that it isn't enough to be able to articulate one's hope in terms of specific practices, although it is a necessary beginning point. One must also be able to say what sorts of general constraints having this particular hope would put on the life of the one who hopes it, what sorts of standards would have to be visible in the economy of the household that anticipates it. In the case of Berry's hope to unhook from the electric company, the generalities that point to that hope are "cheaper, smaller, more modest and preservative of communities," to name a few. Other people who hope other things will live with different constraints and standards, many of which will conflict with Berry's. The evidence of this can be found just about anywhere there's a television, but a more direct indication is in the acerbic letters from readers that Berry's little essay provoked. In them, he was called sexist (because his wife edits his work), judgmental, foolish, and unrealistic because he wants to write with a pen rather than a computer. So even his tiny "I'll keep writing with a pen rather than a computer because electricity has a number of serious drawbacks that my hand doesn't" rebellion was intolerable to many who read of it. Why?

Certainly part of the reason is that, despite the relative obviousness of the fact, people do not like to be reminded that their dependence on coal is also a dependence on violent practices such as mountaintop removal, something that is possible in its current configuration only because of a prior dependence on a great many labor and land injustices. But that is not the whole reason. At least some of the reason for resisting Berry's modest handling of the problem of electricity is that it avoids a couple of false and idolatrous options in confronting violence that, despite the fact that they are false and idolatrous, continue to be the ones with which even Christians are most comfortable. In short, I think that Berry's response to the violence attending coal and electricity is particularly Christian in form inasmuch as it lives out the hope for an alternative without resorting to still further violence.

There are at least two deep temptations for people who take seriously problems like the ones associated with the extraction of coal. One is to regard the violence that we do to one another in the midst of such processes as inevitable in the most straightforward sense. In other words, we say something like, "Well, the world's a fallen and imperfect place. It just seems to be the case that, in order for there to be indispensable good *x*, we're going to have to be willing to face up to suffering *y*." We could even put a really convincing theological spin on it that would make it seem more faithful or at least religious than it really is. We could say that, after all, God is the only one who can act without loss, which is really just a pious admission that nobody's perfect. Or we could say that the cross of Christ and the Kingdom that his life rehearses is an impossible possibility that stands at the edge of history as its judge rather than as its true story. That would give us a kind of Niebuhrian permission to at least feel good about the fact that we regret a thing like mountaintop removal even though there's nothing to be done about it (this always seemed like the only practical point one could take from the so-called serenity prayer). As a practical matter, we'd go on doing mountaintop removal; we'd just regret its necessity. The fact that someone like Wendell Berry has no overarching or wholesale solution to the problem of electricity is an indication of its inevitability, according to this view. This, it seems to me, has been the general mood of the conservative response to radically extractive industry among Christians, and its complacency is legendary.

The other temptation is to believe that, if only the proper legislation were put into place, if only the proper ideological underpinnings could be provided to our ecological policies, the end of the violence we do to one another in the name of energy (and so many other things) would be at hand. Christ has left his work up to us, and we'd better get busy, and the solutions we'd better get busy with had better be global. If the solutions aren't wholesale and programmatic, then they cannot be real solutions. This, we might say, has been the general mood of the liberal response to radically extractive industry among Christians, and the violence of its immodesty is legendary.

But the problem with these two temptations is not that they are false, ineffective, complacent, or immodest, although they are those things often enough for it to be worth saying. Nor is the problem that they are too conservative or too liberal. The problem is, rather, that neither of them is fully Christian in their understanding of the world's violence or what it would mean to live in hope in the face of it.

On the one hand, to regard violence of any kind as somehow ontologically built in to the structure of the world is to despair of Christ's lordship over the world. To say "we must have the coal because we must have electricity because electricity is necessary for life and the coal can be gotten only with violence and therefore violence must inevitably be done and that is simply *how the world is*" is to despair of providing a description of the world as heading toward its redemption in Christ. In the first place, it grants a kind of ultimate significance to something—electricity—that doesn't merit it. We know this because our Lord has taught us that even *food* doesn't have this kind of significance. Our very lives are insignificant in the face of the possibility that we should fail to have them conformed to God's Word, which would mean avoiding as a matter of greatest urgency the kind of violence to our brothers and sisters that electricity production so often entails. There are no good warrants for turning away from this obligation. If food doesn't have this significance, surely electricity does not. Surely it is one of the more silly sorts of idolatry to regard the violence of coal extraction, for example, as somehow sanctified by the fallen condition of the world. It isn't and can't be, to quote John Howard Yoder, "if Christ is truly Lord."[4]

On the other hand, to place faith in a theory of how history can be made to unfold so that the aforementioned violence won't be necessary at all is to deal in fool's gold and worse, once again to rehearse an idolatry. If the previous view fails to understand the *world* (as opposed to individuals' little souls) as heading toward redemption, this one fails to see the world as headed not toward *redemption* but perhaps only toward being repaired. The problems of energy consumption will not be solved in any final or permanent sense by a sweeping or programmatic policy or an ideology or a set of educational reforms of human devising. Why would we trust such an enterprise to *deliver*? The legislation, the government effort that prohibits the type of coal mining that serves as our example here *already exists*. It was passed under the Carter administration in 1977, which is why coal companies must continually appear before federal judges to get special permits to do it. Recently, two such permits were issued for Blair Mountain itself. Now, that ghastly fact might well provide us with another opportunity to speak and act about this problem. The point is that there's no way of knowing, nor any point in trying to guarantee, that such speaking and acting will be efficacious or even knowing what such efficacy would mean. The mistake is to believe that such speech and such action are themselves salvific.

What Christians are awaiting is Christ's return, which means that they live in a hope that, like Wendell Berry's hope, provides them with standards for discernment now even if the fullness of that hope isn't here *yet*. Because the object of our hope isn't yet here in its fullness, we may well get worse than nasty letters for letting the standards it provides guide us into electricity or draft or Wal-Mart resistance. The world doesn't share these standards with us most of the time, which is why it needs a witness rather than a strategy for social engineering. Christians ought not to be awaiting a further set of technologies or ideologies that will end the *apparently* inevitable violence to which we are hooked up. Wholesale attempts to fix those problems simply reenact the same impatience with the world that mountaintop removal does with a coal seam. The refusal to recognize that some seams should remain beyond our reach drives us to tear open the mountain because we regard *some kind* of violence as inevitable in defiance of our claim to faith in Jesus.

There is no inevitable violence. Even if it seems to be so for now, those whose hope is in Christ cannot ever grant such inevitability to anything other than the redemption of the world. Nonetheless, the world is violent, and there is often very little that we know to do about it *for now*, which doesn't yet mean that we do nothing. It's not an easy or comfortable position to be in, I grant. But it's difficult to see what else Christian faithfulness in the face of lives shaped by such violence could demand if it wants to respond to evil in the way God has—with patience.

Let me put some flesh on that abstract description by offering up an example from the small-town Appalachian church of which my wife is the pastor. Recently, in that church of about fifty people, there was a mild controversy about the possible purchase and installation of air-conditioning for the sanctuary (which is positively sweltering in the summer months). The opposition to this expensive proposal came largely from older members of the congregation. I unfairly assumed they objected to it because of the kind of too-fresh memories of bygone harder times that make any expenditure suspicious.

At the meeting in which the proposal was discussed, one of these older members stepped forward to say a word. Max, a man in his late seventies whose family has been living in this part of West Virginia for generations and many of whose children and grandchildren attend that church, mildly asked permission to share with the rest of the congregation some of his memories of its history. He quietly pointed out the place in the sanctuary where the wood-fired furnace, which had at one time been the sanctuary's only source of heat, once stood. He also explained how fans (the kind powered by hands and wrists) had once occupied every hymnal slot in the pews to stave off the heat of worship in July. In his humble way, he was able to remind us that, within the span of his memory, the notion that the worship of God would require electric-powered comfort would have seemed obviously absurd. Only a deep confusion about what is really necessary in our response to the good news of Jesus Christ could possibly make something called *electricity* seem so very urgent. We do not require large amounts of electric power (or any amounts—but that may be too ambitious just yet) in order to be faithful to God on Sunday mornings. If we don't need electricity for that most important of activities, then how could it possibly be indispensable in *any other* context? Max reminds us of this question, and that reminder liberates us from having to take such power seriously.

I don't know whether Max is conservative or liberal in his politics, although I suspect the former. I don't know whether he thinks of himself as an environmentalist, although I suspect not. What I do know is that his hope for Christ's return, his commitment to love God above all things, rightly relativizes the importance of electric power in his life in a way that allows him to be a nonviolent witness against that particular idolatry. Max's testimony (and what else would we call it?) invited those of us in the room to join him in responding to the violence of electricity production and other violence in the way that God has—with patience. It clarifies the church's mission to be Max for the world, which of course really means being Christ for the world. The only way to refuse the violence of energy production without resorting to still more violence is to show the world an alternative. Such an alternative witnesses to the redemptive possibility that we don't need to live violently.

Notes

1. http://www.ilovemountains.org/resources.

2. Wendell Berry, "Why I Am Not Going to Buy a Computer," in *What Are People For?* (New York: North Point, 1990), 170.

3. Ibid., 171–72.

4. John Howard Yoder, "If Christ Is Truly Lord," in *The Original Revolution: Essays on Christian Pacifism* (Eugene, OR: Wipf & Stock, 1998).

L. Roger Owens

Let the Place Judge
Healing the Division between Theology and Practice

Living the Divide—a Personal Preface

I have lived and continue to live the fissure between theology and practice. The work of Wendell Berry has helped me begin to heal that divide in my life and in my theological work, which are little by little becoming a unity.

I felt called to pastoral ministry when I was seventeen. This caused an abrupt change in my college plans. Instead of going to a secular liberal arts university to study music, I headed to Anderson University, a Christian liberal arts university. There I studied Bible, religion, and philosophy and fell in love with the academic life. I remember the day I learned that the differences among the accounts of Jesus' life in the first three Gospels constituted a "problem." Far from being horrified, as were many of my classmates, I was fascinated. I was also fascinated by my philosophy professor's articulation of process theology's solution to the "problem" of evil, which I learned was another fascinating intellectual problem. I purchased with eagerness Charles Hartshorne's *Omnipotence and Other Theological Mistakes,* while the woman at the check-out register expressed dismay that professors at a Christian university would have students read such books.[1]

I went on to enjoy the pleasures of academic life in seminary. After graduation from seminary, I earned a Ph.D. in theology and ethics. In the meantime, I continued to pursue ordination as a United Methodist minister, imagining that I would live out my call to ordained ministry as a college or seminary professor. While various ordination committees along the way expressed reservations about my intentions to teach, doubting my commitment to pastoral ministry, I progressed along the path toward ordination.

During the years of my doctoral work it became clear that about the time I would finish there would be a position in my alma mater's religion department. The other option would be for me to take a pastoral appointment. I had a foot in both worlds—the academic and the pastoral, the world of the theologian and the world of the clergyman—and I had to pick one. All the indications seemed to point me in the direction of the academy. I eventually had a campus interview at Anderson University. My old professors there assured me I would be offered the job in a few weeks.

Then I read Wendell Berry's *Hannah Coulter,* where I saw in the protagonist's description of her son Caleb a mirror of my own life. Caleb grew up on the Coulter farm and loved farming more than any of his siblings. He seemed at home on the farm, and his parents assumed that he would return from college to continue the work. But things changed for him at college. His mother imagines what he might have encountered there: "And I know, I can almost hear, the voices that were speaking to him, voices of people he learned to respect, and they were saying, 'Caleb, you're too bright to be a farmer.' They were saying, 'Caleb, there's no future for you in farming.' They were saying, 'Caleb, why should you be a farmer yourself, when you can do so much for farmers? You can be a help to your people.'" I had heard very similar voices myself: "You can have a much greater impact on the church by teaching people who want to be pastors than you can by being a pastor yourself." Hannah continues:

> And what of Caleb? Caleb eventually became Dr. Coulter. He became a professor, teaching agriculture to fewer and fewer students who were actually going to farm. He became an expert with a laboratory and experimental plots, a man of reputation. But as I know, and as he knows in his own heart and thoughts, Caleb is incomplete. He didn't love farming enough to be a farmer, much as he loved it, but he loved it too much to be entirely happy doing anything else. He is disappointed with himself. He is regretful in some dark passage of his mind that he thinks only he knows about, but he can't hide it from his mother. I can see it in his face as plain as writing. There is the same kind of apology in him that you see in some of the sweeter drunks. He is always trying to make up the difference between the life he has and the life he imagines he might have had.[2]

When I read those words, Berry's novel became for me *lectio divina,* "sacred reading," through which I was given a glimpse of what my own life might become. I did not want anyone to be able to say of me, "He is always trying to make up the difference between the life he has and the life he imagines he might have had." This passage returned me to that sense of vocation I had when I was seventeen. Taking an appointment as a local church pastor was threatening for me—after all, I hadn't taken any "practical" courses in seminary—but it was also the path that seemed the most faithful.

That night I called my friend, the chair of the Religion Department at Anderson University. "I'm surprised I'm calling you," I said. "But I won't be taking a job at Anderson. I'll be asking for an appointment in a local church." He replied, "I'm not surprised. When you were at our house visiting a few months ago, after you left, my wife said to me, 'Don't be disappointed or surprised if Roger decides to go into the local church.' We saw it coming."

I do not want to suggest that I could not have found a way to heal in my life the division between theology and practice as a college professor, or that I will never find myself as a teacher, or that others have not found faithful ways to heal this division as academics. I am only saying that, in my case, the pastoral setting seemed to be the place where theology and practice might find a unity in my life.

This division, which I continue to experience, runs deep. It is embodied in the academic divisions in seminaries between the theological disciplines (biblical studies, theology, history) and the practical disciplines (ethics, pastoral care, ministerial formation, spirituality, preaching, worship, and evangelism). And, just as the theological disciplines often make up the majority of courses in the first years of a seminary education, to provide both a foundation for the practical disciplines and the storehouse of theory to be applied, this division—and hierarchy—is often reproduced within the practical disciplines themselves. We are constantly asking how to "apply" theology in practice. How in a homiletics course is a theology of preaching put into practice? How in worship does a theoretical understanding of worship take shape in the actual liturgy? How in evangelism is a theological account of the Gospel and the church's mission put into practice? These questions, often explicit, sometimes not, create the governing, if unmentioned, framework in which these disciplines operate.

In this essay, I will address one instance of this division—the tendency to apply the doctrine of the Incarnation to questions of enculturation in the field of evangelism—before showing how what Wendell Berry has written on breeding sheep can point toward a healing of that divide through the pastoral work of shaping communities. I hope, however, that its usefulness is broader, for I hope that the other disciplines, even theological education as a whole, can learn from this glance at a single instance of the division between theology and practice in a theological discipline and a vision of its healing.

Division in a Discipline—Incarnation and Enculturation in Evangelism

It is announced so often that it is almost a platitude in the literature on evangelism to say that, to be effectively proclaimed and faithfully embodied, the Gospel must become enculturated. The Gospel, as God's universal grace, requires translation into the various languages and customs of the culture in which it is hoped that Christianity will take root and flourish. This important point was missed by Western missionaries of centuries past, who assumed that the spread of the Gospel meant the spread of Western civilization as well. In the wake of such colonialism masking as evangelization, writers on evangelism are quick to point out that the Gospel and the Christian practices it implies cannot be identified with any one culture but, because of the very universal nature of the Gospel, can be at home in any culture.

In one sense, such claims seem almost obvious. One can see empirically that the Gospel can and has taken root in numerous cultures. The Gospel itself does not dictate such things as styles of worship or dress. Go to any country in the world or any town in North America, and you can witness empirically the truth that the Gospel and the Christian practice it implies can be embodied in the indigenous ways of a culture. As an empirical reality, enculturation seems obvious and unavoidable. It was precisely the mistake of Western missionaries to assume that their Gospel, and its embodiment in practice, was *not* enculturated but that their form of Christian expression was identical with the Gospel itself.

But the claim that the Gospel must be enculturated is more than an empirical claim—it is also a missionary strategy. Those engaged in ministries of evangelism are charged with enculturating the Gospel well to facilitate its taking root in a host culture. They must be trained to recognize which aspects of their own expression and embodiment of the Gospel are essential to its core and which are expressions of their own cultural situation. Thus, the missionary strategy of enculturation involves a balancing act. As Dana Robert says: "The gospel takes shape from the local setting or else it cannot be understood by people in the particular culture. Fixing upon a balance between contextualization and remaining faithful to the core of the gospel is an ongoing strategy in missiology."[3]

Writers on evangelism point to the Incarnation as the theological rationale for the missionary strategy of enculturation. Scott Jones puts the rational most succinctly: "Since Christ is God put into human flesh, the gospel can be put into other languages and cultural forms as well."[4] When evangelists imagine ways to enculturate the Gospel in a particular culture, they are performing a missiological *imitatio Dei*—the Incarnation itself being God's own missionary strategy, God's own way of enculturating the Gospel.

Tex Sample, in a book about ministry in the culture of working-class whites, also points to the Incarnation as the model of enculturation:

> [Jesus] was a carpenter, an occupation of his time. He went to the marginal people of his world, who were illiterate, and he taught them in parables. He was a faithful Jew and participated in central practices of his faith, although he also opposed some of those practices. He spoke Aramaic, thus taking up the language of his people. His teaching used images from that world in terms of lilies, fish, sowing and reaping, mustard seeds, the weather, and much more. . . . I contend that there has never been an authentic expression of Christian faith that was not also indigenous. In fact, serious tragedy attends the missionary work of the church when it refuses to be indigenous. . . . To pitch tent is intrinsic to the incarnate activity of the Triune God made known in Christ who works through the Spirit. One task of the church as the body of Christ in the world is to instantiate such incarnational activity.[5]

From this, it can be seen that the Incarnation works in two ways as a rationale for enculturation. First, the very *fact* of the Incarnation points to the *necessity* of enculturation—the Son's becoming human points to the possibility of a universal Gospel being incarnated in different cultures—and the *way* Jesus expressed his humanity—through the cultural practices of his day, especially his Jewishness—provides theological rationale for modern-day *strategies* of enculturation. This is what Darrell Guder calls the "incarnational principle"—"the humanness of Jesus, and the example of his life, are seen as paradigmatic for the mission activity of the church."[6] In some ways, I suppose all this seems obvious.

Yet it is precisely this notion of the "incarnational principle" with its use as a theological rationale for the missionary strategy of enculturation that I suggest recapitulates the divide between theory and practice that haunts the so-called practical theological disciplines. When the Incarnation is used this way, as a rationale for missionary strategy, I think two mistakes are being made that make the pastoral question, "How can the Gospel be effectively enculturated in this context?" exactly backward.

Stripping Jesus

The first mistake is that this use of the Incarnation as a rationale implies a universal, un-enculturated Gospel that needs to be enculturated; such a universal Gospel does not exist. The very grammar of the question—"How do you enculturate the Gospel?"—points to a pure Gospel essence that needs to be enculturated. The quotation from Dana Robert given above about how to enculturate the Gospel while staying true to the core of the Gospel points to just such an essence. But it would be impossible to name or articulate such an essence because the very instance such an essence is named it is named in a particular language. This fact cannot be gotten behind or around. As Lesslie Newbigin has written: "The idea that one can or could at any time separate out by some process of distillation a pure gospel unadulterated by any cultural accretions is an illusion. It is, in fact, an abandonment of the gospel, for the gospel is about the word made flesh."[7] The attempt to name the essence of the Gospel usually requires abstractions like *love* and *grace* that God expressed in the language of the Incarnation and that we express in our own enculturation of the Gospel. When this happens, however, the particularity of the story of Jesus becomes one cultural expression of the Gospel, even if the paradigmatic one, that itself must be left behind if the Gospel is to take root in ever new situations. For instance, Terry Persha writes:

> Jesus Christ, after all, was an historical being bound to one culture and one society in a given time and moment of history. Because of that, he could not possibly have expressed the mystery of grace in all its historical unfolding and multifaceted dimensions. He could only have expressed the meaning of God's involvement with humanity through the limits of his culture, language, and symbols. Everything, in fact, that the early Christians themselves learned of God in Jesus Christ was shaped by the linguistic, moral, spatial, political, and psychological structures of their time-bound, spatially situated condition in history.[8]

Here, *grace* is a universal abstracted from the story of Jesus and the particularity of his life—from the Incarnation—the cultural particularities of his own day being something that need to be abandoned as the Gospel is proclaimed in ever new and different cultures so that grace might find expression in them as well. For true enculturation to take place, the Gospel itself must be unbound, it seems, from Jesus' own cultural limitations. Jesus must be stripped to his naked, untarnished, universal humanity so that he might then be redressed in new cultural clothes as the proclamation of the Gospel encounters new cultures.

But the Gospel is and has always been enculturated all the way down, so to speak. To assume that there is a pure or essential Gospel that needs to be enculturated ironically repeats the very mistake of the imperialist missionaries who assumed their expression of the Gospel *was* the pure version, untarnished by culture. It repeats the move of liberal Christianity, most clear in von Harnack's *What Is Christianity?* that a core of Christianity can be identified when the layers of cultural husk are stripped away. But this essence does not exist. We are stuck with Jesus, bound as he is "to one culture and one society in a given time and moment of history." When this is realized, the missiological question can no longer be how to maintain a balance between enculturation and staying true to the core of the Gospel. A much more fundamental and startling question takes its place: "What in the world do we do with the Jew Jesus?"

The second mistake is that, when the Incarnation becomes a rationale and model for the missionary strategy of enculturation, the Jewishness of Jesus becomes accidental to the Gospel and to the Incarnation itself. Using the doctrine of the Incarnation as a missiological strategy answers the question, "What in the world do we do with the Jew Jesus?" by stripping him of his Jewishness. This second mistake is the necessary corollary of assuming a universal Gospel. As we have seen Tex Sample suggest above, Jesus' Jewishness was a tactic, a way of embodying the culture in which he found himself. Now, in order to find out how to embody the Gospel in other cultures, Jesus must be stripped of his Jewishness. This way of applying theology in evangelism, this way of turning the Incarnation into a principle to be applied, saves missionaries, evangelists, and pastors from facing the embarrassing fact of Jesus' Jewishness by making it merely tactical and, thus, accidental to the Gospel rather than constitutive of the Gospel itself. Consider Persha again: "Here the universality of Christ can best be appreciated. By virtue of his resurrection, Jesus is no longer bound by time, history, or culture. He becomes, in fact, the totally transcultural one, present to all of creation through the grace of his Spirit."[9] Here, I think, one should read *transcultural* to mean "no longer Jewish."

When, however, the particularity of Jesus as the Jewish Messiah is acknowledged and affirmed as constitutive of and not accidental to whatever we mean when we say *Gospel,* then Jesus no longer needs to be unbound or freed from his cultural particularity. His being Jewish can no longer be viewed as an embarrassment to be overcome, for, when he is stripped of that Jewishness, when the Gospel as the "mystery of grace" is freed from *this* particular culture, then there is no Gospel left. As John Howard Yoder puts it:

> It was the Jewishness of Jesus, the rootage of his message in the particular heritage of Abraham, Moses, and Jeremiah, which as we have seen made it good news for the whole world. . . . Only the Jew Jesus, by announcing and accomplishing the fulfillment of God's promises to the Jews, could send out into the world a people of peace open to the Gentiles. Only the Jewish claim that the one true God, known to Abraham's children through their history, was also the Creator and sustainer of the other peoples as well, could enable mission without provincialism, cosmopolitan without empire.[10]

When the use of the doctrine of the Incarnation implies a universal Gospel, untouched by culture, a naked Gospel that needs to be dressed in the indigenous forms of a particular culture, then of course the most pressing pastoral question will be how to go about such cultural undressing and dressing of the Gospel. But, when we resist, as I think we should, such an application of the Incarnation, when we deny the division between theology and practice that makes it possible, and when we see the Incarnation, not as a rationale to justify a strategy or a paradigm to be imitated, but as the preeminent fact of Christianity—as God's way of opening the blessing of his covenant with the Jews to Gentiles through the flesh of Jesus, the Jewish Messiah, without requiring those Gentiles themselves to become culturally Jews—then the most pressing pastoral question changes. The question is no longer, "How do you enculturate the Gospel?" but, "How do you en-Gospel the culture?" The surprising fact of the Gospel is not that it is capable of wearing any cultural dress but that cultures being confronted with the Gospel do not themselves have to strip in order to participate in the blessings of the body of Christ, God's covenant people.

And that surprising fact leads to the pastoral question, "How do you shape communities faithful to the shape of the life of Jesus the Jewish Messiah without requiring the community to abandon its own cultural particularity?" The Incarnation is not a principle to be applied; it is a reality to be participated in. And the reality in which we are able to participate is the humanity of the Jewish Jesus.

Let the Place Judge

The healing of the divide between theology and practice in evangelism will begin when evangelism as the discipline of disciplemaking and community formation makes this realization and begins to address the more fundamental—and difficult—questions that I have suggested above.

One of the reasons I have been able to find a healing between theology and practice in my life as a pastor is because I have found that theological work in a parish setting is not about getting theology right and then applying it but about shaping a community to conform to the life of the one in whom it participates without forcing that community to abandon its own local identity. It is the particularity of Jesus that secures the particularity of the community and the positing of a universal Gospel that puts such communal cultural particularity in jeopardy—as history has shown. The pastor who tries to shape a community faithful to the Jewish Messiah whose life they embody must think carefully about which aspects of that community's culture—its particular and manifold ways of speaking, acting, relating, and gathering—are consistent with the shape of the life of Jesus and which are not, but the emphasis must be on letting the particularities of the place take the lead in how the shape of the life of Jesus will take local shape in that place if that cultural situation is going to be appropriately en-Gospeled.

And that brings me back to Wendell Berry, whose account of breeding sheep in the essay "Let the Farm Judge" can serve as a metaphor for the pastoral work of shaping communities that conform to the humanity of Jesus in which they participate. In that essay, Berry expresses delight over the fact that, in Great Britain, there are more than "sixty-five British sheep breeds and 'recognized half-breeds'" and wonders what such a fact says about agriculture and

230 L. Roger Owens

the importance of place.[11] The success over hundreds of years of British farmers to adapt sheep so beautifully to their specific localities points, for Berry, to the core work of good farming: "The goal of intelligent farmers, who desire the long-term success of farming, is to adapt their work to their places" (57). Intelligent pastoral workers who want to learn faithfully to shape Christian communities have something to learn from intelligent farmers like Berry who take seriously the need for local adaptation.

In this extended metaphor, let *place* stand for *culture*. Often, culture is thought of in broad terms, as in, "One must understand North American culture to effectively proclaim the Gospel"—but I have learned that, as it is often painted in large brushstrokes, North American culture has little to say about the shape of life in rural communities like the one where I pastor in northern Franklin County, North Carolina. *Place* as *culture* helpfully limits the scope of what we are talking about. So, when Berry says that the farm, the place itself, must "enforce its judgment" (58), he is helping us see the implication of the fact that, as I have already argued, *Gospel* means at least that a particular place does not need to abandon its particularity in order to be en-Gospeled. When one is trying to help Christianity take root and flourish in a place—doing the pastoral work of shaping a community to conform to the shape of the life of the Jewish Messiah, Jesus—the place itself will be respected and listened to; it cannot be stripped, but its own particularities—its indigenous practices—will go a long way toward determining the shape of the community's health and faithfulness. This is not a question of balancing faithfulness to the core of the Gospel with the need for enculturation, for the Gospel itself demands that the place not be stripped of its particularity. Rather, the embodiment of the life of Jesus will be done through that place's particularity. As Berry puts it: "But the farm too must be permitted to make and enforce its judgment. If it is not permitted to do so, then there can be no local adaptation. And where there is no local adaptation, the farmer and the farm must pay significant penalties" (58).

For Berry, a particular phenomenon of the commercial demand for "ideal" animals militates against letting the farm judge. "In our era," he writes, "because of commercial demand and the allure of the show ring, livestock breeding has tended to concentrate on the production of outstanding individual animals as determined by the ideal breed characteristics or the ideal carcass" (58). The production of such an ideal animal—judged by the unplaced standards of the show ring—requires standards of production that are not in harmony with what most farms are capable of sustaining without detriment to the farm. This reminds me of the tendency in the literature of evangelism to think that one size fits all—to try to reproduce in a particular place what has produced outstanding results in another place, which usually means reproducing techniques that helped make another church big. The show-ring church has tricked the rest of us into thinking that the shape of faithfulness to the life of Jesus in which we share is to get bigger and look as much as possible like the most talked-about church of the decade. But becoming that church, for most of us, would require the application of techniques at odds with the way of life embodied in the culture of our particular places. It would require the stripping of the culture—which, as we have seen, is opposed to the story of Jesus. I might be able to produce a show-ring community in the place where I am, but I doubt that I can do it while respecting the place's right to judge, to have its say—and that is a judgment both the place and Jesus demand the place have. As Berry puts it: "I am saying only that the show ring alone cannot establish and maintain adequate standards for livestock breeders. You could not develop locally adapted strains if your only standards came from the show ring or from breed societies" (61). And, when it comes to the Gospel as embodied in particular communities, local adaptation is all there is.

The show-ring sheep or cow also reminds me of the so-called universal Gospel—Persha's mystery of grace—because it is an animal abstracted from any locality. It does not bear the marks of a place but seems to have derived from no place whatsoever. And so it could likely not live well in any place without accounting for the enormous cost of maintaining its viability and the cost that maintenance would have on the farm.

When "Let the Farm Judge" turns to the Berrys' own work of breeding sheep on their farm in Kentucky, I see a beautiful image of the patient, pastoral task of shaping evangelistic communities that are conformed, precisely in their particularity, to the life of the Jewish Messiah, Jesus, a life that made possible these communities' participation in the body of God's people without needing to abandon their own particularities and cultural identities. Berry recounts the problems of adapting a flock of Border Cheviot ewes to a farm in the lower Kentucky River valley. Because heavier animals often damage the hillsides, the Berrys decided that their farm needed sheep. In 1978, they bought six Border Cheviot ewes and a buck. In 1997, they had thirty ewes. He notes: "Our choice of breed was a good one. The Border Cheviot is a hill

232 L. Roger Owens

sheep, developed to make good use of such rough pasture as we have. Moreover, it can make good use of a little corn, and our farm is capable of producing a little corn. There have been problems, of course. Some of them have had to do with adapting ourselves to the breed. These have been important, but just as important have been the problems of adapting our flock to our farm" (59).

To the extent that raising sheep is like cultivating Christian communities in a particular place, Berry helps us see that the adaptation is mutual. While the Gospel does not require a place to strip itself of its particularity in order for it to participate in Christ's body, the Gospel also has a judgment of its own to make. The community being cultivated is a *Christian* community, and the shape of that community will challenge some indigenous practices of any culture. But the important point here is that, even with those cultural practices challenged, the community itself will still be recognizably of that place.

Berry continues:

> Our farm, then, is asking for a ewe that can stay healthy, live long, breed successfully, have two lambs without assistance, and feed them well, in comparatively demanding circumstances. Experience has shown us that the Border Cheviot breed is capable of producing a ewe of this kind, but that it does not do so inevitably. In eighteen years, and out of a good many ewes bought or raised, we have identified so far only two ewe families (the female descendents of two ewes) that fairly dependably perform as we and our place require. The results of identifying and keeping the daughters of these ewe families have been very satisfactory. This year [1997] they made up more than half of our bred ewes. Presumably because of that, our lambing percentage, which previously hovered around 150 percent, increased to 172 percent. This year we also reduced our winter hay-feeding by one month, not beginning until the first of February.

Over almost twenty years of watching and careful breeding, the Berrys have shaped their own flock of sheep to be healthy and productive by the standards of their farm. These sheep would not be healthy or productive on a farm anywhere else. But in that place they are just right. Neither would these sheep win prizes in show-ring competitions: "Some of the qualities we are after simply are not visible to show ring judges" (60).

Berry is offering what philosophers would call a *nonfoundationalist* approach to breeding sheep. There is no universal, perfect sheep, no Platonic ideal sheep—not even a blue-ribbon winner in the show ring—that can be a standard for health and productivity of all sheep everywhere. Health is largely relative. It is determined by how particular sheep fare under the circumstances of a particular place. And, with patience, over several years, the health and productivity of the sheep in a particular place can be improved by adapting the sheep to the local conditions and by adapting, when possible and necessary, the local conditions to the sheep. Saying that there is no universal healthy sheep by which to judge the health of other sheep is not the same thing as saying that the health of sheep cannot be judged. But that judgment will be made by the wisdom of a practitioner and not against the standards of an archetype.

I am suggesting that we should think of shaping Christian communities like adapting sheep to a farm. This image of adapting sheep to a place is more helpful to Christian mission and the pastoral work of shaping missional communities than is the language of enculturation. As we saw above, the language of enculturation implies a universal Gospel, itself untouched by any culture (a show-ring Gospel), that can wear the dress of any culture. But, just as there is no universal standard for a healthy sheep, so too there is no Gospel or Christian community that is not always and already enculturated. The health and productivity of a Christian community can be determined only with reference to its place and not to a universal Gospel or show-ring church. And, as with the health of sheep, so it is with the health of communities. Saying there is no universal expression of Christianity by which to judge the health of a Christian community is not the same as saying such health cannot be judged. But the judgment will be made by the wisdom of the pastor who knows the place, not against the abstract standards of a putative un-enculturated Gospel.

Evangelism in Place

How have we come from how writers on evangelism use the Incarnation to justify certain accounts of strategic enculturation of the Gospel to talk about raising sheep as a metaphor for the pastoral work of shaping communities of faithfulness? We got here by changing the pressing question. After we have abandoned the hope of locating a universal Gospel essence, the pressing practical question can no longer be, "How do you balance the need to enculturate the Gospel with the need to maintain the core of the Gospel?" Since the

Incarnation does not provide a principle to be applied but is a reality to be participated in, the pressing question becomes, "How do you shape communities faithful to the shape of the life of the Jewish Messiah, Jesus, in whose body they participate?"

Christianity has a Jewish Messiah who was and is still Jewish—a fact of embarrassment to some. Theologians of Christian evangelism have argued that Jesus needs to be unbound from his Jewishness so the universal Christ can be enculturated everywhere. We should no longer allow this mistake to be made. We should begin to wrestle with the fact that, whatever we mean by *Gospel,* Jesus' Jewishness is not accidental to it. It is not that, once you strip early Christianity of its Jewishness, you find that it can wear any cultural dress—that Jesus means something other than or beyond his being Jewish. Rather, the good news is that Gentiles have been invited to participate in the body of the Jewish Messiah without themselves having first to be stripped of their own cultural particularity.

Since this is the case, I want to offer one final reformulation of the guiding question for pastoral shapers of Christian communities: "What will be the communal shape of our faithfulness to and participation in the flesh of the Jew Jesus, given the particularities of this place, so that ours will not be a *mis*placed faithfulness?" Incarnation means it makes little sense to say that the Gospel must be enculturated because there is no unenculturated Gospel to enculturate. If I proclaim the Gospel in English to a group of Spanish speakers, the problem is not that the Gospel I am proclaiming is not enculturated—it certainly is. The problem is that it is the wrong sheep on the wrong farm. It is a misplaced Gospel embodiment. When this new question becomes the most pressing question for theologians of the church's evangelistic task—as it is now for me as a pastor and a theologian—then what I called the *divide between theory and practice* will have no place. Our modus operandi will no longer be making theological principles relevant to our practice. We will either be shaping or giving guidance to those who shape communities as they try, not to apply theological principles, but to embody the life of Jesus the Messiah.

Notes

1. Charles Hartshorne, *Omnipotence and Other Theological Mistakes* (Albany: State University of New York Press, 1984).

2. Wendell Berry, *Hannah Coulter* (Washington, DC: Shoemaker & Hoard, 2004), 128, 131.

3. Dana Robert, *Evangelism at the Heart of Mission,* Mission Evangelism Series, no. 1 (New York: General Board of Global Ministries of the United Methodist Church, 1997), 5, quoted in Scott J. Jones, *The Evangelistic Love of God and Neighbor* (Nashville: Abingdon, 2003), 121.

4. Jones, *Evangelistic Love,* 124.

5. Tex Sample, *Blue Collar Resistance and the Politics of Jesus: Doing Ministry with Working Class Whites* (Nashville: Abingdon, 2006), 4.

6. Darrell Guder, "Incarnation and the Church's Evangelistic Mission," *International Review of Mission* 83, no. 330 (1994): 421, 422.

7. Lesslie Newbigin, *Foolishness to the Greeks: The Gospel and Western Culture* (Grand Rapids, MI: Eerdmans, 1986), 4. Elsewhere he has written: "If we accept the fact that the gospel is a factual story about what God has done, we have immediately to say that that story has to be told in human language. And language is the very heart of culture. It is the key to culture. And therefore there is no gospel which is not already embodied in a culture" (Lesslie Newbigin, *Signs amid the Rubble: The Purposes of God in Human History,* ed. Geoffrey Wainwright [Grand Rapids, MI: Eerdmans, 2003], 116).

8. Jerry Persha, "Toward Developing an Adequate and Comprehensive Understanding of Evangelization," *Missiology* 14, no. 3 (1986): 284.

9. Ibid., 278.

10. John Howard Yoder, *The Jewish-Christian Schism Revisited,* ed. Michael G. Cartwright and Peter Ochs (Grand Rapids, MI: Eerdmans, 2003), 75.

11. Wendell Berry, "Let the Farm Judge," in *Citizenship Papers* (Washington, DC: Shoemaker & Hoard, 2003), 57. Page numbers for subsequent citations will be given parenthetically in the text.

Part 4

Moving Forward

Charles R. Pinches

Democracy, America, and the Church

Inviting Wendell Berry into the Discussion

The question of how Christians should participate in the politics of America has been posed lately with a special urgency, although with little clarity. Almost everyone has something to say on the matter. Yet, if one listens a while, the talk seems to break apart into little bits of propaganda, drawn from one or the other side of the culture wars. In theological circles, however, the discussion has taken a particularly interesting turn of late, after the publication of Jeffery Stout's *Democracy and Tradition*.[1] Stout sets about to ask the big question, What, after all, is democracy in America? And he answers that it is not a great idea, or even a system of government, but rather a *tradition*. An important result of his defense of the tradition of democracy in America is his call for Christians, particularly Christians like the well-known American theologian Stanley Hauerwas, to participate in the tradition.

To be honest, Stout does more than invite Hauerwas into the democratic tradition; he excoriates him for criticizing democracy (and liberalism) in a reckless way so as to diminish a tradition that Stout himself loves dearly and thinks needs strengthening, particularly at this time in American history. All this has not been lost on Hauerwas, who has responded to Stout's critique at some length. In this essay, I want critically to consider both Stout's and Hauerwas's viewpoints on America and democracy. As Hauerwas has responded to Stout, another big question has risen to the surface: Who are Christians, and what is the church? This, actually, is a bigger question than Stout's, What is (American) democracy? We cannot hope to settle it in the few pages that follow. Yet it is important to get both questions out on the table, for they are what is at stake in the current discussion, not just between Stout and Hauerwas, but in the cacophony of voices one hears today swirling around them. With regard to these other voices, this essay has another point than carefully considering what Stout and Hauerwas have to say. One voice in particular—that of Wendell Berry—stands apart from the sloganry and folderol about America, democracy, and the Christian church. I hope to move the discussion in Berry's direction. Doing so will correct and sharpen what both Stout and Hauerwas have to say about the big questions posed above.

Discussing *Democracy and Tradition*

In *Democracy and Tradition,* Stout opposes what he calls the "anti-modern traditionalist" critique of modern democratic societies, namely, that these societies have become "morally and spiritually empty."[2] The "traditionalism" whose criticisms of democracy Stout means to oppose encompasses the likes of Edmund Burke and Pope Pius IX but also the "new traditionalists," in particular the triad of John Milbank, Alasdair MacIntyre, and Stanley Hauerwas. Of these, Hauerwas seems a special target. With him, Stout's critique takes on a personal urgency and extends over almost two chapters, while Milbank and MacIntyre get only one apiece. As Hauerwas later says in response: "Stout's criticisms of Milbank and MacIntyre serve to introduce his critique of my position."[3]

Stout's strategy to oppose these three so-called traditionalists is to show that democracy in America is, in fact, a morally substantive tradition, one that remains alive today, even if in need of the concerted attention of civically minded Americans. If Stout can convincingly show this, he can blunt the criticisms of democracy from the traditionalists—since, after all, democracy in America has what they think is necessary for a viable social community. Moreover, he can turn round to generously offer the traditionalists a place at the democratic table, where, he thinks, their voices are both welcome and needed.

Stout's defense of democracy in America is an interesting one. He accepts the postmodern critique of an Enlightenment rationality that sees history or tradition as a moral encumbrance to the establishment of a good and just society. Like his three stated opponents, Stout believes that "tradition"— which is to say, roughly, the passage of a body of virtues and moral practices and a discourse about human life and society from one generation to the next—is essential to the establishment of a just and proper social order. Furthermore, like Hauerwas and the others, Stout acknowledges that many defenders of democracy have missed this point and, armed with a skewed and narrow understanding of what "reasonable persons" believe, have tried to dismiss religious traditions from the democratic conversation. Finally, Stout's defense of democracy in America is interesting because it is honestly critical of it. While he defends it against the attack of the three theologians, Stout acknowledges that the modern democratic tradition is not presently in the best shape in America, where the plight of the poor is largely being ignored and we are retreating into enclaves defined by race or lifestyle.[4]

Perhaps partly because of this last point, Stout chastises the new traditionalists, not only for failing to identify democracy as a rightful tradition, but also for thoughtlessly damaging its best elements by refusing, as religious thinkers, to take a place within it as valuable members of a coalition for a better American society. Stout recalls such coalitions personally:

> I came of age ethically, politically, and spiritually in the Civil Rights movement, where I acquired my democratic commitments from prophetic ministers. In college, when I moved rapidly down the path that leads from Schleiermacher to Fauerbach, Emerson and beyond, I found myself collaborating mainly with dissenting Protestants, secular Jews and members of the radical Catholic underground in the struggle against U.S. involvement in the Vietnam War. I have known since then that it is possible to build democratic coalitions including people who differ religiously and to explore those differences deeply and respectfully without losing one's integrity as a critical intellect. This book is offered in the hope that similarly diverse coalitions and equally full expression of differences remain possible in democratic culture today, if we can only summon the will to form them.[5]

This is the problem with Stanley Hauerwas—and perhaps the main reason Stout's criticisms are directed principally at him. He is not summoning his will. If he would, he could do a great deal of good since he is, according to Stout, "the most influential theologian now working in the United States."[6] But he is not using this influence in America rightly. To the contrary, in his teaching and writing, he is turning out a generation of students and readers whose attentions have been taken in other directions entirely, some of them apparently quite antithetical to the democratic hope that Stout so personally and poignantly expresses.

One might be surprised after reading Stout's book that he and Hauerwas are friends. In Hauerwas's most developed response to Stout, he reports that, when he finished reading the book in manuscript form, he "called Jeff asking where I could possibly find his democracy materially instantiated. He replied I could find his democracy instantiated in the same place you could find my account of the church."[7]

I take it as interesting that these two could have this conversation and that both could laugh knowingly. In the conversation, each presses the other for concreteness, albeit at different locations. "Show me the body!" they say to each other. It is interesting because each is otherwise known, indeed, seems to want to be known, as a sort of pragmatist who champions the concrete and particular.

Hauerwas otherwise offers *Democracy and Tradition* high praise. Indeed, he suggests a practical outcome, a sort of next step: "Put bluntly, this is a position with which we Christians not only can, but should want to, do business. Stout does try to give an account of democratic life that is not in the first place state theory. I am extremely sympathetic with that project. Stout's understanding of practical reason, the centrality of the virtues, as well as the democratic tradition not only makes it possible for us to have a conversation, but makes such a conversation imperative."[8]

Hauerwas reminds us here of the significance of what Stout has done. His defense of democracy in America does not rest on nebulous terms like *freedom* or *individual rights*. Rather, Stout tells a story of a democratic tradition in America that he self-consciously and passionately claims. He believes as well that this tradition is at least partly sustained by Christians who think and act as if theology matters, and he welcomes their voices, even solicits them. Philosophically, he avoids such invented ideas or terms as the *original position* of John Rawls, turning instead to a historically continuous community that carries along a triad of virtues (piety, hope, and love), a company of heroes (Emerson, Whitman, and Dewey), and a variety of practices, including playing and coaching athletics in places like Princeton, New Jersey. (Stout, in fact, dedicates his book to a soccer coach in that place.) Christians in America need such an account, not only to compare with their own commitments— for instance, Christians might ask how the love in Stout's triad relates to Paul's account in 1 Corinthians 13 or Aquinas's in the *Summa*—but also to remind them of the many ways their own lives are sustained by good and concrete American practices they neither invented nor exclusively sustain.

That Hauerwas considers Stout's position one Christians need to do business with suggests that more talk is yet to come. American democrats and Christians should welcome the prospect that the likes of Stout and Hauerwas will continue their discussion. But the point remains from the phone conversation. What could it mean for Hauerwas to ask, with sense, for the "instantiation" of Stout's democratic tradition? And why could Stout turn this around, also with some success, and ask for something similar from Hauerwas about the church? It is on these points that I think help is needed from Wendell Berry. To extend the doing-business metaphor, if Stout and Hauerwas decide to sit down to share a business lunch, I should like to see whether I can get Wendell Berry invited. There is indication that both Hauerwas and Stout would welcome Berry's presence. Hauerwas's recent writing is dotted with positive references to Berry.[9] In *Democracy and Tradition*, Stout offers Berry's work high praise, calling him "a gifted practitioner of observational social criticism."[10] Yet, despite this awareness and good feeling, there is less evidence in Stout's and Hauerwas's work that they have listened to Berry as carefully as they might, as I hope we shall see in what follows.

Piety and Memory in America—Stout to Berry

Throughout his book, Stout works to disassociate the democratic tradition he defends from the broad scope of the term *liberal;* indeed, he wishes that Hauerwas and others would simply stop using the word. Yet the connection may not be so easy to break. In his response to Stout, Hauerwas sees fit to recall two points that he came to understand about liberalism in his own intellectual journey—both still relevant. The first point is about the disembodiment implied by the liberal understanding of human agency whereby an actor's bodily actions and his agency could be held at a distance. The second point, linked to the first, is about the irrelevance of *memory* to what he calls "liberal politics and ethics." He speaks biographically about coming to see this point:

> I became convinced that any attempt to recover the significance of the virtues required a moral psychology that displayed how our actions are constituted by our agency. It seemed to me at the time that most accounts of moral action, accounts I think that reflected a moral psychology thought necessary to sustain liberal regimes, made it also impossible to recover Aristotle's understanding of activity. This is because most liberal theory, both political and ethical, depended upon being able to *separate action from agent.* That separation, moreover, had everything to do with the liberal attempt to form a *politics and ethics without memory.*[11]

Hauerwas does not systematically pursue his comments about disembodied agency and memory and never takes them directly to Stout's text. However, he makes a further remark about each that helps fill out the picture. Regarding embodiment, he observes:

[The] problem was not whether liberalism could give some account of the virtues, but rather what virtues were recommended. I long ago suggested, for example, that one of the primary intellectual virtues for liberalism is cynicism. I thought such a virtue to be correlative of the demand for autonomy that assumes I must always be able to step back from my engagements. What I "do" is, therefore, not "who I am." As a result my body is only secondarily "me" because my body is primarily something I use. To be habituated to be "free" in this sense makes it difficult for those so formed to recommend how they have learned to live to others. We each have to become the managers of our lives.

With regard to memory, he comments further:

The fundamental problem with liberalism, and I suppose I mean by liberalism primarily liberal theory, has been the attempt to suppress memory in the interest of eliminating conflict. Yet I believe it impossible not to be what we were made to be, whether we are Christian or not, which means we cannot live without memory. Indeed I think there is a kind of "natural law" effect—that is, there will be negative results—when people attempt to suppress the wrongs of the past in the interest of cooperation. I do believe, after all, that the cross is the grain of the universe.[12]

Somewhat surprisingly for him, in these comments Hauerwas suggests that certain things are natural about us as human beings—and, therefore, irrepressible. We suppress them to our great peril. And the two liberalism suppresses are our bodies and our memories. Put in relation one to the other, if we hope to remember well, we will need first to recall that we are more than mere spirit: we are body.

Memory and embodiment both are necessarily communal. As Alan Verhey marks: "The body itself links us to others, first on the level of natural relationships. Everyone is someone's child. No one is a self alone."[13] Verhey worries that, as we have forgotten that we are bodily in the modern world, so we have forgotten our connectedness to one another. Recollection of ourselves as bodily creatures keeps our delusions of self-sufficiency and independence in check since it is impossible to think that we are the makers of our own bodies. Indeed, we receive our bodily life not from just anyone but from two particular people, namely, our mother and father. And this connection to our parents reminds us that we are the inheritors of a past, a specific past, to which we are linked throughout our lives by memory. Memory, in fact, begins in family and extends outward to clan, tribe, and people. Hauerwas's comments suggest that the liberal self disconnects us from these things, from the concrete communities that tie us by our bodies to a particular past. So liberalism will of necessity encourage in us a fundamental forgetfulness of what has gone before.

The relevance of this point to Stout's democracy is simply that we shall need to check its body and memory, especially if, as Stout hopes, it styles itself as a tradition. Specifically, we shall have to check its connection to a past. Stout is aware of this and addresses it in the final section of his first chapter, a section entitled "Piety Reconceived." As he tells us, of the three cardinal democratic virtues—piety, hope, and love—piety is the one that "looks toward the past."[14]

Piety has traditionally related to what we owe to specific parties who have gone before us in life, such as our parents. Aquinas takes it to be about our parents and, he adds, "our country" since both have given us "birth and nourishment."[15] The relations of piety in Confucianism are even more specific and elaborate. Piety, or *hsiao* in that tradition, extends over the father-son, the brother-brother, the prince-subject, the friend-friend, and the husband-wife relations. It governs these relations in subtly different ways, although, as Herbert Fingarette notes, they all are "ultimately sanctified by virtue of their place in *li*," which is, as he elaborates, a kind of ceremonial performance that gathers up social relations, bestowing on them a sacred and transforming power. Piety in Confucianism, therefore, regards not only specific relations but also how gifts are given and received within them in such specific settings as a family meal. Fingarette quotes Confucius in the *Analects*, "merely to feed one's parents well . . . even dogs and horses are fed" (2.7), and adds this gloss: "To be devoted to one's parents is far more than to keep the parents alive physically. To serve and eat in the proper way, with proper respect and appreciation, in the proper setting—this is to transform the act of mere nourishment into the human ceremony of dining."[16]

The specificity of Aquinas or Confucius is lacking in Stout's account of democratic piety. He gives no clear direction about to whom piety binds us, nor does he say how it governs and directs what is done in our relations with them. Rather, he opens his discussion by telling us that Walt Whitman was much concerned with "how the poets of democracy ought to conceive, and respond to, the sources of our existence and progress through life. This constituted much of his literary business. Hence, he has much to say about piety. For piety, in the sense at issue here, is virtuous acknowledgement of dependence on the sources of one's existence and progress through life. When traditionalists conclude that democracy is antithetical to piety itself, they must be assuming that piety consists essentially in deference toward the hierarchical powers that be."[17]

Stout makes two unfortunate moves in this passage; even more unfortunately, they stay with him throughout his treatment of democratic piety. First, he settles on the phrase "sources of our existence and progress through life," which becomes almost formulaic in the section, never admitting of substitution or further elaboration. Its meaning is actually quite difficult to decipher. For instance, how are we to understand what he means by "progress through life"? Is it simply that we are making it along the way, from birth to death? Or are we progressing in the sense that we are getting better, better than when we ourselves began, and better, progressively, than those who went before? Beyond this, however, the phrase specifies no one in particular to whom our piety is owed. As we have been discussing, piety needs specification. Who or what are these "sources" toward which democracy trains me to be pious?

This lack of specificity is accented later when Stout relates piety to gratitude: "Gratitude, not loyalty or deference, is, for the tradition of Emersonian perfectionism, the better part of piety."[18] This move, from piety to gratitude, seems fitting. In the *Summa,* for instance, Aquinas turns to gratitude almost immediately after discussing piety. They are related. Yet, perhaps even more than piety, gratitude requires a target. We are grateful for specific gifts given. But, since Stout's vague "sources of our existence and progress through life" have guided piety, they must stand in as well for gratitude. But what does gratitude offered to these sources mean, concretely? And, moreover, does gratitude or piety offered to these "sources" bind us communally in any clear way?

There is a second problem. In the quote given above (and elsewhere), Stout sets his democratic, self-reliant piety over against another sort of piety that he thinks includes "deference towards the hierarchical powers that be." Democratic piety is "a kind of piety entirely distinct from acquiescence in the dominant practices and institutions or their natural setting simply because they are there. It is a self-conscious identification, undertaken on the part of the individual who, thinking for him- or herself, acknowledges that on which his or her self-reliant judgment depends."[19] Moreover, Stout assumes that his three new traditionalists operate with a notion of piety that is of the second sort, the "deference piety." As the quotation given above reads: "When traditionalists conclude that democracy is antithetical to piety itself, they must be assuming that piety consists essentially in deference toward the hierarchical powers that be."

Stout operates here with a caricature of traditionalist or religious people that has nothing to do with his three opponents. Anyone who knows them or their work also knows that it is simply impossible to find Stout's kind of deference in anything Milbank, MacIntyre, and Hauerwas have said or done. Stout here falls into conventional assumptions all about power and subservience and authoritarianism by means of which he dismisses what he takes to be an overly traditionalist outlook on the past. A corrupt "hierarchical power" might try to use piety to family or country or church to make his minions serve his every whim. But that is *not* how piety works in Confucius, or in Aquinas, or, for that matter, within any vital religious tradition. Rather, such relations—including the deference shown within them, which is always subtle and varied—matter because they sustain the rich and specific moral landscape in which the particularities of human relations of various sorts can be worked through. As a start, they sustain the relations between parents and children that enable moral training to occur, wisdom to be passed on, and gratefulness to be specifically extended.

In sum, Stout's portrayal of democratic piety heightens rather than allays concerns expressed by Hauerwas about liberalism's loss of embodiment and memory. It deepens worries that Stout's democratic tradition will treat the past as largely faceless, gathering it into time-honored principles like respect for persons or gratitude for vague companies who contributed to our "progress through life." Put another way, if the alleged democratic tradition does not tie each of us to embodied human beings who have given us our lives, it is difficult to imagine what piety or gratefulness can even mean. Such looseness and lack of specificity among a people can easily be turned, as one might argue has occurred in America, to talk about personhood or freedom that can be shouted but never parsed. Hauerwas's cleverly titled article "My Uncle

Charlie Is Not Much of a Person but He Is Still My Uncle Charlie" is pointed exactly at this faceless tendency in modern life.[20] We need a way to speak about what we owe to Uncle Charlie, and Stout's democratic piety does not provide it.

If both piety and gratitude need specific targets, memory also does, even more so. Memory, after all, is carried by story, and vague principles or unspecified allegiances carry no memory at all.[21] For Wendell Berry, healthy human living must connect to the remembered past, a past that is not ours to make or reform as we see fit but rather a story to which we belong: "If we were lucky enough as children to be surrounded by grown-ups who loved us, then our sense of wholeness is not just the sense of completeness in ourselves but also the sense of belonging to others and to our place; it is an unconscious awareness of community, of having in common. It may be that this double sense of singular integrity and of communal belonging is our personal standard of health as long as we live."[22] If we are to belong in Berry's sense, our ties to the past through memory must be particular and direct. We must be able to name the ones who hold us in this pattern of timeful human life. We belong not to everyone but to our family, our neighborhood, and our people. We belong not to any place but to a specific one.

In Berry's novelette *Remembering*, Andrew Catlett loses his right hand in a picker when he and other men from Port William are harvesting corn for a neighbor in need. The loss wounds him deeply, as it should. He needs to find his way back to wholeness, health, although this obviously cannot happen by the restoration of his hand. In this state of bodily loss, Andy is tempted by another kind of loss or alienation. Although he remains tied by family and land to Port William, he is an academic agriculturalist who travels in the floating world of academic papers and conferences that could be held anywhere. Much of the story takes place in a hotel room in San Francisco—although it could have been anywhere. Here, Andy is tempted to translate his rage at the loss of his hand into the modern alienation from body that occurs in strange hotel rooms and cities across America where countless, nameless men and women traverse back and forth, back and forth, without leaving footprints.

A decisive turn in the story comes when the organizer of an academic agricultural conference Andy recently attended (he remembers all this in his troubled sleeplessness in the hotel) introduces him as from "Fort" rather than Port William. This unleashes Andy's anger, and he begins his speech as follows: "What we have discussed here this morning is an agriculture of the mind. No farmer is here. No farmer has been mentioned. . . . The real interest of this meeting is in the academic careerism and the politics and the business of agriculture, and I daresay that most people here, like the first speaker, are proud to have escaped the life and work of farmers, whom they do not admire." He goes on to tell the conference participants about his grandmother, Dorie Catlett, who, together with her husband, had received a bill from the warehouse for $3.57 at the end of the farming season of 1906. A year's hard work on the land, and they earned a negative $3.57. Dorie had turned this bill over, the same bill Andy later found in an old bureau drawer, and written, "Oh, Lord, whatever is to become of us?" and then, "Out of the depths have I cried to thee, O Lord."[23]

Andy concludes his speech with a list of names that those who have read Berry's many novels immediately recognize: "I speak for Dorie Catlett and Marce Catlett. I speak for Mat and Margaret Feltner, for Jack Beechum, for Jarret and Burley Coulter. . . ."[24] The point that Andy (and Berry) is making is that he is not Andy alone but with all these others; he does not live and farm in any place but rather Port (not Fort) William. What Andy cannot initially see, what Berry takes the novelette to show him and us, is that sharing with these others means also sharing in their deep disappointments and grief. He must learn to cry out with his grandmother "Out of the depths have I cried to thee, O Lord"—that is, if he is once again to become whole without his right hand. He can do this only as he learns to remember not only his own history but also that of those who went before, stretching back to his grandparents, who had lost $3.57 for the year, but also to the generation before that had first come to the land and worked it.

It is the specificity of this story remembered, and its location in the life of particular bodies and land, that keeps memory from being cheapened into nostalgia. (Indeed, if there is a "natural law" outcome to the loss of memory in our modern context, it is this: the growth of nostalgia.) Moreover, as Berry's story suggests, as specified, truthful memory cannot but enter into the loss, failure, disappointment, and even sinfulness that is part of human life and community. For Andy in *Remembering*, the connection to this past brings him round to recognizing his own sin, his failure, for instance, to trust his wife, Flora, who held their life together as Andy in his anger was strongly tempted to sink into the modern sea of forgetfulness surrounding him.

One might suppose that the sort of connection to the past that Berry portrays in his story *Remembering* is only about farming life, where particular families pass on particular land. Yet this is a mistake about what I believe Berry is pressing in all his Port William stories. Without Port William, there is no America—which is to say, not merely that America is built on places like Port William (which is true enough), but, more significantly, that participation in the place we call *America* is facile, unreal unless one does it in and through a place such as Port William.

So this is what I wish Stout would learn from Wendell Berry. Insofar as democratic piety requires us to name no names, to connect with no specific neighbors or parents or grandparents or children, it floats over the land that is America like the disembodied spirits we have seen Hauerwas earlier mention. The democrat who is grateful for no more than the "sources of [his] progress through life" dangles detached, even cynical, imagining that, with a brief bow and a wave to the past, he can get on with that progress as he himself defines it.

Moreover, such a person will be tempted to smugly imagine that the conflict of the past can be kept there, and, thus, as Hauerwas worried, democracy will "suppress memory in the interest of eliminating conflict." Wendell Berry's book about racism in America, *The Hidden Wound*, has rightly caught Jeffrey Stout's attention as exemplary.[25] Stout has throughout his career spoken out against the evils of slavery in America. And, to his credit, the second chapter of *Democracy and Tradition* deals not with Emerson, Whitman, and Dewey but with James Baldwin and Ralph Waldo Ellison, black storytellers who, Stout thinks, fit squarely within the democratic tradition. Theirs are stories that arise in the midst of suffering, the specific and named suffering of slavery and racism that was visited on one people by another in America.

However, Stout has not learned from Berry's book as he might. His interest in Ellison or Baldwin is less about how they might help us remember and name a great sin whose effects we have all endured and more about how Ellison and Baldwin show that democracy makes room for measured critique, a critique that does not go so far that it cancels itself in a contraction. It does this by holding on to a "hope of making a difference for the better by democratic means."[26] But what sort of hope is this? Like Stout's piety, this hope names no names, refers to no bodies. It seems to dangle in the air, perhaps the stale air of an academic meeting room in a hotel somewhere in America.

Stout has missed that the reason Berry's *Hidden Wound* is "the best book on race by a white writer" is because it does not speak in abstractions about race but is rather Berry's quite personal attempt to understand his own and his family's complicity in the sin of racism, primarily through the quite real person of Bart Jenkins, a violent slave trader to whom Berry's great-grandfather once sold a slave and who later was eulogized by a white Southern writer named Mosgrove as a model of the best in Southern virtue.[27] Included within it is the story of the quite real black man named Nick Watkins who came to work on Berry's grandfather's farm when Berry was three years old. Berry came to love Nick, although even as a young lad he felt the sad racist distance that separated them.

In sum, if democracy in America is, indeed, a tradition (Stout does well to try to show that it is one, less well in actually convincing us on the points mentioned), it cannot be carried along in our minds by an unspecified gratefulness for our "progress through life" but must rather draw us into direct contact with what we have inherited, the good and the bad, from particular people to whom we are connected (like it or not) by story. Short of that, piety and memory in a democratic society are ripe for takeover by formal and vacuous ideas or sappy and nostalgic sentiments. Both will bar the door to either gratitude for the good gifts we have received from those who have gone before or truthfulness about what curses we bear.

Body and Work in the Church: Hauerwas to Berry

Stout is deeply distressed that his friend Stanley Hauerwas, with his resounding critique of liberalism and his talk otherwise about "letting the church be the church," has in effect convinced Christians to retreat into the church, setting aside any sense of responsibility for the state of democracy in America. While it is clear throughout Hauerwas's corpus that he wants to convince American Christians that their principal loyalty must be to the church and not to America, he does this a good bit because they seem to think otherwise. Or, perhaps better put, they have, many of them, even forgot that the church is a distinct community at all whose charge is to be the body of Christ in the world.

Hauerwas's principal questions—about what it means for the church to be the body of Christ in any place and how, in a particular place like America, it should join in the people's life—are intrinsically more difficult and theologically intricate questions than those Stout asks about democracy in America. Moreover, initially, it is less clear what he might learn from Wendell Berry about what the church is, especially since Berry does not seem to belong to one.

Nevertheless, his writing is actually full of insights about the church that Berry presents by criticizing it—what one might call a sort of *negative ecclesiology.* He shows us churches in America that have failed. Or, alternatively, he shows us vital communities that aren't the church but might be.

In *The Unsettling of America,* which Stout calls the "most important book on environmental ethics ever written," in the extraordinary essay at the center of the book entitled "The Body and the Earth," Berry refers once again to health—the same health to which, after losing his hand, Andrew Catlett must be restored by remembering.[28] Here, he draws out the connection between the human body and the body of the earth: "If the body is healthy, then it is whole. But how can it be whole and yet be dependent, as it obviously is, upon other bodies and upon the earth, upon all the rest of Creation? . . . Our bodies are also not distinct from the bodies of other people, on which they depend in a complexity of ways from the biological to the spiritual."[29]

For Berry, the abuse and waste of the environment is tied directly to the waste of the physical human body. Moreover, this is tied to a mentality (perhaps even a tradition) that he associates with "institutional religion":

> It is clear to anyone who looks carefully at any crowd that we are wasting our bodies exactly as we are wasting our land. . . . Our bodies have become marginal; they are growing useless like our "marginal" land because we have less and less use for them. . . . This separation of the soul from the body and from the world is no disease of the fringe, no aberration, but a fracture that runs through the mentality of institutional religion like a geographical fault. And this rift in the mentality of religion continues to characterize the modern mind, no matter how secular and worldly it becomes.

These comments remind us that (as Hauerwas agrees) the loss of memory and the loss of body are related losses. Both also include a loss of the deep dependency we have one on another, by body and through time. On Berry's view, the geologic fault in modern thought and life separating body from soul accounts for both. And their division has deep root in religious faith of one kind or another. Berry goes on to make his point more exactly and also to qualify it vis-à-vis the Bible:

But I have not stated my point exactly enough. This rift is not like a geological fault; it is a geological fault. It is a flaw in the mind that runs inevitably into the earth. Thought affects or afflicts substance neither by intention nor by accident, but because, occurring in the Creation that is unified and whole, it must; there is no help for it. The soul in its loneliness hopes only for "salvation." And yet, what is the burden of the Bible if not a sense of the mutuality of the influence, rising out of the essential unity, among soul and body and community and world? These are the works of God, and it is therefore the work of virtue to make or restore harmony among them.[30]

Berry's alienation from institutional religion may rest somewhat uneasily with his love for the Bible. Yet we can see what has offended him. The salvation that Christians have sometimes offered has been a kind of death precisely as it detaches the saved soul from body and land. Healthy people whose lives depend on one another and the land will resist it.

Berry's novel *A Place on Earth* is a long and subtle story of how the people of Port William cope with sad losses that come with drastic disturbances such as war or flood or even those that come more quietly like the loss of strength in old age. Mat and Margaret Feltner are at the center of the story; early on in it their son Virgil is reported missing in action in World War II. Shortly after the news comes, they are visited in their home by Brother Preston, the local minister. They greet him warmly, as is their way, and sit with him politely as he offers words of consolation. Yet they do not really listen:

The preacher's voice, rising, rides above all chances of mortal and worldly hope, hastening to rest in the hope of heaven. In the preacher's words the Heavenly City has risen up, surmounting their lives, their house, the town—the final hope, in which all the riddles and ends of the world are gathered, illuminated and bound. This is the preacher's hope, and he is moved to it alone, outside the claims of time and sorrow, by the motion of desire which he calls faith. In it, having invoked it and raised it up, he is free of the world.

This is neither Mat's nor Margaret's faith or hope. The conversation, such as it is, stalls and mercifully ends. After it, Brother Preston returns to his church: "Unviolated now by any presence but his own, the old church seems to Brother Preston to stand erect and coherent, enclosing him. As though the racket he made opening the door signaled a division between the church and the town, the sanctuary is now filled with quiet. He returns to his church where he can be alone." He senses that the visit has not gone all that well. What he hoped would be a conversation had become a sermon: "This was the history of his life in Port William. The Word, in his speaking it, fails to be made flesh. It is a failure particularized for him at the church door every Sunday morning—the hard dark hand taking his pale unworn one in a gesture of politeness without understanding. He belongs to the governance of those he ministers to without belonging to their knowledge, the bringer of the Word preserved from flesh."[31]

Berry is speaking as a theologian in these passages but also in criticism of the church. Many of us will receive his critique gladly, accustomed as we are to the critiques of individual soul salvation. And it is a critique of that. Yet there is something more here. As Berry believes, the body is land. If the Word became flesh, it also became soil, dirt. And this means that the Word must work with the dirt, share the toil of the day—which is the difficult but redeeming work of caring for the land and for one another in our local communities. This is what Brother Preston holds himself above, with his pale, unworn hands. Burley Coulter later reports in a letter to his nephew Nathan, who is also at war in Europe, that he knew all of what Brother Preston had to say to Mat and Margaret, and its emptiness, since the minister had visited him before when his own son Tom had died: "None of it quite fit. . . . Here in a way he'd come to say the last words over Tom. And what claim did he have to do it? He never done a day's work in his life, nor could have. He never did stand up in his ache and sweat and go down the row with us. He never tasted any of our sweat in the water jug. And I was thinking: Preacher, who are you to speak of Tom to me, who knew him, and knew the very smell of him?"[32]

The church is not the land, but it must work with the land if it is to speak to the people whose lives depend on it. If, indeed, as Hauerwas rightly sees in his critical comments about liberalism in response to Stout—that it is an attempt "to form a politics and ethics without memory" and, thus, also without embodiment—then he may need to consider more thoroughly how the body and the land come to play in Christian memory.

One thing this will involve is that Christians will need to confess, with others, their complicity in the abuses of the land, which is not merely an environmental point. As Berry does in *The Hidden Wound*, Christians in America will need to ask about their own participation in racism. Insofar as one is born on and nourished daily by the land that is America, the same land whose wealth in Lincoln's time—and, thus, also even yet today in our own—was "piled by the bondsman's two hundred and fifty years of unrequited toil," then the remembering is also not only participatory but required for all who continue to live on this land.[33] If you are an American, you are obliged to know and care about American slavery and its deep and scarring effects. The church cannot insulate or hold us aloof from this.

To return to the debate between Hauerwas and Stout, here is where Stout has a point. Hauerwas's fiery and trenchant critique of liberalism sometimes seems to hold him aloof from accounting for America as a history and a land, as if the two, liberalism and America, could be dismissed as a twin set of bad ideas, perhaps even as the same bad idea. (Indeed, at one point in his book *A Better Hope*, Hauerwas follows MacIntyre in labeling America as "not just a country but a metaphysical entity.")[34] Stout is better off chiding him on this point, rather than that he should feel obliged to join in the democratic process in order that we can together "make a difference for the better by democratic means."[35] The appeal must be that, insofar as Hauerwas has lived his whole life long off the soil of this land, insofar as he was, like Berry, born a white man in the American South, insofar as he today crisscrosses this wide but bounded land speaking in each engagement to an assortment of locals who are not just church people but American teachers or businesspeople or doctors and nurses who daily live and remember the particular American story of that particular locale, then he cannot opt out of what one might simply call his *patriotic obligations.* (Here I leave what is patriotic open, for there is great danger in circumscribing it too narrowly. The best way to put it is that, as an American, Hauerwas owes other Americans an explanation of how what he says and does contributes to America's common life.)[36] It seems to me, in other words, that Hauerwas is tempted—as I have also suggested Stout is tempted, although in a different way—to forget that his body is part of America's body.

Hauerwas is not unaware of this challenge. In the first few pages of *A Better Hope*, he says: "I am also an American. As much as I might like—as a Texan or as a Christian—to deny or avoid that I am an American, I know that such denial would be self-deceptive."[37] This seems like a genuine and moving profession. Nevertheless, as Stout observes, the index of that book "contains more than twenty listings under the term 'liberalism.'"[38]

Hauerwas has claimed, with some sense, that liberalism is actually not his main target, even in his attacks against liberalism: "The object of my criticism of liberalism has never been liberals, but rather to give Christians renewed confidence in the convictions that make our service intelligible. From my perspective the problem is not liberalism but the assumption on the part of many Christians that they must become liberals or, at least, accept liberal political principles and/or practices to be of service in America."[39]

I do not mean to imply that Hauerwas, a churchman, should not try to protect the church by opposing certain ideas or people who threaten its life. But it seems to me that he can and should do so directly, without the excursion that draws up different standards for who can be expected to think what. Features of what Hauerwas calls *liberalism* are dangerous to our common life, at various levels, and ought to be opposed in the various ways they threaten, both in and outside the church. When we do this, however, it seems unnecessary to accent that the origin of the dangerous idea is in liberalism. Perhaps the best, most embodied thing to do is simply to name the person carrying the idea and try to show him and others why it is wrong.

In Berry's story "Fidelity," a man named Kyle Bode comes sniffing around Port William. He is a cop who has come to investigate the disappearance of Burley Coulter (in his eighties in this story), who was vegetating helplessly in a hospital and so has been taken secretly (and illegally) by his remaining son, Danny, back to his own place, where he can die in peace and communion. Burley's relatives, friends, and neighbors in Port William resist Bode's intrusions. Better put, they resist the terms in which his intrusions are phrased. Bode is full of what Hauerwas would call *liberal moralisms*, all about violations of rights and the following of proper procedures.[40] The people of Port William do not like him one bit. Yet they endure him. When he visits their homes, they answer his questions and extend to him the courtesies of a guest—albeit without great enthusiasm. They even welcome him to their final gathering in Wheeler's law office after Danny, hidden from the view of the intrusive Bode by the community's resistance, has laid Burley to rest in a grave he dug for him by hand. During the gathering, Bode forgets himself for a moment as he glimpses the deep humanity that runs round the circle of gathered family and friends. He is drawn in by the memories they share of Burley's life, each remembered story lovingly yet also truthfully told—important since Burley was no saint. This way of speaking, of a people gathered together to remember in words the real life of a man lived out in the community and on its land, is all new to him, but also somehow familiar.

These Port William citizens treat Kyle Bode directly as a human being, one who has come into their neighborhood. To be sure, they bristle at his stupidities that show how wildly he misunderstands their lives, and they mark quite directly where and why they cannot adopt his language. He is a liberal in the sense that he carries with him a notion of individual freedom and rights that makes Burley's death a murder, one nameless person of another, rather than an act of faithfulness of a son and his community to a dying father and friend. But they do not think of him first as a liberal; rather, he is Kyle Bode. As his weakening in the last scene shows, perhaps he is less liberal than he appears.[41] Insofar as he is an embodied human being here in the midst of this circle of friends, that is enough; it is the basis, anyway, on which they will deal with him. The greatest resource that holds him and them in this position is that they share a common life on the land and the memory of what has gone before that holds them in this place.

The embrace that Bode feels in this final gathering is evangelical. Indeed, the gathering in Wheeler's office is ecclesiological. Unlike Brother Preston, all those who gather here (save Bode) knew Burley, as he once knew Tom. That is how they can speak truthfully, one by one, out of their memory of his particular life. Theirs is an embodied love; their words are made of flesh.

Christians in America would do well to aspire to the sort of church that is not really a church but behaves like one, namely, Berry's Port William community. As Berry believes, they are knit together in body, which is possible only as they share local work, work that connects them together to the land. If they know that land well and the local community, they will also know how its story is truthfully told, including the contributions made to its life by those who have gone before (and now rest in its earth), and what are its particular local sins. If America is not merely an idea but a collection of local communities, and if democracy within America is really a living local tradition, then the church in those communities will need to speak not only to them but within them, and in so doing they will speak to and within America. Hauerwas is right that the church needs to be the church. As I think Wendell Berry helps us see, the church in America needs to be the church in (various local places in) America.

Notes

A different version of this essay was published as Charles R. Pinches, "Stout, Hauerwas and the Body of America," *Political Theology* 8, no. 1 (January 2007): 9–13.

1. Jeffery Stout, *Democracy and Tradition* (Princeton, NJ: Princeton University Press, 2004). Stout's text has garnered considerable attention since its publication, including seven critical essays in the *Journal of Religious Ethics* (vol. 33, no. 4 [December 2005]), coupled with his lengthy response.

2. Stout, *Democracy and Tradition*, 2.

3. Stanley Hauerwas, *Performing the Faith: Bonhoeffer and the Practice of Nonviolence* (Grand Rapids, MI: Brazos, 2004), 223.

4. Stout, *Democracy and Tradition*, 24.

5. Ibid., 91.

6. Ibid., 140.

7. Hauerwas, *Performing the Faith*, 237.

8. Ibid., 223.

9. For instance, in *A Better Hope* (Grand Rapids, MI: Brazos, 2000), 141–44, Hauerwas uses Berry's *The Hidden Wound* (1970; reprint, San Francisco: North Point, 1989). Most recently, he has engaged a broad range of Berry's works in "What Would a Christian University Look Like? Some Tentative Answers Inspired by Wendell Berry," in *The State of the University: Academic Knowledges and the Knowledge of God* (Oxford: Blackwell, 2007), and reprinted in this volume.

10. Stout, *Democracy and Tradition*, 134.

11. Hauerwas, *Performing the Faith*, 224 (emphasis added).

12. Ibid., 236, 238.

13. Alan Verhey, *Reading the Bible in the Strange World of Medicine* (Grand Rapids, MI: Eerdmans, 2003), 79.

14. Stout, *Democracy and Tradition*, 9.

15. Aquinas, *Summa theologiae*, trans. Fathers of the English Dominican Province (New York: Christian Classics, 1948), 101 (II-II).

16. Herbert Fingarette, *Conflicius: The Secular as Sacred* (New York: Harper & Row, 1972), 75, 76.

17. Stout, *Democracy and Tradition*, 30.

18. Ibid., 38.

19. Ibid., 37.

20. Stanley Hauerwas, "My Uncle Charlie Is Not Much of a Person but He Is Still My Uncle Charlie," in *Truthfulness and Tragedy* (Notre Dame, IN: University of Notre Dame Press, 1977), 116–26. The argument I am making here also, I think, gives support to Hauerwas's concern expressed in another equally provocative but ultimately less successful article titled "Why Justice Is a Bad Idea for Christians" (in

After Christendom [Nashville: Abington, 1991], 45–68), the very article Stout later roundly criticizes (see Stout, *Democracy and Tradition*, 149). As Hauerwas says in his response to Stout's critique: "What concerned me about liberal accounts of justice is their unwillingness to describe the practices that make the language of justice concrete" (*Performing the Faith*, 231). If justice is about what is owed to whom, then we need to know who is the *whom*. As Hauerwas suggests, this is increasingly difficult in a culture where the *whom* is anyone at all.

21. We remember particular things—as Jews, e.g., remember the crossing of the Red Sea or Christians remember the last meal Jesus ate with his disciples. For more on how Jews and Christians remember, see my *A Gathering of Memories: Family, Nation and Church in a Forgetful World* (Grand Rapids, MI: Brazos, 2006), esp. 123–56.

22. Wendell Berry, "Health as Membership," in *Another Turn of the Crank* (Washington, DC: Counterpoint, 1995), 87.

23. Wendell Berry, *Remembering*, in *Three Short Novels* (New York: Counterpoint, 2002), 138, 139.

24. Ibid., 140.

25. Wendell Berry, *The Hidden Wound* (1970; reprint, New York: North Point Press, 1989).

26. Stout, *Democracy and Tradition*, 58.

27. Ibid., 134.

28. Ibid. Here again, I wish Stout would more carefully consider why it is such a good book. *The Unsettling of America* is not really about environmental ethics at all; rather, it tells the story not just of our environmental abuse but of our forgetfulness of the fact that we are embodied creatures whose life is built on the land.

29. Wendell Berry, "The Body and the Earth," in *The Unsettling of America: Culture and Agriculture*, 3rd ed. (San Francisco: Sierra Club Books, 1997), 108.

30. Ibid., 108, 109.

31. Wendell Berry, *A Place on Earth* (Washington, DC: Counterpoint, 1983), 98–99, 101.

32. Ibid., 104.

33. Abraham Lincoln, Second Inaugural Address (March 4, 1865), available at http://avalon.law.yale.edu/19th_century/lincoln2.asp.

34. Hauerwas, *A Better Hope*, 31. Alasdair MacIntyre's use of the phrase is in "The American Ideal," in *America and Ireland, 1776–1976: The American Identity and the Irish Connection*, ed. David Noel Doyle and Owen Dudley Edwards (Westport, CT: Greenwood, 1980), 58–59.

35. Stout, *Democracy and Tradition*, 58.

36. In my *A Gathering of Memories*, esp. chaps. 4–6, I consider in more detail how patriotism might rightly go for Christians in America.

37. Hauerwas, *A Better Hope*, 24.

38. Stout, *Democracy and Tradition*, 140.

39. Hauerwas, *A Better Hope*, 24.

40. Berry stops to describe Bode's life for us. It is a comic description, including this: "Kyle Bode's father had originated in the broad bottomlands of a community called Nowhere, three counties west of Louisville. Under pressure from birth to 'get out of here and make something of yourself,' Kyle's father had come to Louisville and worked his way into a farm equipment dealership" (Wendell Berry, "Fidelity," in *Fidelity: Five Stories* [New York: Pantheon, 1992], 145–46). With this "heritage," it is no wonder that Detective Bode understands so little about the people of Port William.

41. Ibid., 189.

Contributors

ELIZABETH BAHNSON is a musician and runs a cottage farm in Orange County, North Carolina.

FRED BAHNSON is a W. K. Kellogg Food and Society Policy fellow. His poems and essays have appeared in *Orion,* the *Sun, Best American Spiritual Writing, 2007,* and the *Christian Century.*

KYLE CHILDRESS is pastor at Austin Heights Baptist Church in Nacogdoches, Texas.

RICHARD P. CHURCH is an attorney and farmer living in Chatham County, North Carolina.

ELLEN F. DAVIS is the Amos Ragan Kearns Professor of Bible and Practical Theology at Duke University Divinity School in Durham, North Carolina.

STANLEY HAUERWAS is Gilbert T. Rowe Professor of Theological Ethics at Duke University Divinity School in Durham, North Carolina.

D. BRENT LAYTHAM is professor of theology and ethics at North Park Theological Seminary in Chicago, Illinois.

PHILIP A. MUNTZEL is professor of theology at King's College in Wilkes-Barre, Pennsylvania.

L. ROGER OWENS is pastor of Duke Memorial United Methodist Church in Durham, North Carolina.

CHARLES R. PINCHES is professor and chair of the Department of Theology at the University of Scranton.

JOEL JAMES SHUMAN is associate professor and chair of the Department of Theology at King's College in Wilkes-Barre, Pennsylvania.

BRIAN VOLCK is a physician and writer living in Cincinnati, Ohio.

SCOTT WILLIAMS is instructor in philosophy at Waynesburg College in Waynesburg, Pennsylvania.

NORMAN WIRZBA is research professor of theology, ecology, and rural life at Duke University Divinity School in Durham, North Carolina.

Index